CONGRESS, THE BUREAUCRACY, AND PUBLIC POLICY

The Dorsey Series in Political Science

Consulting Editor   Samuel C. Patterson   *The University of Iowa*

~ Congress,
the bureaucracy,
and public policy ~

RANDALL B. RIPLEY
Professor and Chairperson
Department of Political Science

GRACE A. FRANKLIN
Research Associate
Mershon Center

both of
The Ohio State University

 1980 ~ Revised Edition

THE DORSEY PRESS   Homewood, Illinois   60430
Irwin-Dorsey Limited   Georgetown, Ontario   L7G 4B3

JK
1067
.R53
1980

ISBN 0-256-02256-9
Library of Congress Catalog Card No. 79–89263

Printed in the United States of America

1 2 3 4 5 6 7 8 9 0 ML 7 6 5 4 3 2 1 0

Preface

WE EXPECT A STUDENT USING THIS TEXT to come away with an understanding of the critical nature of the relationship between Congress and the federal bureaucracy. The examples we have used should give the student a feel for part of the substantive business of the United States government and should also give the student a better sense of how and where to seek additional examples of that business. We also think the student who uses this book will be able to use simple English to explain to herself or himself and to others a number of patterns in American policy-making.

Public policy-making at the national level in the United States is both important and complicated. It is important because it affects the daily lives of all residents of the United States and sometimes affects the lives of people in other nations. It is complicated because of the vast number of substantive areas on the agenda of the national government and because of the large number of individuals and institutions that get involved in decisions about public policy.

Central to the complex and important business of public policy-making is the interaction between Congress and the federal bureaucracy. Existing books about public policy usually either ignore this relationship or merely allude to it, implying that it is too mysterious to be comprehended. In fact, it is comprehensible and—happy thought!—there are patterns in the relationship that help reduce the confusion surrounding national policy-making. We have sought to portray those patterns in clear terms. And, above all, we have sought to give concrete, interesting, and timely examples of the relationships that illustrate the patterns rather than producing a sense of confusion of their own.

We do not intend to describe all that either Congress or the bureaucracy do with regard to public policy. Our focus is on those areas and activities in which constant interaction occurs between them and has at least the potential for major substantive results. Our attention, therefore, is primarily directed to *policy formulation and legitimation.* The *implementation* of policy by bureaucracy is a vast and important topic by itself, but congressional input into the details of implementation is limited and sporadic (although it may be quite important in any individual case). We address implementation questions occasionally in some of the examples we use and in our discussion of oversight, but the major part of implementation is simply beyond the scope of this book.

We are grateful to the Mershon Center at Ohio State University for providing a good location in which to write and think and interact with other people interested in public policy. This book stems both from a number of projects on policy-making sponsored in part by Mershon, in which we have been involved throughout the 1970s, and from our teaching—both formal and informal and to a number of audiences—about public policy.

In preparing this revised edition we had the benefit of thoughtful reviews of the first edition by Samuel C. Patterson and David W. Rohde.

December 1979   **Randall B. Ripley**
                                                       Grace A. Franklin

Contents

List of tables

List of figures

~1~

The nature of policy and
policymaking in the United States

Policy is a common word, one that you encounter frequently—you hear it on the radio and TV, you use it in conversation, you read it in the press—but it is a difficult concept to define, despite its familiarity. Political scientists have filled many pages defining and arguing about the meaning of policy and its relatives—policymaking and policy process. That policy is complex, both conceptually and substantively, is undeniable. Nor should the importance of government policies be underestimated; one reason you hear about policy so frequently in the news is that the policies of government are pervasive in their direct and indirect impact on you and all citizens.

To help sort out the complexities, we offer the following very simple statements, based on our reading of the literature and our empirical research:

Policy is what the government says and does about perceived problems.

Policymaking is how the government decides what will be done about perceived problems.

Policymaking is a process of interaction among governmental and nongovernmental actors; policy is the outcome of that interaction.

Figure 1–1 presents a highly simplified model of the policy process, the chain of activities in the making and implementation of policy.

1

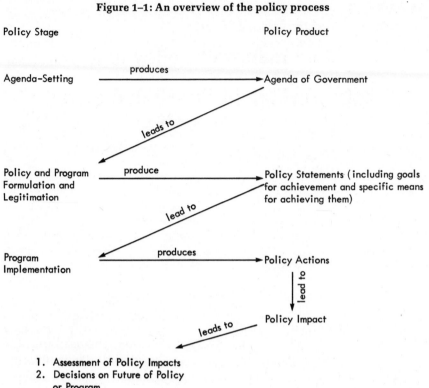

Figure 1–1: An overview of the policy process

1. Assessment of Policy Impacts
2. Decisions on Future of Policy
   or Program

In the first stage of the policy process—*agenda-setting*—a problem exists in society, and through various means it comes to the attention of government actors, who perceive it to be an issue that should be addressed by government. In short, in agenda-setting some parts of the government recognize that an issue or problem should receive attention. The agenda of the government can be thought of as the sum of all the issues and problems that the government is addressing at any given time. In the 1970s, for example, some of the issues on the government agenda included environmental preservation, energy resources, unemployment, and inflation.

Having acknowledged that a problem deserves governmental attention, government must say what it is going to do, and specify how it plans to accomplish its goals. In the stage of *formulation and legitimation,* government and nongovernment actors propose alternative methods of problem solution, and they choose a course of planned action. The presence of competition among different, often vehement, points of view necessitates negotiation and compromise if a decision is to be reached in formulation and legitimation. The typical product of this stage of policy process is a congressional statute creating a new program or amending an existing one.

Once a plan of action has been selected, the decisions must be *implemented* by responsible individuals and agencies. The agencies must acquire resources, interpret the legislation, write regulations, train staff, and deliver services to carry out the purposes of the legislation.

The actual operation of a program designed to address a problem will have some kind of *impact* on society. It may achieve its intended purposes or not (assuming those were clear), or it may achieve other purposes. The assessment of policy impact is an important feature of the policy process, but it is unfortunately a part that is largely ignored by government actors. When assessment of government policies and their impact is undertaken, the results can lead to changes in the operation of the program (reimplementation) or to renewed formulation and legitimation as revised programs are debated. It can occasionally, but very rarely, lead to termination of existing programs. It most often, however, results in no change, or only minor change, in the existing policies.

A treatment of the entire policy process is beyond the scope of this book (see Jones, 1977, for an excellent introduction to the policy process). In this book, we are going to focus on one part of the policy process—the formulation and legitimation of public policies and programs. At the heart of the policymaking process lies the relationship between Congress and the bureaucracy, a relationship that is not usually given sustained attention in the literature on American government and policymaking. That relationship is the focus of this book. In order to set the relationship in perspective, we will first describe policymaking in American national government in terms of major actors, relationships, and characteristics.

Before turning to that discussion, we should offer a few of our personal observations about the policy process. The model portrayed in Figure 1–1, the definitions of policy, and the brief description of the policy process we presented above must, of necessity, vastly simplify the rich variety of the real world. Our scheme offers generalizations about and imposes an order on a very complex world whose activities and interactions are not as neat and orderly as a model suggests. In short, they should be treated as a starting point, but not as the ultimate description of reality.

Furthermore, there are many facets of the policy process that cannot be captured in any model but that are important nonetheless to an understanding of public policy. Charles Jones (1977: 7–8) has produced a list of propositions about the characteristics of the policy process in the United States that we feel accurately reflects the incremental, pluralistic nature of much public policy. We are repeating his propositions here, both because we feel they are important and true, but also because an understanding of them helps to provide a context for understanding the interaction of Congress and the bureaucracy in shaping public policy.

1. Events in society are interpreted in different ways by different people at different times.

2. Many problems may result from the same event.

3. People have varying degrees of access to the policy process in government.

4. Not all public problems are acted on in government.

5. Many private problems are acted on in government.

6. Many private problems are acted on in government as though they were public problems.

7. Most problems aren't solved by government though many are acted on there.

8. Policymakers are not faced with a *given* problem.

9. Most decision making is based on little information and poor communication.

10. Programs often reflect an attainable consensus rather than a substantive conviction.

11. Problems and demands are constantly being defined and redefined in the policy process.

12. Policymakers sometimes define problems for people who have not defined problems for themselves.

13. Many programs are developed and implemented without the problems ever having been clearly defined.

14. Most people do not maintain interest in other people's problems.

15. Most people do not prefer large change.

16. Most people cannot identify a public policy.

17. All policy systems have a bias.

18. No ideal policy system exists apart from the preferences of the architect of that system.

19. Most decision making is incremental in nature.

AN OVERVIEW OF THE
GOVERNMENTAL POLICY PROCESS

Actors and relationships

The core of the American national governmental policy process is located in Congress and in the executive branch. Each of these institutional entities can be understood in terms of key component parts. In Congress there are party leaders, committee and subcommittee leaders (typically, committee and subcommittee chairpersons and ranking members), and rank-and-file members of the House and Senate. In the executive branch there are the President personally, the presidency collectively in the form of the Executive Office of the President and the presidential appointees, and the civil servants throughout all of the agencies.[1] Each of these six component parts of the central Washington policymaking institutions interacts with every other part, but all of the relationships are not equally important. Figure 1–2 indicates the interactions most important to national governmental policymaking.

Within the executive branch two relationships are critical—that of the President with Executive Office personnel and presidential appointees throughout the government (the institutional presidency in a broad sense), and that of Executive Office personnel and presidential appointees with civil servants throughout the government. The bureaucracy is so vast that the President cannot hope to have direct relationships with civil servants (except for a few career civil servants in the Executive Office and a few career ambassadors in the foreign service). Thus, the Executive Office personnel and presidential appointees scattered throughout the various departments and agencies take on special importance in serving as links between the President and his programmatic ideas and the development of and implementation of those ideas in the bureaucracy.

**Figure 1–2: Critical relationships for policymaking
in the national government**

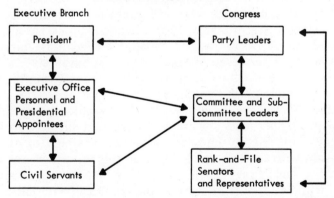

---

[1] That part of the federal bureacracy in which we are most interested are those career officials—both civilian and some military equivalents—who are high enough in grade or rank to be considered as involved in national policymaking. Typically, this would mean individuals who are supergrades (GS 16, 17, or 18) or equivalents in other career services, including the military.

Three relationships are critical within Congress. Committee and subcommittee leaders play an intermediary role between party leaders and rank-and-file members, but party leaders also need and maintain direct ties to the rank and file; this is relatively easy to achieve in physical terms, given the limited size of the House and Senate. The committee and subcommittee leaders are typically the most important individuals in deciding what emerges from Congress in substantive terms. The party leaders make the strategic and tactical decisions about how best to get the work of committees and subcommittees approved by the full House and Senate. The rank and file are approached by both committee and subcommittee leaders and party leaders in their respective spheres of expertise.

There are also three critical relationships between the executive branch and Congress: those between the President and the party leaders (largely on strategic and tactical matters), between the Executive Office personnel and presidential appointees and committee and subcommittee leaders (on substantive matters), and between policy level actors in the civil and military service and committee and subcommittee leaders in Congress (on substantive matters).

To get very dramatic policy movement out of the government, the eight relationships portrayed in Figure 1–2 must all be marked by a high degree of mutual confidence and trust, and there must also be a high degree of agreement on the nature of the problems facing society and the nature of proper solutions to those problems. These conditions are absent more than they are present, which helps to explain the normal posture of the government as moving very slowly on only a few problems at a time. Rapid movement on major issues occurs, and when it does it is unusual enough to warrant special notice.

This book focuses primarily on the relationship between civil servants (and equivalent military officers) and committee and subcommittee leaders as portrayed in Figure 1–2. The other relationships included in the figure will be discussed as necessary to set the context for the central relationship to be examined.

In some policy areas the other actors and relationships will appear more frequently because they are very important. In addition, some of the unportrayed relationships that occur more rarely (for example, a relationship between the institutional presidency and committees or bureaucracies and rank-and-file members or bureaucracies and party leaders) will also appear in some of the empirical materials in subsequent chapters.

In general, the role of the President personally will receive attention only when it becomes critical. Given the vast workload of the federal government and the limits on any one individual, the President may personally become involved only rarely. The institutional presidency has more routine contact with Congress, and so parts of it—especially the White House office and the Office of Management and Budget—will receive more frequent attention. (Chapter 2 contains a discussion of the roles of these actors.)

Principal characteristics

Policymaking in the U.S. government is an extremely complex phenomenon. This complexity results from a variety of factors—the sheer size of the government, the number of participants (both governmental and nongovernmental) that can become involved in policymaking, the proliferation of specialization within agencies and committees and subcommittees, the involvement of various levels of government, the separation of institutions that share powers as outlined by the Constitution, and of course, the vast range of substantive issues to which government addresses itself and the complexity of most of those issues. Four of the most important characteristics, each of which contributes to complexity, are described in the following paragraphs.

The first characteristic is the widespread occurrence of *subgovernments* in commanding or at least important positions in various issue areas. Subgovernments are small groups of political actors, both governmental and nongovernmental, that specialize in specific issue areas. Subgovernments in part are created by the complexity of the national policy agenda and they help sustain that complexity. They are also most prevalent and influential in the least visible policy areas.

A second major characteristic of policymaking is the great variety of governmental institutions—federal, state, and local—that share the responsibility for developing and implementing a number of policies and programs as well as having some programs exclusively their own. Thus a national program is very likely to involve actions not only in Washington but also throughout a number of states and cities in both federal field offices and offices of state and local government.

A third important characteristic of federal policymaking is separated institutions (the legislative, executive, and judicial branches) that share powers. The separation of institutions stems from a decision by the founders not to place all powers of government under a single body or person—hence, the basic governmental functions were subdivided and delegated to three distinct branches. However, in order to limit the autonomy of each branch a variety of checks and balances were written into the Constitution that force the institutions to share their powers to some extent. The separation makes some jealousies and conflicts over "turf" inevitable. The sharing necessitates cooperation among the branches to prevent the whole governing apparatus from ceasing to function with any effectiveness. In addition to the separation and sharing of powers prescribed in the Constitution, a commingling of legislative, executive, and judicial powers has evolved as the branches have interacted over time. Congressional delegation of authority to the executive branch is a particularly notable example of this sharing.

A final characteristic of national policymaking is the tremendous variety and volume of issues facing government. The substantive spectrum of government policy ranges from acreage allotments for cotton, wheat, and corn growers to child care and legal assistance for poor people to military and economic aid for developing nations. The relative specificity of governmental policy also varies greatly—a law may spell out in infinite detail every guideline, or it may be highly general and nonspecific. Naturally, different types of policy have different rewards and penalties for various groups, and the anticipated outcome of a proposed policy can affect the process by which the policy is made.

The remainder of this chapter will explore the above four characteristics of policymaking and the policy process in national government—the subgovernmental phenomenon, the commingling of governments, the separation of institutions that share powers, and the policy arenas with which government deals. In this discussion several broad themes are introduced that will be developed and examined throughout the book.

THE SUBGOVERNMENT PHENOMENON

Subgovernments are important throughout a broad range of American public policy. They afford an important channel by which nongovernmental actors help determine policy and program content. They are not equally dominant in all policy fields and their level of influence changes from time to time within a single field. (Later in this chapter we suggest that the level of subgovernment dominance varies in a predictable way depending on which of several broad policy types is involved.)

Subgovernments are clusters of individuals that effectively make most of the routine decisions in a given substantive area of policy. The existence of subgovernments has been noted and documented in a number of studies of American government (see, for example, Cater, 1964; Davidson, 1977; and Freeman, 1965). A typical subgovernment is composed of members of the House and/or Senate, members of congressional staffs, a few bureaucrats, and representatives of private groups and organizations interested in the policy area. Usually the members of Congress and staff members are from the committees or subcommittees that have principal or perhaps exclusive jurisdiction over the policy area dominated by the subgovernment. The congressional members of the subgovernment are also usually the few most senior members of a relevant committee or subcommittee. The bureaucrats in a subgovernment are likely to be the chief of a bureau with jurisdiction paralleling that of the congressional committee or subcommittee and a few of his or her top assistants. The nongovernmental members of a subgovernment are most likely to be a few lobbyists for interest groups with the heaviest stakes in the nature of governmental policy in the area.

Most of the policymaking in which subgovernments engage consists of routine matters. "Routine" policy is simply policy that is not currently embroiled in a high degree of controversy. The substance of routine policy does not change very much over time, and the participants most interested in it are also thoroughly familiar with it and quietly efficient in its implementation and minor alterations.

Since most policymaking is routine most of the time, subgovernments can often function for long periods of time without much interference or control from individuals or institutions outside the subgovernment. If the members of a subgovernment can reach compromises among themselves on any disagreements about policy they can reduce the chances of calling a broader audience together that might become involved in their activities and output. When more participants enter, the chances of basic policy realignments increase because there are a greater number of interests to satisfy, and such realignments might not be perceived to be in the best interests of the members of the subgovernment. Thus there is strong incentive for them to reach compromises and avoid broadening the number of participants.

In general, there are three ways that the normally closed, low-profile operations of a subgovernment can be opened up to "outsiders." First, as just indicated, if the subgovernment participants themselves disagree on some point fundamentally, this disagreement may become publicized and stimulate attention and intrusion from nonmembers of the subgovernment.

Second, the President, other high administration officials, and members of Congress can draw on a variety of formal and informal resources if they choose to be aggressive in inquiring into the functioning of a subgovernment. Formal resources include budget limitations, staff size limitations, vigorous legislative oversight of program activity, and restraints on agency communications (Freeman, 1965: 62). Informal resources consist mainly of using personal influence selectively on an individual-to-individual basis. This is especially true for the President, who can exert influence on persons he has appointed. Whether the President, administration officials, and congressional members will be aggressive with respect to subgovernments depends on the extent to which they perceive interests important to them to be threatened by the subgovernment's behavior. For example, the President or a department Secretary may be stirred to an aggressive stance if the bureau chief member of a subgovernment strays too far too often from officially announced administration policy.

Third, a new issue that attracts the attention of outsiders can be introduced into the subgovernment's jurisdiction. The new issue can upset normal decision making if it is more important or different in character from the issues the subgovernment is used to dealing with, especially if the issue involves regulation of private activities or redistribution of wealth to one group at the expense of another. In recent years, for example, both the increased concern for the environment and the "energy crisis" have intruded into the world of the various subgovernments dealing with oil, coal, and natural gas. Now the subgovernment must handle major regulatory issues as well as the familiar issues of subsidy.

The "rules of the game" of American politics and policymaking minimize the distinction between governmental and nongovernmental institutions. Any line between the two is easily crossed, and this situation is thought to be proper. It is also thought quite appropriate for the individuals and groups that are most affected by governmental actions to have almost continual access to governmental officials during the policymaking process (Lowi, 1979).

Not only are the lines between governmental and nongovernmental institutions blurred by the norm of open, continual access during policymaking, but there is also a constant flow of personnel between governmental and nongovernmental institutions that further blurs the distinctions. People from Congress (both the members and staff) and the executive branch agencies move into jobs in the private sector to work in the same substantive policy areas they worked in during their government tenure. This flow of personnel enhances the importance and stability of subgovernments, and the magnitude of this type of personnel interchange is so large that subgovernments have also been called "incest groups" (Lewis, 1977).

It is worth underscoring that participation in subgovernments offers the most pervasive and effective channel for interest group participation in policy and program decisions. But the impact of interest groups will not be uniformly important—rather they will have a great deal of importance in some areas and minimal importance in other areas (see Hayes, 1978). In part their varying impact is due to the fact that the impact of subgovernments themselves varies depending on the policy area (this is a point we will develop later in the book), and in part it is due to the varying strengths and resources of different interest groups.

When all organized interest groups are considered together a strong "business or upper class bias" becomes evident (Schattschneider,

1960). That is, the more well-off in society, especially the private business sector, are particularly strongly represented. This helps explain why much substantive policy that emerges is favorable to these interests.

FEDERALISM IN POLICYMAKING

Geographic dispersion of the national government

Washington, D.C., is synonymous with the national government, and it is true that much of the decision-making apparatus of the government is concentrated there. But Washington contains only a small part of federal employees—in 1976, of all federal civilian employees (a total of over 2.8 million persons) only 12 percent were stationed in the metropolitan Washington area. Eighty-three percent were stationed elsewhere in the United States, and 4 percent were stationed outside of the United States entirely, either in U.S. territories or in foreign countries. In terms of putting federally subsidized, regulated, or redistributed bread and butter on the plates of citizens, it is the regional and local outposts of the federal government where the primary responsibility for delivery of benefits and services resides.

Nearly every federal agency has some regional and local field offices. Unfortunately there is no standard summary of agency field offices, and the patterns among agencies vary widely—some have a profusion of installations in every state, while others have very few. Even at the regional level, there is considerable variation among agencies, despite the Standard Federal Regional Boundary System established in 1969 that prescribes ten standard regions to which agencies should conform. But a glance through any telephone book of reasonable size under the heading "U.S. Government" will reveal how extensively the federal government is represented on the local and regional level.

Federal, state, and local government interaction

In addition to being complicated by the dispersion of purely national institutions and employees, policymaking and implementation in the United States is also complicated because there are numerous state and local governments that are important in their own right and are also important in implementing national programs. Numerous ties bind federal, state, and local governmental units and employees together: federal money, limited exchanges of personnel, and daily interaction on programs.

State and local government employment is much larger than federal government employment. In 1977, for example, there were 15,075,000 governmental employees in the United States. Of these, only 19 percent were federal while the remainder were state and local. The federal share of total civilian governmental employment has been shrinking: in 1950 it was 32 percent and in 1960 it was 28 percent.

The financial impact of the federal government on state and local governments has been growing, however. Table 1–1 summarizes the changing situation. As this table shows, the amount of federal aid to states and localities has risen enormously—more than twelvefold between 1960 and 1979, for example. These expenditures also represent a constantly increasing percentage of all federal spending and of all state and local expenditures. In 1979 it is estimated that over one quarter of all so-called state and local spending will come directly from federal grants-in-aid.

Table 1–1: The growth of federal grants-in-aid to state and
local governments, 1950–1979

Fiscal year	Amount (millions)	Federal grants as a percent of	
		Total federal outlays	State-local expenditures
1950	$ 2,253	5.3	10.4
1960	7,020	7.6	14.7
1965	10,904	9.2	15.3
1970	24,018	12.2	19.4
1975	49,723	15.2	23.2
1979 (estimated)	85,020	17.0	26.2

Source: *Special Analyses, Budget of the United States Government, Fiscal Year 1979* (Washington: Government Printing Office, 1978), p. 184.

In addition, the purposes for which these federal grants-in-aid to states and localities are spent have changed considerably. Table 1–2 summarizes these changes from 1957 to 1979. General purpose fiscal assistance reported for 1977 and 1979 is primarily general revenue sharing. These funds have been used preponderantly for education by state governments and for public safety and transportation (mass transit) by local governments. Various forms of specific revenue sharing are also beginning to emerge to replace some of the categorical programs. Most employment and training and community development funds are now handled through variants of special revenue sharing.

The form that federalism takes in actual operation has varied greatly depending on time, place, and policy. Perhaps the most common pattern has been that of categorical federal assistance, where the federal government agency, represented by its national or regional office, retains extensive control over the allocation and expenditure of federal dollars through planning requirements, reports on program operation

Table 1–2: Percentage distribution of federal grants to states and localities
by function, 1957–1979

Function	1957	1962	1967	1972	1977	1979 (est.)
Natural resources and environment	1	2	2	2	6	7
Agriculture	9	6	3	1	1	*
Transportation	24	36	27	15	12	12
Community and regional development	1	3	6	10	7	7
Education, training, employment, and social services	8	8	25	26	23	26
Health	4	5	10	17	18	17
Income security	49	38	25	26	18	17
General purpose fiscal assistance	3	2	2	1	14	11

Note that columns do not add to 100 because of rounding and because a small "other" category is omitted.

* = Less than 0.5 percent.

Source: *Special Analyses, Budget of the United States Government, Fiscal Year 1979* (Washington: Government Printing Office, 1978), p. 182.

and evaluation, and performance standards. The state and local governments serve as conduits for the money but have not traditionally had a great deal of input regarding how the money is spent. An interesting variation of this pattern occurred following passage of the Economic Opportunity Act of 1964, when the federal government gave its grants directly to nongovernmental units at the local level, including community action agencies. This approach bypassed the state and local agencies, much to the latter's displeasure.

A pattern of federalism that has recently received a great deal of rhetorical attention, and some actual implementation, is the block grant or revenue sharing approach to federal assistance. Under this approach, grants are given to state and local jurisdictions with fewer federal restrictions on how and for what the money is to be spent. The keywords of this approach are decategorization and decentralization. The elimination of federal categorical grant programs allows local officials to design programs that presumably closely match the needs of their areas, while the reduction of federal standards and requirements gives local officials greater flexibility and freedom in designing and administering their programs. The cost to state and local officials of this greater flexibility is that often the total amount of federal money coming into a community for a cluster of grant programs is reduced when a revenue sharing or block grant approach is implemented. And, in general, it can also be said that the federal bureaucracy does not usually give up a substantial role for itself. Nor will Congress cease to review such programs frequently. Thus the congressional-bureaucratic interaction remains at the heart of policymaking even when authority granted to state and local governments is increased. And the "natural" pressures are for members of Congress and the bureaucracy to keep states and localities dependent on them in many ways so that they can continuously claim credit for programs for their various constituencies.

SEPARATE INSTITUTIONS, SHARED POWERS

Cooperation and conflict

The Constitution created three branches of government that have distinct identities in terms of their powers and in terms of their source of holding office. Yet it also distributed powers in such a way that interaction and at least some cooperation is necessary if anything is to be accomplished. Institutional jealousies about preserving powers and competition to serve different constituencies mean that the three branches will inevitably have some conflicts. But an overriding desire and necessity to achieve some policy goals also means that most participants in all three branches understand and operate on the values of cooperation and compromise. The existence of subgovernments serves to reinforce the values of cooperation and compromise for the participants (Morrow, 1969: 156–158). Institutional jealousies and competition for constituencies remain within the subgovernmental system, but their effects are muted in its day-to-day operations. The premium is placed on the production of policy (the policy being usually an extension of the status quo or some incremental variant of it). More policy production also creates more bureaucracy, which in the course of implementing programs creates more occasions for members of Congress to serve their constituents in dealings with the bureaucracy. Such service generates benefits to the members at election time (Fiorina, 1977).

Most of the literature dealing with Congress and the bureaucracy usually focuses on the conflictual aspects of the relationship because conflict is a more exciting topic than cooperation. But the bulk of policymaking is based on cooperation. One of the tasks of this volume will be to develop suggestions in the literature (Bernstein, 1958; Bibby, 1966; Fiorina, 1977; Morrow, 1969; Scher, 1963; Sharkansky, 1965a, 1965b) about the conditions that promote cooperation or conflict. The following brief survey indicates some of the conditions to be addressed:

First, personal compatibility between key congressional (usually committee) personnel and key agency personnel is important. A high degree of compatibility will promote cooperation and lesser amounts of compatibility (or greater amounts of hostility) will promote conflict.

Second, the degree of ideological and programmatic agreement between key individuals in Congress (usually on the relevant committee) and in the agency is important. A high degree of agreement will promote cooperation; a low degree of agreement will promote conflict. Similarly, if there is a high degree of unity *between* different individual members of Congress thought by bureaucrats to be important this is likely to make the bureaucrats less inclined to pursue their own interests that may conflict with united congressional opinion. Disunity among members of Congress may tempt bureaucrats to form alliances with those agreeing with them, thus provoking conflict with the other congressional faction.

Third, the amount of genuine participation by Congress (generally, members of a committee or subcommittee) in the development of programs is important. If executive branch officials simply present Congress with finished products—either in the form of proposed legislation or in the form of major administrative decisions—conflict may result. If the executive officials adopt a style of consulting as they undertake either legislative or administrative courses of action they enhance the chances of cooperation.

Fourth, if an issue is of relatively low salience to constituents and/or interest groups then the chances of congressional-bureaucratic cooperation are enhanced. However, if constituents and/or interest groups are heavily involved the potential for conflict increases.

Fifth, agencies that are highly aggressive in seeking to expand their authority and their funding run a greater risk of conflict with Congress (committees and subcommittees) than agencies that are less aggressive.

Sixth, if the presidency and Congress are controlled by the same political party the chances for cooperation are enhanced. If different parties control the two branches the chances for conflict increase.

Delegation of authority

Delegation of authority is an instance of shared powers that occurs when Congress allows the executive branch freedom to specify policy content of legislation. In theory, Congress sets clear regulations, standards, and guidelines in its legislation for the bureaucracy to use in administering programs. In practice, the clarity and specificity of those regulations, standards, and guidelines vary a great deal. For example, Congress may direct the National Labor Relations Board (NLRB) to ascertain that "fair standards" in labor negotiations are adhered to and leave the determination of what constitutes fair standards up to the agency. The interpretation of "maximum feasible participation" of the poor in the Economic Opportunity Act of 1964 was similarly left up to the Office of Economic Opportunity (OEO) and its local branches. On the other hand, Congress may specify extremely precise standards that eliminate agencies' discretionary power, as it did in the Securities Act of 1933. The existence and size of the *Federal Register* testify to the amount of freedom agencies have in making formal (i.e., recorded) interpretations of congressional intents. In that daily document agencies are required to file the rules and guidelines they use in administering their programs. The amount of informal (i.e., unrecorded) administrative rule making of a specific character that occurs is no doubt equally voluminous.

Delegation of authority to the executive branch allows Congress to keep its workload manageable. Government has assumed increasing responsibility in an ever-expanding number of issue areas in the 20th century, and Congress of necessity has delegated a great deal of authority vested in it by the Constitution to various parts of the executive branch. The sheer volume and technical complexity of the work is more than Congress with its limited manpower can manage alone.

Congress sometimes intentionally uses delegation to delay making a final decision. A clear-cut policy decision may result in penalizing or angering some groups, which can manifest their unhappiness by withdrawing their support from members of Congress. If the members perceive that they would lose a great deal of support, they may choose not to state a clear policy, and leave the policy outcome ambiguous by delegating decision making to parts of the bureaucracy, or to regulatory commissions, or to the courts, with only vague congressional guidance. Thus the winners and losers affected by the policy are less clearly defined, and the responsibility for decision making is deflected from Congress to other agencies.

The propriety of congressional delegation of authority was challenged during the New Deal, and the Supreme Court ruled on a few occasions that certain delegations were unconstitutional because of vagueness, but that check has not been exercised since. In effect, Congress can follow whatever course it wishes with respect to delegation —its form will change only when Congress decides to rewrite the legislation containing the delegation. In summarizing this fact and the continuing trend toward very broad delegations Woll (1977: 170) says that "It is possible to conclude that there are no constitutional or legal restrictions that have impeded in any substantial way the trend toward greater delegation. This situation has not, of course, resulted from administration usurpation, but from congressional desire." Delegation, in sum, is a result of necessity, but it is also a matter of will, not coercion.

If the principle of delegation of authority is well established, the question of what form delegation ought to take is not so well settled. Some scholars, like Harris (1964), argue explicitly that Congress should be only minimally involved in administration, and by implication, that its delegations of authority should be broad and vague to allow the bureaucrat to make interpretations best suited to meeting the problems faced in program administration. Others, like Lowi (1979), argue that delegation of authority without accompanying clear guidelines limits congressional policy impact to relatively marginal details and is, in effect, an abdication of responsibility by Congress. By implication, Congress should publish clear expectations and guidelines along with its delegations.

It is clear from examining legislation that the forms of delegation do vary, although the trend has been toward broad, unrestrictive grants of authority. The reasons for relatively clear guidelines in statutory language in some cases and very broad and vague language in other cases are numerous and, no doubt, vary from case to case. One important consideration may be the mood of Congress at any given time with reference to the agency to which the delegation is being made. Or, more to the point, the most important consideration may be the attitude of the congressional committees responsible for the legislation toward the relevant agencies.

An example of how patterns of delegation are affected by changing congressional attitudes is evident in the degree of discretionary power allocated to the Federal Trade Commission in the Securities Act of 1933 and the Securities and Exchange Commission in the Securities and Exchange Act of 1934 (Landis, 1938: 52–55). The FTC's discretionary power was severely limited in part because of congressional distrust and lack of confidence in the membership of that body. Its duties were defined so precisely that administration was almost a matter of mechanical routine. In contrast, attitudes toward the FTC had changed by 1934, and the new confidence was reflected in the broader administrative authority granted to the new SEC.

The type of issue area involved also affects the nature of congressional delegation. In highly complex issues, particularly those in the jurisdictions of the regulatory agencies, Congress is often unable or unwilling to make specific judgments. As a result, the area of discretion, and the accompanying set of political pressures in the regulatory commissions, such as the Federal Trade Commission, Securities and Exchange Commission, Federal Communications Commission, and Federal Power Commission, are unusually large.

A desire to shift responsibility for decision making may also be a factor in congressional delegations of authority to the bureaucracy. Unpopular decisions can be laid at the bureaucracy's door, rather than that of Congress. Landis (1938: 55–60) makes the point that to the extent that Congress avoids making clear pronouncements of policy in its statutes the conflict over which policy will in fact be enforced is shifted from Congress to the administrative agencies involved. This congressional stance seems particularly prevalent in the entire area of regulation of business.

The implication of congressional delegation of authority is that a good deal of public policy gets made by the bureaucracy without any explicit attention from Congress. Congressional access to the routine matters of public policy is in practice, although not in theory, limited. Even in initiating new formal statutes the bureaucracy is important and sometimes dominant (Woll, 1977: 170–200).

Legislative oversight

Congressional delegation of authority does not necessarily mean congressional abdication, however. Congress still has access to administrative policy making through a variety of activities that are collectively known as legislative oversight. In effect, legislative oversight could be construed as a counterbalance to congressional grants of policymaking authority to the bureaucracy. On the one hand Congress gives away parts of its own powers to the executive branch, but on the other hand it reserves the right to monitor the way the executive branch is exercising that authority. In this volume we will use "oversight" as a neutral term, avoiding any implication that it is good or bad. We certainly do assert that oversight in general is necessary in a representative government, but we do not want to prejudge any given exercise of it as either "proper" or "improper."

Legislative oversight is not just a single activity that occurs on a regular basis. In fact, oversight, broadly conceived, consists of all of Congress' involvement in the affairs of the bureaucracy (see Keefe and Ogul, 1977: chapter 12; and Ogul, 1973). The oversight activities of Congress fall into five categories: concern with the substance of policy, concern with agency personnel, concern with agency structure, concern with agency decision-making processes, and concern with agency budgets. A brief survey of the techniques of oversight follows and will receive further treatment in Chapter 3.

Congressional concern with the substance of policy is manifested at any of the three stages: passage of legislation, application and implementation of legislation, and societal impact of legislation. The content of legislation at the time of its passage identifies congressional intents as modified during the legislative process. As indicated in earlier paragraphs, the legislation may allow the bureaucracy considerable discretion in interpreting and applying the law. To monitor administrative interpretation, Congress can hold regular hearings (for both authorization and appropriations) and focus on aspects of this issue, it can hold special investigations, or it can exercise a variety of informal contacts (phone calls and visits with bureaucrats, lobbyists, and affected constituents, for example). If Congress determines that it has overdelegated or underdelegated, it can rewrite a statute to include additional and clearer guidelines. To monitor the impact of legislation on clients in society, Congress can require program evaluations, either done by itself, by an outside body (for example, the General Accounting Office), or by the agency itself. The findings of evaluations will suggest how legislation, or administrative patterns, could be altered to improve the fit between intended and actual impact.

The personnel who develop and apply government programs are just as important to policy impact as the content of legislation. Congress is involved with a variety of agency personnel matters—size of total staff or certain staff components, confirmation of top administrators (civil service, foreign service, and military officers) who are appointed by the President, compensation for federal employees, and the conduct of personnel (political activity, loyalty, and conflict of interest).

Congress is also involved in agency structure and organization in a fundamental life-and-death sense in that it is responsible for creating new agencies or for granting the President reorganization powers, usually with provision for possible congressional disapproval. Congress also controls the life blood of all agencies—their budget—and could kill an agency by refusing to fund it. This happened, for example, when Congress killed the Area Redevelopment Administration in 1963. In addition, Congress becomes involved in the details of agency organization when the President submits executive reorganization plans for congressional approval. A congressional veto can kill the reorganization. Congressional action killed President Kennedy's proposed department of urban affairs in 1962.

Congress inserts itself into the decision-making processes of agencies in at least two ways—by requiring reports and other data to be submitted by the agency, and by the use of the legislative veto, which in essence requires the executive branch to submit its proposals either to the whole Congress or to a particular committee for approval before acting on them. Both of these techniques allow Congress to maintain at least the form of reviewing bureaucratic activities in a regularized fashion, especially in legislative areas involving substantial delegation of authority.

Congressional oversight occurs at all stages of agency budgets—authorizations, appropriations, and expenditures. Authorizations establish the legitimacy of a program and set a ceiling on appropriations for subsequent years; authorizations must be passed before a program can receive appropriations. The authorization process for a new or existing program consists of hearings before the relevant legislative committee in the House and Senate, at which the past and expected program performance is reviewed. The frequency of authorization hearings varies from yearly to longer periods, depending on the program. The appropriations hearings are an annual event for most agencies, and they occur before the relevant subcommittee of the House and Senate Appropriations Committees, where, among other things, the performance of the agency's program is reviewed. Unfortunately it has been difficult for Congress to coordinate the program reviews that occur in the separate authorization and appropriations hearings, and the quality of the oversight, if not its quantity, has been criticized for focusing too much on detail and too little on program effectiveness and impact. Congress is also concerned with expenditures made by an agency after the appropriations process. This concern manifests itself during the appropriations hearings ("How did you spend the $10,000 for chicken wire at the ASCS field office in Ogden?") and also in special audits and investigations by the Government Accounting Office (GAO) commissioned by Congress. Congress has removed considerable federal funding from the appropriations process, thus further dispersing responsibility for fiscal oversight among a greater number of committees.

TYPES OF POLICY

The national government has assumed responsibility for a mushrooming variety and volume of issues over the years. Trying to discuss and analyze governmental policy without a classifying scheme can be confusing and misleading, and many scholars have proposed different schemes to ease the task of analysis. Policies have been categorized in many ways: by the substantive matter involved (education, agriculture, environment); by the relative size of the budgets of different policies (presidential requests, congressional appropriations, agency expenditures); by the beneficiary or target group affected (students, farmers, consumers); by the impact on society or some other outcome measure; or by the process through which the policy is made.

The key to any useful typology is to identify characteristics that components of the policy type share. We have developed a sevenfold classification scheme for governmental policy based on our reading of the policy literature (particularly Lowi (1964); see also Froman, 1968; Hayes, 1978; Huntington, 1961; Lowi, 1967, 1972; Salisbury, 1968). In our scheme there are four types of domestic policy: (1) distributive; (2) competitive regulatory; (3) protective regulatory; and (4) redistributive. We identify three types of foreign and defense policy: (1) structural; (2) strategic; and (3) crisis.

The basic notion behind our categorizations is that each type of policy generates and is therefore surrounded by its own distinctive set of political relationships. These relationships in turn help to determine substantive, concrete outcomes when policy decisions emerge. Table 1–3 summarizes the characteristics of the political relationships surrounding policymaking for each type of policy. The main features of the political relationships that we are concerned with in Table 1–3 are the identity of the primary actors, the basic nature of the interaction among those actors, the stability of their interaction, the visibility of the policy decisions to individuals not immediately involved or concerned, and the relative influence of different individual actors.

We have excluded competitive regulatory policy from Table 1–3 because it is a type of policy that is rarely formulated and legitimated; rather competitive regulatory policy is concerned primarily with issues of implementation. Responsibility for competitive regulatory policy is almost totally delegated to bureaucratic agencies, regulatory commissions, or courts for implementation. It focuses on decisions about individual cases, and the actors involved are limited to relevant bureaucratic, judicial, or quasi-judicial agencies, the individuals competing for benefits being awarded, and occasional members of Congress who have a specific interest in the outcome. We have included a discussion of competitive regulatory policy in the sections immediately following to contrast it with the other types of policy, but because this book focuses on the formulation and legitimation of policymaking, we have not included competitive regulatory policy in the analysis in the remainder of this book.

Domestic policy

Distributive policy. Distributive policies and programs are aimed at promoting private activities that are said to be desirable to society as a whole and, at least in theory, would not or could not be undertaken otherwise. Such policies and programs provide subsidies for those private activities and thus convey tangible governmental benefits to the individuals, groups, and corporations subsidized. (A subsidy is a payment designed to induce desired behavior.) Many governmental policies turn out to be subsidies, even if they do not seem to be subsidies at first glance. Decisions about subsidies are typically made with only short-run consequences considered. The decisions are not considered in light of each other; rather they are disaggregated. Thus there appear to be only winners and no losers.

The cast of characters (usually individuals or groups that comprise a subgovernment) involved in distributive decisions in a particular field (such as agricultural price supports, water resources, or subsidies for health research) is fairly stable over time, and their interactions are marked by low visibility and a high degree of cooperation and mutually rewarding logrolling. The congressional subcommittee generally makes the final decisions after receiving input from the other actors. The recipients of distributive subsidies are not aware of each other, and there is no sense of competing for limited resources—anyone can potentially be a recipient, and resources are treated as unlimited. Distributive decisions embody the federal pork barrel in its fullest sense,

Table 1–3: Political relationships for policymaking

Policy type	Primary actors	Relationship among actors	Stability of relationship	Visibility of decision
Distributive	Congressional subcommittees and committees; executive bureaus; small interest groups	Logrolling (everyone gains)	Stable	Low
Protective regulatory	Congressional subcommittees and committees; full House and Senate; executive agencies; trade associations	Bargaining; compromise	Unstable	Moderate
Redistributive	President and his appointees; committees and/or Congress; largest interest groups (peak associations); "liberals, conservatives"	Ideological and class conflict	Stable	High
Structural	Congressional subcommittees and committees; executive bureaus; small interest groups	Logrolling (everyone gains)	Low	Stable
Strategic	Executive agencies; President	Bargaining; compromise	Unstable	Low until publicized; then low to high
Crisis	President and advisers	Cooperation	Unstable	Low until publicized; then generally high

giving many people a bite of the federal pie. Distributive decisions, both within a field and between different substantive fields, are made individually, without consideration for their interrelation or overall impact—they are decentralized and uncoordinated. Chapter 4 will discuss the nature of the congressional-bureaucratic relationships when distributive policies are being made.

Examples of distributive policies include direct cash payments for purchase of agricultural commodities; grants for scientific research in universities and private laboratories; grants to localities for airport

		Influence of		
President, presidency, and centralized bureaucracy	Bureaus	Congress as a whole	Congressional subcommittees	Private sector
Low	High	Low (supports sub-committees)	High	High (subsidized groups)
Moderately high	Moderate	Moderately high	Moderate	Moderately high (regulated interests)
High	Moderately low	High	Moderately low	High ("peak associations" representing clusters of interest groups)
Low	High	Low (supports sub-committees)	High	High (subsidized groups and corporations)
High	Low	High (often responsive to executive)	Low	Moderate (interest groups, corporations)
High	Low	Low	Low	Low

construction, hospital construction, sewage facilities, and mass transit facilities; promoting home ownership through tax provisions allowing deductions for interest on home mortgages and local property taxes; and issuing low-cost permits for grazing on public lands.

Competitive regulatory policy. Competitive regulatory policies and programs are aimed at limiting the provision of specific goods and services to only one or a few designated deliverers who are chosen from a larger number of competing potential deliverers. Some of the potential deliverers who want the business win; some lose. Some decisions allocate scarce resources that simply cannot be divided, such as television channels or radio frequencies. Some decisions maintain limited rather than unlimited competition in the provision of goods and services by allowing only certain potential deliverers to provide them and excluding other potential deliverers. Some decisions are aimed at regulating the quality of services delivered through choosing the deliverer periodically and imposing standards of performance. If those standards are not met, a new deliverer can be chosen. This type of policy is a hybrid, which subsidizes the winning competitors and also tries to regulate some aspects of service delivery in the public interest. Examples of competitive regulatory policies include the granting and review of licenses to operate television and radio stations; authorizing specific airlines to operate specified routes; and authorizing specific trucking companies to haul specified commodities over specified routes.

Decisions on basic overall policy in this area are rare. Most decisions are delegated to bureaus, regulatory commissions, and courts. The influence of the competitors is high and over time most of them can be expected to get some benefits. Thus in application at the general level the policy resembles one of subsidy, especially for the largest competitors that can enter many specific competitions. For example, a major airline will not win every route from the Civil Aeronautics Board for which it competes but it will win enough routes over time to enhance its profitability. Congressional influence on individual decisions is present but usually in the form of intervention from specific Senators and Representatives. Given the lack of very much policymaking at a level comparable to the other policies we consider we have omitted competitive regulatory policy from the remainder of the book.

Protective regulatory policy. Protective regulatory policies and programs are designed to protect the public by setting the conditions under which various private activities can be undertaken. Conditions that are thought to be harmful (air pollution, false advertising) are prohibited; conditions that are thought to be helpful (the publication of interest rates on loans) are required.

Protective regulatory policies are not as disaggregatable as distributive decisions because they establish a general rule of law and require that behavior among a certain segment of the population conform to the law. The actors (coalitions of members of the full House and Senate, executive agencies, and representatives of trade associations) involved in protective regulatory decisions are much less stable than in the distributive arena, partially because of constantly shifting substantive issues. The ultimate decisions get made on the floor of the House and Senate. Chapter 5 examines the congressional-bureaucratic relationship in shaping the protective regulatory policy.

Examples of federal protective regulatory policies include the requirement that banks, stores, and other grantors of credit disclose true interest rates; prohibitions of unfair business practices, unfair labor practices, and business combinations that lessen competition; limits on the conditions under which strip mining can be undertaken and requirements for the postmining restoration of land; the prohibition of harmful food additives; and high taxation to reduce the consumption of scarce commodities such as gasoline.

Redistributive policy. Redistributive policies and programs are intended to manipulate the allocation of wealth, property rights, or some other value among social classes or racial groups in society. The redistributive feature enters because a number of actors perceive there are "winners" and "losers" in policies and that policies transfer some value to one group *at the expense of* another group. Thus the more well off sometimes perceive themselves to be losers in relation to a program that seeks to confer some benefits on the less well off. Whites sometimes perceive themselves to be losers in relation to a policy or a program that confers special benefits on minority groups.

Redistribution runs in several directions. Some programs redistribute items of value from the less well off to the more well off or from minorities to whites, but usually such programs are not perceived as redistributive. They do not generate the hot political controversy that is associated with redistributive attempts in the other direction. Thus the politics of redistribution almost always involves situations in which the intended beneficiaries are the relatively disadvantaged in society.

Since redistributive policy involves a conscious attempt to manipulate the allocation of wealth, property, rights, or some other value among broad classes or groups in society, the actors perceive that there will be distinct winners and losers. The stakes are thought to be high and this fact means that the policymaking process will be marked by a high degree of visibility and conflict. The coalitions that form over any redistributive issue may change in composition depending on the issue (integrated schools, open housing, public welfare programs) but they can generaly be identified as a proponent ("liberal") group and an opponent ("conservative") group. Their debate on the issue at hand is cast in ideological terms. Whether redistributive policy will emerge from the coalitions' conflicting viewpoints depends on the presence of strong presidential leadership and the willingness of participants to retreat from ideological stances and adopt compromises. The principal political consideration among the participants during the process is who gets what at the expense of whom. Chapter 6 focuses on the congressional-bureaucratic relationship when redistributive issues are at stake.

Examples of redistributive policy include setting progressive personal income tax rates so that more affluent people pay a higher percentage of their incomes in taxes than do less affluent people; requirements that housing, public accommodations and facilities, and public education be available to all, without racial discrimination; requirements of affirmative action in hiring by federal contractors to increase the employment of women and minorities; the provision of employment and training programs, food stamps, or special legal services for the disadvantaged; and government-sponsored health insurance to help the elderly meet the costs of medical care.

Foreign and defense policy

Policy typologies in nondomestic issue areas are less clear-cut than in domestic areas. Lowi (1967: 324–325) suggests that there are three distinctive patterns of politics in foreign policy. The first is crisis foreign policy. In this situation the perception of a threat to the national security cuts across normal channels of decisions, and an elite of formal officeholders within the executive branch makes the decisions with a minimum of conflict. In the absence of a crisis, there is time for "normal" patterns and concerns to emerge. Institutions become involved and interactions occur over a number of questions. Foreign policy then is basically either distributive or regulatory, with much the same sets of characteristics as domestic distributive or regulatory policy types.

In the area of defense policy, which has both domestic and foreign policy aspects, Huntington (1961) has identified two types—strategic and structural defense policy. Strategic defense policy is oriented toward foreign policy and international politics, and it involves the units and uses of military force, their strength, and their deployment. Structural defense policy focuses on domestic politics and involves decisions about the procurement, allocation, and organization of personnel, money, and materiel that constitute the military forces. Structural decisions are made primarily within the context of strategic decisions and are made to implement those decisions.

We have drawn on both Lowi and Huntington in developing our ideas about the three categories of foreign and defense policy: structural, strategic, and crisis. All three types will be examined in more detail in Chapter 7.

Structural policy. Structural policies and programs aim primarily at procuring, deploying, and organizing military personnel and materiel, presumably within the confines and guidelines of previously determined strategic decisions. Since the federal government has no competitors in providing defense, the element of total subsidy for the enterprise is a given. But the details of that subsidy can vary greatly.

Thus, as indicated in Table 1–3, structural policies are closely related to distributive policies. The process is characterized by the presence of subgovernments, by decentralized decision making, by nonconflictual relationships among the actors, and by decisions that treat internal resources as unlimited and separable. Policy decisions emerge from the formal legislative process (bill introduction, committee hearings, passage by the House and Senate). Although Congress is generally responding to executive requests rather than initiating policy in this area, it nonetheless has final decision power.

Examples of structural policies include specific defense procurement decisions for individual weapons systems; the placement, expansion, contraction, and closing of military bases and other facilities in the United States; the retention, expansion, or contraction of reserve military forces; and the creation and retention of programs that send surplus farm commodities overseas.

Strategic policy. Strategic policies and programs are designed to assert and implement the basic military and foreign policy stance of the United States toward other nations. Policy planning and proposals resulting from that planning stem primarily from executive branch activities. A number of executive branch agencies compete, bargain, and sometimes engage in conflict during policy development. Decisions are made by these agencies, with the final approval of the President. Public debate and congressional involvement usually occur after the formal decisions are announced. Congress may get involved in several ways—committees or individuals may lobby executive agencies for particular decisions, Congress may respond to an executive request for legislation to implement a decision already made, or Congress may protest and alter an action already completed. Congress does not make strategic decisions by itself; thus the influence of Congress as a whole can be high, but that potential influence is often used to respond supportively to executive branch initiatives.

Examples of strategic policies include decisions about the basic mix of military forces (for example, the ratio of ground-based missiles to submarine-based missiles to manned bombers); foreign trade (tariffs and quotas for specific goods and nations); sales of U.S. arms to foreign nations; foreign aid; immigration; and the level and location of U.S. troops overseas (both in general and in relation to specific "trouble spots").

Crisis policy. Crisis policies are short-run responses to immediate problems that are perceived to be serious, that have burst on the policymakers with little or no warning, and that demand immediate action. The occurrence of crisis situations is unpredictable and tied to external (nondomestic) events. The principal actors are elite officeholders who work cooperatively together with a minimum of publicized conflict. Visibility of the decision-making process is also low, except to the extent that press releases and press conferences inform the public. The involvement of Congress is informal and limited and is usually made in the mode of consultation with key individuals. The full body may get involved formally, usually after the crisis, to make the action legitimate or to forbid similar exercises of executive power in the future.

Examples of crisis policies include decisions about the U.S. response to the Japanese attack on Pearl Harbor in 1941; the impending French collapse in Indochina in 1954; the Soviet Union's placement of missiles in Cuba in 1962; the North Korean seizure of a U.S. Navy ship in 1968; and the Cambodian seizure of a U.S. merchant ship in 1975.

THE REST OF THE BOOK

In the remainder of this volume we will develop the notions that have been introduced in this chapter—especially the involvement of subgovernments in policymaking, the need for cooperation and the potential for conflict between Congress and the bureaucracy, and the presence and effect of different policy types. Chapter 2 will discuss the actors in the congressional-bureaucratic relationship: members of the House and Senate, congressional staff, politically appointed members of executive branch agencies, and civil servants (and their military and foreign service equivalents) in policy-making positions in agencies.

Chapter 3 will focus on the occasions for interactions among the actors and will describe the resources available to Congress and the bureaucracy in those interactions.

In Chapters 4 through 7 we will use empirical case studies to illustrate congressional-bureaucratic relations in each of the six policy areas identified above. We will focus on the subgovernment phenomenon where it is present. In the absence of a subgovernment, we will describe the broader congressional-executive interactions that do occur. A caveat might be offered at this point regarding the policy categories we use. Reality in government is never as simple or clearcut as analysts and students might wish. The policy categories we have suggested are not mutually exclusive—some policies will display attributes of more than one category. We have selected examples that best fit each policy type, and where individual policies fall into more than one category, we have distinguished the different parts.

In Chapter 8 we will summarize our findings about congressional-bureaucratic interactions in the various policy arenas and make an overall assessment of the substantive policy impact of the relationship between Congress and the bureaucracy.

~2~

Actors in the relationship

AS CONGRESS and the bureaucracy interact on policy matters, it is clear that there are a number of actors involved and that they behave differently from one another in a variety of general and specific ways. For example, members of authorizing (legislative) committees and appropriations committees behave differently. Staff members in the two houses vary in their approaches to legislation as do staff members serving a committee as opposed to those working in individual members' offices. Presidential appointees in the White House or Office of Management and Budget may act quite differently from presidential appointees at the cabinet and subcabinet level. Civil servants may take very different views of the policy world depending on whether their assignment places them in a line operating position, a staff position (especially one dealing with budgetary matters), or a legislative position. Their attitudes and activities may also vary with their assignment to a Washington office or to a field office.

Differences in behavior not only distinguish different groups of actors, but also have important implications for the nature of the relationship among the actors (the degree of cooperation or conflict) and for the policy emerging from that relationship (its substance, direction, and magnitude). In this chapter we will begin to make some observations about the nature of the relationships among congressional and bureaucratic actors and about the effect of those relationships on policy and policy change. The next two sections present a description and comparison of four major classes of actors—members of the House and Senate, congressional staff members, political appointees in the executive branch, and civil servants. The elements described, when taken together, present a picture of the institutional setting in which the actors work, as well as a portrait of traits that characterize them in the aggregate. The various elements described—political expertise, method of selection, loyalties, demographic factors, and so on—were selected for two principal reasons: their demonstrated importance as evidenced by their treatment in the literature, and their comparability across at least several classes of actors.

These profiles of institutional setting and group characteristics of actors are presented not only to familiarize the reader with the actors by conveying basic descriptive information, but also to serve as an aid for subsequent analysis of factors that explain the cooperation or conflict present in their relationships and the policy that results from those relationships. In the concluding section the impact of specific role orientations on the likelihood of conflict or cooperation and the nature of that conflict or cooperation is assessed. Various institutional and role constraints suggest that some conflicts between various individuals in different positions and roles are almost surely going to crop up, because institutional loyalties sometimes push in different directions and because the scope and substance of policy interests are likely to be different.

It should be noted that some institutional changes (often called "reforms") were made in Congress in the first half of the 1970s. The following discussion takes account of those changes where they seem to have had an impact, although in many cases the impact has been somewhat minimal. (On these changes see Davidson and Oleszek, 1977; Dodd and Oppenheimer, 1977; Rieselbach, 1977; and Welch and Peters, 1977.) In 1978 Congress passed a civil service reform bill that might, ultimately, have some impact on the way the bureaucracy conducts business, although it will take a number of years for any such impact to develop. (For a summary of the new law see Cooper, 1978.) Change does occur in congressional and bureaucratic institutions, but it is usually slow. New forms are often absorbed into customary modes of conducting business with only minor adjustments.

THE INDIVIDUALS INVOLVED

This section presents aggregate profiles of major clusters of participants in the relationships between Congress and the bureaucracy: members of Congress, congressional staff members, political appointees in the executive branch, and civil servants.

Geographical representation

Congress, by definition, is geographically representative. Since the reapportionment decisions of the federal courts applying to the House of Representatives in the 1960s, rural, suburban, and urban areas are all represented roughly in accord with their proportion of the total population. If there is any geographical bias in Congress it may be in the overrepresentation of smaller towns in terms of where members were born and raised. This is true of House leaders, for example (Nelson, 1975).

Many congressional staff members, particularly those on personal staffs, come from the state of their first employer. Once established, however, they may well go to work for a member from a different state. A recent study showed that close to two thirds of personal staff members in the Senate retained a legal residence in the same state as the senator for whom they worked (Fox and Hammond, 1977).[1] Although reliable figures are scarce, it is reasonable to conclude that staff members in Congress come from all over the United States (with a few from foreign countries) and are probably broadly repesentative in geographical terms. Regardless of their own place of birth and upbringing, some personal staff members will have concrete responsibility for tending to the welfare of the geographic constituency of the legislator for whom they work—assignment to constituency work is not limited to staff who come from the same geographic area as their employing legislator.

Federal political executives—that is, the major appointed figures in the executive branch—are also generally geographically representative of the entire population (Stanley, Mann, and Doig, 1967: 9–12, 110).[2] Compared to the general population in terms of birthplace, political appointees were underrepresentative only of the East South Central cen-

---

[1] Fox and Hammond, 1977, is the main source of data on congressional staff members. Their samples vary in size depending on the characteristic they discuss and their method of data collection; the samples range between about 160 and 480 Senate personal staff members, between about 50 and 450 House personal staff members, and about 300 committee staff members. They focus on staff professionals (omitting clerical and secretarial positions). That focus is useful for our purposes since it is the staff professionals that are in a position to have some impact on the shaping of policy.

[2] Stanley, Mann, and Doig, 1967, will be used frequently in the following pages. Their study is based on data on about 1600 appointments made to about 180 top federal positions from early 1933 through part of 1965. These positions include the secretaries, undersecretaries, assistant secretaries, and general counsels of the cabinet level departments and the three military services; the administrators and deputy administrators of a number of major independent agencies; and the members of seven regulatory commissions and boards. We shall use their terminology of "federal political officials" when presenting their results.

sus region (Kentucky, Tennessee, Alabama, Mississippi). Compared on the basis of legal residence at the time of the appointment, only the South Atlantic census region was overrepresented (simply because Washington, D.C., is in this region). And on the basis of location of principal occupation at the time of the appointment, the distribution for political appointees again roughly mirrored that of the general population, although the Washington area overrepresentation was even more pronounced.

Federal political executives did heavily overrepresent larger cities, however, when the size of their city of principal occupation at the time of appointment is compared to the general population. Individuals from Washington (28 percent of all those appointed) and New York City (14 percent of all those appointed) dominated.

Members of the higher civil service (defined as GS 14s and above in this instance)—the policy level of the civil service—overrepresent the East and urban backgrounds when compared to the general population. The South is underrepresented. The Midwest and West are represented almost perfectly (Meier, 1979: 171). Thirty-nine percent of the higher civil servants in 1974 came from the East and 22 percent from the South. The population in general was located 28 percent in the East and 31 percent in the South. In terms of birthplace 51 percent of the general population had an urban birthplace but 76 percent of the higher civil service had urban birthplaces.

Education

Virtually all of the principal actors in Congress (both members and professional staff) and the actors in the policymaking positions in the executive branch have a considerable amount of formal education, and all groups are about equally well-educated. Table 2–1 summarizes data

Table 2–1: Formal education of policymakers and the general public

Group	Date of data	Less than college	Some college, no degree	College degree or more
U.S. Representatives	1966	7	14	79
U.S. Senators	1966	4	13	83
Congressional staff (professionals)	1972	6	5	89
Federal political executives	1961–65	2	5	93
Higher civil service (GS 14+)	1974	1	3	96
General adult population	1974	69	18	13

Sources: For Representatives and Senators, Jones, 1967: 49; for congressional staff, compiled from data in Fox and Hammond, 1977: 175; for federal political executives, Stanley, Mann, and Doig, 1967: 18; for higher civil service and general adult population, Meier, 1979: 171.

on specific groups and compares them to the general population. Note that the data come from slightly different periods of time so they are not precisely comparable, but they certainly sustain the point that by any standard the policymakers are very well-educated. A very large proportion of these groups have education beyond the college level— either in graduate school or in law school. This held true, for example, for 60 percent of the Representatives, 69 percent of the Senators, 46 percent of higher civil servants defined as GS 15s and above (Stanley, Mann, and Doig, 1967: 18; data for 1963), and 63 percent of "supergrades" (GS 16, 17, and 18 and equivalents) in the civil service (Corson and Paul, 1966: 166; data for 1963).

Occupation

Reliable comparative figures on occupation of various policy-making groups *before* they attained their present position are hard to come by for several reasons. First, many individuals begin their careers in public service, either elected or appointed, and so their occupation is simply one of public service/politics. Second, when asked, many individuals, particularly in Congress, list several occupations. But examination of various figures leads to support for some general statements (although a table with nice percentages would be misleading):

In Congress about half of House members are lawyers and about two thirds of Senators are lawyers. About one quarter of each house comes from a business background (some of them are also lawyers). Educational backgrounds are well represented too (17 percent of House members and 12 percent of Senate members in 1977–78). (See Ripley, 1978: 94–97.)

Most committee staff members (no data are available on personal staff members) come from other public service positions (35 percent in the executive branch and 30 percent from other congressional positions, mostly positions on personal staffs). Only a few come from business (3 percent) or from the private practice of law (9 percent). (See Fox and Hammond, 1977: 175.)

Federal political executives between 1933 and 1965 came to their government positions predominantly from business or law backgrounds (about one quarter from each category). Another 7 percent came from educational backgrounds (Stanley, Mann, and Doig, 1967: 34).

A sample of higher civil servants analyzed since 1967 shows that most higher civil servants (GS 15s and above and their equivalents) begin their careers in public service (40 percent); a large proportion come from business (30 percent); and a smaller but sizable proportion come from educational backgrounds (15 percent). (See U.S. Civil Service Commission, 1976: 35.)

What stands out in a comparative review of the backgrounds of the four groups of actors is (1) the public service orientation of all categories of actors except federal political executives, (2) the dominance of a legal background in Congress, (3) the importance of a business background in all groups, and (4) the sizable representation of education (both public and private schools, colleges, and universities) in all groups of actors. Thus it is not fanciful to imagine that in discourse among these groups the concepts and language of the law and business are often predominant, with some familiarity with the concerns peculiar to educational institutions. It also seems likely that because of their much weaker public service orientation and experience federal political executives probably find it most difficult to become accepted as fully legitimate (see Heclo, 1977, for considerable confirmation of this speculation).

Age

Members of Congress and others in top level policymaking positions in the executive branch do not differ greatly in terms of average age. Only congressional staff members are somewhat younger, although not enough to put them clearly in a different "generation" (a vague notion at best). In 1977 the average age of Senators and Representatives together was 48 (about 54 for the average Senator and 47 for the average Representative). (See Ripley, 1978: 96–97.) Federal political executives averaged 48 years of age when appointed, and higher civil servants (GS 15s and above) averaged 48 years of age when appointed (Stanley, Mann, and Doig, 1967: 28). (The average age of all civil servants was 43 in 1973.) Congressional staff members, rather than being in their late 40s, tended to be just about 40 in the mid-1970s (Fox and Hammond, 1977: 173). Whatever difficulties individuals on the Hill and both career and appointed bureaucrats have in communicating with each other would not seem to stem from a "generation gap."

Sex and race

All of the groups we are discussing are dominated by white males. The 96th Congress (1979–1980) had only one woman and no blacks in the Senate (out of a total of 100 members), and only 16 women and 15 blacks among the 435 voting members of the House (there are two non-voting delegates in the House).

There are relatively few women in top congressional staff jobs at the professional level. One survey of professional staff (Fox and Hammond, 1977: 174) showed that 23 percent of Senate personal staffs, 31 percent of House personal staffs, and only 11 percent of committee staffs were women. A *Washington Post* story in 1976 (June 8) showed that only 6 percent of the 644 best-paying Senate staff positions were held by women. There are also relatively few blacks in these positions.

The higher civil service (GS 14s and above) is even more the preserve of white males. In 1974 96 percent were white and 98 percent were male (Meier, 1979: 171). No systematic data on sex and race are available for political appointees, but it is accurate to say that the numbers and percentages of women and minorities remain very small.

Previous governmental and political experience

Individuals in the highest positions—Senators, Representatives, and federal political appointees—are highly experienced in government and political service before they reach their positions. Congressional staff members are less experienced, and higher civil servants gain experience during their careers. Ripley (1978: 97–98) summarizes some of this experience for members of Congress:

> ... of the 179 senators who served between 1947 and 1957 only 10 percent of them had never held public office. Almost 80 percent of them had held public office for more than five years before coming to the Senate and 55 percent of them had held public office for more than ten years. Twenty-eight percent of them had been governors immediately before coming to the Senate and 28 percent came to the Senate directly from the House. ... A sample of members of the House in the 88th Congress showed that almost three-quarters of them had held a state or local party position, almost half of them had served in a state legislature, and only 6 percent had no discernible political experience.

Most congressional staff members, in large part because they are often younger than the other groups, have had less governmental experience before joining a personal staff (although those on committee staffs are more likely to have had such experience). Many congressional staff members will have had considerable political experience, however, usually through working in political campaigns, before joining a staff on the Hill.

Higher civil servants are not likely to have much governmental or political experience except that gathered through their careers, usually just in their own agency and, less frequently, in several federal agencies. But their experience in their own agency is likely to be spread over many years.

Of all federal political executives appointed between 1933 and 1965 only 15 percent had had no federal service of any kind prior to assuming office and more than three out of five had had federal administrative experience (Stanley, Mann, and Doig, 1967: 42, 45).

Beliefs

Although there is a lot more to learn, some research has been done that characterizes both the beliefs about government and the political ideology of the groups of policymakers being considered here (Aberbach and Rockman, 1976, 1977, 1978; Meier, 1979; Meier and Nigro, 1976; and Fox and Hammond, 1976).

Members of Congress, federal political executives, and higher civil servants all seem to believe in the legitimacy of subgovernments. They also generally believe that interest groups should have a high degree of access to both Congress and the bureaucracy (Aberbach and Rockman, 1977, 1978). No specific examination of congressional staff attitudes has been undertaken but it would be surprising if they held attitudes on these points differing from their appointing members.

The political ideology of members of Congress can be expected to change, probably slowly, over time depending on the outcome of elections. There is some evidence that at any given time that ideology is probably not too far out of line with that held by higher-level officials in the bureaucracy (Aberbach and Rockman, 1977). The higher civil service levels of the bureaucracy seem to hold abstract beliefs slightly more liberal than the general public but not far different from the public on specific issues (Meier, 1979: 172–173).

The ideology of congressional staff members, not surprisingly, mirrors rather closely the individuals in Congress for whom they work and by whom they were appointed (Fox and Hammond, 1977). The ideology of federal political executives, in theory, reflects that of the appointing president but, in practice, probably comes to mirror that of the agency or department in which they work.

Thus, there is widespread agreement among different groups of actors with regard to some key beliefs about the functioning of government. And, even with regard to political ideology, there are forces that minimize differences between groups, although party affiliation may still divide Democrats from Republicans and may make relationships between a president and political executives of one party and a Congress controlled by another party somewhat difficult.

Summary

Table 2–2 summarizes the personal characteristics just discussed. When added to the information in the following section, a composite picture of the various groups of policy actors begins to emerge that shows that these characteristics can have some impact on the nature of relations between the groups as they labor on public policy.

Table 2–2: Personal characteristics of major congressional and bureaucratic policy actors

Characteristics	Senators and Representatives	Congressional staff members	Higher career civil servants	Federal political executives
Geographical representativeness	Broadly representative geographically; overrepresentative of small towns	Broadly representative geographically	Broadly representative	Broadly representative geographically; overrepresentative of large cities (especially New York and Washington)
Education	Highly educated	Highly educated	Highly educated	Highly educated
Occupation	Heavily in law and business; some educators; many professional politicians	Occupational specialty tied to job; many professional public servants; some generalists	Occupational specialty tied to job; many professional public servants; many with business background; some educators	Heavily in business and law; some educators
Age	Median: late 40s (senators slightly older)	Median: about 40	Median: late 40s	Median: late 40s
Sex and race	Mostly white males	Mostly white males	Mostly white males	Mostly white males
Previous governmental and political experience	High experience in both government and politics	Limited government experience; more political experience	High government experience through civil service career	Moderately high experience in federal service
Beliefs	Believes in subgovernments and interest group access; ideology shifts with election results	Believes in subgovernments and interest group access; ideology reflects that of congressional employer	Believes in subgovernments and interest group access; ideology reflects that of agency	Believes in subgovernments and interest group access; ideology reflects that of agency

THE INSTITUTIONAL SETTING

The institutional setting in which congressional and bureaucratic actors function is simply the general work environment that serves as a framework for any person in a particular job. A member of Congress operates in a different job environment from an agency head, as does a staff member for a congressional committee from a Secretary of a department. The literature suggests a number of factors important in the institutional setting or job environment for each of the four groups of actors being examined. These include method of selection, job tenure and orientation, principal loyalties and representativeness, substantive specialization, professionalism, political expertise, and anonymity. In general, these factors are relatively unchanging over time, regardless of the individuals holding the positions.

Method of selection means simply how actors achieve the positions they hold. The principal options are election, political appointment, or merit advancement. *Job tenure and orientation* is related to the means of selection and involves the length of service and careerist aspirations associated with different actors. *Principal loyalties* involve the actors' perceptions of the entity to which they feel they owe primary service. *Representativeness* of various actors varies both according to the geographic area represented (national versus local) and the breadth of interests represented (broad-gauged interests versus narrow, special interests). Do actors tend to become expert in a few issues (specialists) or do they tend to have a general understanding of many issues (generalists)? The notion of *degrees of substantive specialization* addresses these questions. An actor's identification with a profession, in addition to identification as a government employee, is the focus of the discussion of *degree of professionalism*. The *degree of political expertise* inherent in different actors' jobs involves how political those jobs are and how much political skill is necessary for successfully holding them —skills in bargaining, negotiations, and competing for limited amounts of power and resources. The final factor presented to describe the institutional setting is the *degree of anonymity* (or conversely, visibility) associated with the actors—how publicly visible are different groups as they perform their daily routines?

Method of selection

Of the four groups, only one—members of the House and Senate— is elected. This simple fact makes an enormous difference in the kinds of considerations that are most salient to members as they deal with policy. Concern for job security nurtures a predisposition for congressmen to provide the voters back home with sufficient tangible benefits that they will reelect the providers. Congressmen usually evaluate their behavior, either consciously or unconsciously, in terms of the impact it will have on the electoral constituency and the constituency's reaction to it (Mayhew, 1974).

Once in Congress, members seek appointment to specific committees and subcommittees for a variety of reasons (see Fenno, 1973). A number of members consciously seek positions because of the electoral advantage it can bring them. Even those who pursue memberships primarily because of their policy interests and because of their interest in increasing their influence within their chamber are mindful of opportunities a given assignment might afford them to serve their constituents. As members become more senior, they are generally less vulnerable at election time and can afford to pursue policy views that are particularly congenial to them as they work in committee and subcommittee settings.

The congressional staff is appointed by members of Congress and so reflect some of the members' concern with reelection and constituents. But, given the fact that an experienced staff member with an individual Senator or Representative can probably find another such job with a different member if his employer should lose an election, his or her personal stake is not nearly as strong as the member's own stake.

Political appointments in the executive branch are made by the President. At least in theory, he is responsible for selecting the appointees, but in practice many appointees are chosen by other high-ranking officials in his administration, either because they know and want a particular individual or because he or she comes highly recommended by an important party figure—such as a major contributor of funds or an important Senator or Representative.

Civil servants and their military and foreign service equivalents are appointed on the basis of competitive examinations in the first instance and they advance on the basis of merit after that.

Job tenure and orientation

Not surprisingly, job tenure and orientation are related to the way an actor acquires his office. Personnel turnover in positions dependent on electoral results is greater than in nonelective positions among civil servants. The shortest length of service occurs among political appointees in the executive branch. Median tenure in the mid-1960s was only 28 months in a position and 31 months in an agency (Stanley, Mann, and Doig, 1967: 57; see also Heclo, 1977: 104). Because of their short tenure, political appointees generally have their careers in some field other than government service.

Tenure for individual congressmen will always be uncertain because these are elective positions, but overall length of service in Congress has increased over time (not always steadily, depending on election results). The average number of years of service for members of both houses has dropped a bit in the 1970s but is still high: in 1977 it stood at almost ten years for a Senator and over eight years for a Representative. Careerist aspirations are now well entrenched among most members of Congress. (See Huntington, 1973; Polsby, 1968; Price, 1971; and Witmer, 1964 on the development of a congressional career.)

Although data are relatively scarce, it seems that many congressional staff members have become oriented toward a career in legislative staff work and are able to realize their ambitions, in many cases, for two reasons: First, the long service of the members (the appointing authorities) helps them stay in their positions for a long time. Second, even if their original patron is unseated they are often sought out by new members of the House and Senate and offered jobs because of the high value placed on their experience. (On the development of a congressional staff career see Fox and Hammond, 1977: 62–65.) The size of congressional staff has expanded dramatically in recent years—between 1967 and 1976, for example, Senate personal staff increased by 86 percent, House personal staff increased by 71 percent, Senate committee staff increased by 147 percent, and House committee staff increased by 163 percent. Thus it is not surprising that a number of staff members are still both relatively young and relatively junior in service. Some years from now we will be better able to tell how many of them are making their careers on the Hill.

Careerism among bureaucrats at the policymaking levels is characterized by long service but low mobility in terms of shifting occupational specialties, shifting between agencies, and shifting between Washington and federal field installations (see Corson and Paul, 1966: 22, 175, 176, and Stanley, 1964: 27, 32–34, 102–103). In the early 1960s, for example, the higher civil servants had an average length of service of 23 years. Almost three quarters of these individuals had served for more than 20 years. Over 86 percent of them had spent their entire careers in no more than two departments (almost 56 percent had been in only one department) and over 68 percent had served in no more than two bureaus (over 37 percent had only been in one bureau). Movement between Washington headquarters and field offices was very low (almost 90 percent had never left headquarters to go into the field). Recent figures published by the Civil Service Commission (1976) show the same lack of mobility in the 1970s.

Corson and Paul's figures on supergrades in the civil service in 1963 show the same pattern: two thirds had worked in no more than two bureaus and about 40 percent in only one. About half had worked in the same agency or department for their entire careers. Only 15 percent had ever worked outside the federal government once they had begun service and over three fourths had held all of their federal jobs in the same occupational field.

The civil servants are the most career-oriented of all the four groups and are also most likely to serve a full career wholly within a single institutional location. For example, a sample of federal civil servants interviewed in 1960 and 1961 showed that most were highly intent on staying in federal service; 88 percent of the general employees were very sure or fairly sure they wanted to stay in federal service, and only 7 percent planned to leave. Among executives in the civil service 94 percent were very sure or fairly sure they wanted to stay and only 3 percent planned to leave. Even among professionals (natural scientists, social scientists, and engineers whose major loyalties might be to their professions and not to the government organization with which they were employed) there was a high propensity to stay with federal service. Between 69 and 82 percent of these three professional groups were either sure or fairly sure they wanted to stay in federal service, and only between 10 and 18 percent planned to leave (Kilpatrick, Cummings, and Jennings, 1963: 188). Predictably, civil servants who were older and had more service were the most wedded to remaining.

Principal loyalties and representativeness

The principal loyalties of members of the House and Senate are generally split between loyalty to their constituencies (or, more accurately, to their perceptions of various constituencies—see Fenno, 1978) and loyalty to their congressional parties. In general, congressional life is structured so that the two loyalties do not compete in head-on fashion a great deal of the time. When they do compete directly, a member will ordinarily stick with his perceptions of the constituency's interest.

Congressional staff members are primarily loyal to their appointing authority—that is, to the individual Senator or Representative responsible for having put them in their present jobs. Thus if a staff member's "sponsor" is highly oriented toward constituency interests the staff member is also likely to reflect that concern. If a sponsor is more oriented toward maintaining a given programmatic or ideological stance then the staff member is more likely to take that tack too.

In theory, executive political appointees are primarily loyal to the President, the President's program, and the administration as a collectivity. In practice, political appointees are also at least partially loyal to the organization to which they are appointed. Thus a Secretary of Agriculture will try to be responsive to the President who appointed him, but if career bureaucrats within the department perceive their interests to be at odds with the President's policy initiatives, the Secretary will find himself cross-pressured. Ordinarily he will try to find some compromise that will allow him not to disagree with the President, at least publicly, while still not "selling out" the department.

Civil servants are primarily loyal to the organizations in which they work and in which they are likely to make their career. They are perhaps less cross-pressured than the other major actors. Those in agencies who are also professionals (lawyers, engineers, scientists, etc.) may also feel considerable loyalty to the standards of their profession and may be cross-pressured by the perceived competing demands of profession and agency at times (see Wilensky, 1967).

Members of the House and Senate are concerned with representing their geographical areas—their districts or states—and are usually also concerned with representing a variety of interests they perceive to be important. While the notion of representation may be interpreted differently by different Senators and Representatives, they are virtually all genuinely concerned with being representative. For some this may mean focusing mostly on tangible benefits for the district and for the most important organized groups in the district. For others this may mean thinking about the broader needs of the district and of national interests and groups—both organized and unorganized. For most members representation probably involves a range of activities—from seeking a new post office for some town in the district or state to worrying about the welfare of all poor people or all cotton farmers or all black people or whatever group seems to the member to be important.

Congressional staff members are also interested in representation in the same several senses in which members are interested. Their interest is largely a reflection of the interests of their sponsors, although some individuals personally may also feel strongly about their representative capacities serving in a staff role.

Executive branch officials are also concerned with representation, but they are not concerned with a specific constituency in the same sense as individuals on Capitol Hill. The geographical ties to a local constituency of both political appointees and civil servants stationed in Washington are weaker than those of members of Congress and usually weaker than those of congressional staff members. They may retain some ties to the region in which they grew up, or more likely, their program may have a particular regional focus (an Agriculture Department official working with cotton price supports is, of course, going to be concerned mostly with the cotton growing regions of the South and an official in the Bureau of Reclamation is going to be concerned mainly with the arid lands of the West). But many Washington officials are involved with programs that have a national scope and they are therefore likely to think about the program in national terms.

But 87 percent of bureaucrats in the United States are not located in the metropolitan Washington, D.C., area. These individuals (over 2.35 million of them in 1976) are scattered throughout the country in a variety of federal field installations such as state, regional, and local offices. The bureaucrats who populate these field installations outside Washington have regional and local geographic loyalties tied to their agencies' programs, and they undertake their work in such a way as to maximize the size of their particular operation in their region, state, or locality.

In addition to geographic interests, bureaucrats—both political appointees and civil servants—are also typically concerned with representing interests they perceive to be important to their programs and worthy of their attention. In general, political appointees are expected to be supportive of and sympathetic to the programmatic interests of the President and to represent those interests to Congress. They also may be concerned with representing the interests thought to be important to their political party, and thus their concern with specific representation may not be very well-developed, although it seems reasonable to argue that a Republican Secretary of Labor, for example, will concern himself with representing managerial interests at least some of the time and that a Democratic Secretary of Labor will concern himself with representing organized labor's interests most of the time. To survive politically, appointees in departments and agencies are most likely to be representative of many interests involved with their agencies rather than representing only one or two interests. An appointee who principally advocates a single, narrow interest is apt to be a controversial figure and a political liability for the President's program and in the national electorate.

Political appointees can be representative in the critical sense of allowing competing points of view to be heard in the executive branch on controversial matters before final action is taken. Sometimes policy debates take place almost wholly within the executive branch and the major decisions are made and the major compromises are struck before the matter even becomes an important item on the congressional agenda. This was the case, for example, with the bargaining and arguments that led up to the passage of the Communications Satellite Act of 1962 and the Economic Opportunity Act of 1964 (Davidson, 1967: 390–393).

Civil servants often become very concerned with representing interests and organized groups they conceive to be important in the substantive fields in which they are working. Sometimes this representational activity simply takes the form of advocacy by strategically placed civil servants on behalf of interests and groups. In other cases the advocacy of specific interests by a bureaucracy becomes more institutionalized.

For example, some agencies use a variety of advisory committees to make and enforce decisions at the local level. These committees operate in several policy areas, including agriculture and land use (see Foss, 1960; Lowi, 1973a). A potential problem with advisory committees is that they may become captives of some segment of the served clientele, and bureaucrats, in heeding their advice, are thus responding to only a narrow interest group. This was the case with federal lands grazing policy (see Foss, 1960: chapter 6).

Degree of substantive specialization

Members of the House and Senate are both subject matter specialists and generalists. They are generalists because they are given the constitutional power—which they exercise with considerable, even if uneven, vigor—to oversee the entire range of federal governmental activities. They must consider and vote on literally everything the federal government does, at least in broad outline. Naturally, any individual is going to have a number of substantive areas in which his or her knowledge is minimal, but most Senators and Representatives who serve for more than a short time begin to develop familiarity with and some competence in a wide variety of subject matter areas.

At the same time members have also become specialists through their service on the standing committees and subcommittees of the two chambers. The committee system emerged in large part as the congressional response to a bureaucracy constantly growing in size, specialization, and expertise. Especially in the House—where in the 93rd Congress (1973–1974) the average member had assignments to only 1.6 standing committees and 3.5 subcommittees (Asher, 1974: 68)—members who serve for more than a short period become genuine experts in some piece of the policy world. In the Senate the members are spread more thinly because each Senator has more assignments—an average of 2.6 standing committees and 9.7 subcommittees in 1973–1974 (Asher, 1974: 68).

The congressional urge to specialize in order to compete with the bureaucrats is reinforced by the staff on the Hill. In both houses staff members have become genuinely expert in some bounded portion of the policy universe although staff members working in the offices of individual Senators and Representatives have much less time for work on substantive legislative matters than staff working for committees. Senate staff members—both those on committees and a few working in individual Senators' offices—are particularly important as specialists because of the limited time and attention the typical Senator can give to his committee and subcommittee assignments. Senators often rely principally on a staff member to do most of the substantive work in some subcommittees to which the Senator is formally assigned (Ripley, 1969a: chapter 8). Many staff members, including those on committees, are also expected to attend to political matters and to deal with constituents in a variety of ways.

In the bureaucracy the degree of substantive specialization in the civil service is very high. The main reason for the emergence of a large bureaucracy is, after all, to facilitate dealing with technical and complex topics. On the other hand, the degree of specialization among political appointees is typically very low—much lower than for a member of the House or Senate with even a few years of service. The typical political appointee in the executive branch has little experience in the subject matter with which he or she is expected to deal and usually does not stay in office long enough to develop much expertise through on-the-job training.

Degree of professionalism

"Professionalism" is used to denote allegiance on the part of individuals to a profession other than that of government employee. For example, if a chemist is employed by the Food and Drug Administration he or she may well remain loyal to the norms of the chemistry profession, attend meetings of the American Chemical Society, and subscribe to a variety of professional journals. Such an individual is likely to be equally concerned with national professional standards and judgments as with the narrower interests of the Food and Drug Administration as an agency.

Most professionalism in this sense resides in the civil service. Scattered throughout the bureaucracy are social scientists, natural scientists, engineers, dentists, physicians, and others whose professional identification is very high.

In the rest of the government—the appointed parts of the executive branch and both the elected and appointed parts of the legislative branch—the degree of professionalism is much lower. There are many lawyers, particularly in Congress, but they seem to retain little identification with abstract norms of the profession. For many, law was both a form of academic training and a natural entry into public service but not a profession actively practiced, at least for very long.

Degree of political expertise

By definition Senators and Representatives are and must be politicians. A few may not be, but they are likely to be very transient residents of the congressional institution. Members need the political skill of assessing the mood of their constituency and the amount of latitude they have within that mood. They also are likely to develop considerable bargaining skills as they pursue their daily tasks in Congress. Staff members typically possess a number of the same kinds of political skills. Some are hired expressly for their political skills that can be used to help the member gain reelection and/or have the maximum impact on substantive policy questions.

In the executive branch, political appointees presumably possess considerable political skills—both in advancing the interests of the Administration and the party of the President and in bargaining. Some political appointees are very adroit politically. In fact, some are so skillful that they develop their own constituency and support apart from the President who is presumably their sponsor. A classic case is that of Jesse Jones, Secretary of Commerce under President Franklin Roosevelt (Fenno, 1959: 234–247). His ties with powerful business interests and his excellent relations with Congress allowed him to take policy stands contrary to those desired by Roosevelt. Yet the President tolerated his behavior for over four years because, on balance, he thought his independent strength helped the Administration more than it hurt it.

Some political appointees turn out to be quite inept politically. President Eisenhower's Secretary of Defense, Charles Wilson of General Motors, was usually in hot water with some congressional committee for his seemingly thoughtless remarks ("What's good for the country is good for General Motors, and vice versa.") and behavior. In speaking of the cabinet specifically, Fenno (1959: 207–208) concluded that politically a skillful Secretary "maintains legislative-executive relations in an equilibrium and prevents them from deteriorating to the point where they hurt the President. What the ordinary Cabinet member supplies is a kind of *preventive assistance*. . . . The best that he can ordinarily do is to help the President in small amounts—probably disproportionate to the time he consumes doing it." The same generalization probably applies to the whole range of political appointees in the executive branch.

In theory, civil servants are supposed to be apolitical. They are barred from overt partisan activity by federal statute. The textbooks proclaim them to be "above politics" and concerned only with rational, economical, and efficient implementation of public policy objectives determined by their political superiors.

In the United States, however, the textbook model does not apply in large part. Senior civil servants are fully political actors and in many respects the governmental system in which they work expects that they will be if they are to be successful (see Heclo, 1977).

The political stance of the bureaucracy is the result of several factors—grants of administrative discretion, congressional reliance on the bureaucracy, and competition in advancing the agencies' perceived interests. Broad administrative discretion to fill in the gaps of basic legislation does not promote "neutral" administration. Bureaucrats' decisions have political impact and repercussions, and bureaucrats experience pressure for and against their administrative decisions. Congress relies on the bureaucracy as a primary source of policy ideas and initiatives, and policy is rarely neutral—it almost always conveys benefits to some and deprives others. Who wins and who loses is, after all, what politics is all about. The continuous maneuvering by senior agency officials to maximize the interests of their agencies and programs, especially at budget time, but also throughout daily routines, requires a high degree of political skill. Agency officials cannot afford to be neutral if their agency's interests are to be advanced.

Richard Neustadt has convincingly explained the basic reason for the political nature of our top civil servants: the governmental system puts them in direct competition with other actors and thereby breeds the necessity of developing political skills in order to gain or preserve the resources to perform programmatic tasks effectively. The following excerpt elaborates the idea (Neustadt, 1973: 132):

> . . . we maximize the insecurities of men and agencies alike. Careerists jostle in-and-outers (from the law firms, business, academic life) for the positions of effective influence; their agencies contend with the committees on the Hill, the Office of Management and Budget, other agencies for the prerequisites of institutional survival, year by year. Pursuit of programs authorized in law can be a constant struggle to maintain and hold support of influential clients, or the press. And seeking new authority to innovate a program can be very much like coalition warfare. Accordingly, most agencies have need for men of passion and conviction—or at least enormous powers of resistance— near the top. American officialdom may generate no more of these than other systems do, but it rewards them well: they rise toward the top.

Degree of anonymity

Anonymity is, of course, relative, and it may vary from observer to observer. To even an interested part of the general public, for example, virtually all of the actors being discussed here except some Senators and Representatives are anonymous. To most journalists covering Washington only Senators and Representatives and a few political appointees in the executive branch are consistently visible. A really skillful reporter will also come to know important congressional staff members and, occasionally, even a civil servant or two. Skillful lobbyists will tend to know individuals in all of the major clusters of actors. In general it would be most accurate to say that Senators and Representatives and the major political appointees in the executive branch, such as the President's cabinet, tend to be the most visible to most observers. Congressional staff members and civil servants tend to be relatively unknown to a large number of observers.

Summary of differences

Table 2–3 summarizes the discussion of the institutional work setting for the four major clusters of actors. The impact of these differences will be discussed next.

TYPICAL RELATIONSHIPS BETWEEN CONGRESS AND THE BUREAUCRACY: THE IMPACT OF ROLE

Thus far we have examined the work settings of the principal actors in the congressional-bureaucratic relationship and the aggregate characteristics of individuals in those positions. A third factor that can also help explain cooperation and conflict in the relationship between Congress and the bureaucracy is the actor's role.

Role is a complex concept as used in sociology and psychology, but its essential meaning is the "expected pattern of behavior associated with an actor who is in a particular relationship to a social system" (Davidson, 1969: 73). The role associated with any particular actor derives from several sources—the actor's individual characteristics and disposition, his or her institutional setting, the cumulative history of previous behavior in the position (by the actor and others), and expectations of others about how an actor in the position should act. For purposes of this volume, we will refer to role as regularities in behavior of actors—that is, how actors have tended to behave in the past.

Several well-established relationships between Congress and the bureaucracy that are critical to policymaking occur among various subgroups of actors: between congressional committees and clusters of bureaucrats; between congressional staff and bureaucrats; between executive branch liaison personnel and Congress; and among the institutional presidency, bureaucrats, and Congress. In the following pages, general descriptions of these types of interactions are presented (1) to illustrate the role of the actors (that is, the regularities in their behavior) and (2) to illustrate the kinds of accommodations the actors reach in their interactions. Specific examples of these types of interactions will be presented in Chapters 4 through 7.

Table 2–3: The general institutional setting for congressional and bureaucratic policy actors

Characteristic	Members of House and Senate	Congressional staff members	Executive branch political appointees	Civil servants and equivalents
Method of selection	Election	Appointment by Senators and Representatives	Appointment by President	Competition and merit
Job tenure and orientation	Relatively long service; careerist orientation	Relatively long service; relatively careerist orientation	Short service; noncareer orientation	Long service; career orientation
Principal loyalties	Constituencies and congressional parties	Sponsors (appointing members)	President and agency to which appointed	Agency
Degree of concern with representation	High for geographical constituencies and special interests	Moderately high for geographical constituencies and interests	Low for geographical units; moderately low for special interests	High for special interests; moderate for geographical units among non-Washington based civil servants; low for geographical units among Washington based civil servants
Degree of substantive specialization	Moderately high (especially in House)	Moderately high	Low	High
Degree of professionalism	Low	Generally low	Low	High for major subgroups of employees
Degree of political expertise	High	Moderately high	Moderately high	Moderately high (for highest grades)
Degree of anonymity	Low	High	Moderately low	High

Bureaucrats and the appropriations committees

The interaction between agency bureaucrats and Appropriations Committee members is of critical importance because Appropriations Committees allocate some (although not all) of the resources that enable bureaucrats to carry out their agency's programs. This interaction has been extensively and well studied (see Fenno, 1966; Horn, 1970; Wildavsky, 1974. See also LeLoup, 1977; and Gist, 1978). These studies support several generalizations about the nature of the interaction.

First, there is a great desire on the part of executive branch officials responsible for program operations to build up confidence over time with the members of the subcommittees that have specific jurisdiction over their appropriations. They believe that long-standing relations of good quality between themselves and the members will build a solid reputational base for them and will result in better (that is, larger) appropriations. In fact, there is solid empirical evidence that the longer individuals in an agency interact with its appropriations subcommittee the better their agency will do in its appropriations both in terms of the absolute size of appropriations and in terms of the percentage of its requests that are granted (Moreland, 1975).

Second, the general thrust of the behavior of agency bureaucrats is to reduce uncertainty in the treatment they receive in the appropriations process. They also seek to increase their appropriations and their share of appropriations but they do not usually do so at the risk of alienating subcommittee members and thus jeopardizing even their existing appropriations base. Basically they seek to reduce uncertainty by being solicitous of subcommittee concerns (for example, by following mandates in subcommittee reports scrupulously even though such mandates do not literally have the force of law) and by preparing thoroughly for formal hearings and by maintaining continuing informal contacts so that the subcommittee members always feel fully informed about agency activities.

Third, the basic attitude of most members of the House Appropriations Committee is that agency budget requests always contain some "fat" and that it is the committee's duty to trim the fat. But generally the members are also concerned with providing what they perceive to be enough money for an agency so that its programs are not damaged. And once a subcommittee has made its decisions its members will usually serve as agency defenders in the full Appropriations Committee and especially on the floor of the House.

Fourth, the basic attitude of most members of the Senate Appropriations Committee is even friendlier to the agencies. They think the House Committee usually cuts dangerously deep into agency requests and they are likely to restore a substantial portion of the cuts. They will raise some questions but are more disposed to accept bureaucrats' judgments about necessary resources. The differences in outlook of the House and Senate Appropriations Committees stem from the personnel shortage on the Senate committee, which makes them inclined to accept the executive's vision of what is needed without time-consuming scrutiny, and from the fact that Senators can choose their subcommittee assignments on the Appropriations Committee (in the House until 1975, the chair made the assignments) (see Morrow, 1969: 178). This leads Senators to seek subcommittees where they can dispense "pork" to their areas, and hence they are not keen on eliminating the surplus in requests.

Fifth, neither Senators nor Representatives on the Appropriations Committees seem to have much desire to engage in broad-gauged oversight of committee activities. Their oversight activity is more likely to focus on specific items of expenditure taken singly rather than posing broader questions about the societal impact of the agencies whose proposals are being considered. Members do seem disposed, however, to seek membership on subcommittees overseeing agency budgets that are relatively more "controllable" (that is, the product of annual appropriations, rather than other statutes).

Sixth, interest group representatives have an impact on appropriations decisions—often through the executive branch officials (sometimes at the behest of those bureaucrats) and sometimes through Appropriations Committee members, especially in the Senate. The thrust of such intervention by lobbyists is almost always to preserve advantages with which they are already blessed either in terms of level of support for a program important to them or in terms of specific report language favorable to their interests. Horn (1970: 189–190) cites a classic case of the latter kind:

> In 1965, a nationwide automobile rental firm, faced with competition in the Midwest from a small, subsidized airline that also rented cars to its passengers at various airports, successfully secured report language directing the Civil Aeronautics Board's attention to "the practice of certain air carriers to engage in noncarrier activities. . . ." The Senate subcommittee admonished the board to "continue to supervise these activities vigorously to make sure that such noncarrier operations are not being subsidized."

Finally, in general it can be said that in the appropriations process most of the important actors desire stability above all else, despite the differences in perspective indicated by the fact that members of Congress are directly responsible to constituents and bureaucrats are not. Fenno (1966: 348) summarizes the relationship between bureaucrats and the House committee very persuasively and his description could easily be broadened to cover the Senate committee, too.

The House Appropriations Committee–executive agency relationship is characterized on the one hand by conflict and uncertainty; it
is characterized on the other by a substantial agreement on what
should be done and is being done to minimize conflict and uncertainty
and, hence, to keep the relationship reasonably stable.

The sources of conflict lie in the difference between the program-
oriented goals of the agencies and the combination of economy-over-
sight goals of the Committee. . . . The existence of conflict helps to
promote uncertainty. And the sources of that uncertainty lie in the
difference in the political worlds inhabited by the nonelected executive and the elected Representative. . . .

Both groups, however, want to stabilize the relationship—want,
that is, to keep conflict and uncertainty to a tolerable and predictable
level—because it is in their interest to do so. For the agency, a stable
relationship is an aid to program planning and implementation. For
the Committee, a stable relationship is an aid to adaptation and survival—to its continued ability, that is, to meet House member and
Committee member desires.

Bureaucrats and the Ways and Means Committee

The House Ways and Means Committee has extensive and important jurisdiction: it contributes to congressional input into governmental tax policy, the source of revenue for all agencies; it oversees the
entire Social Security system, including Medicare; it legislates welfare
policy; and it makes trade policy, including tariffs and import and export quotas.

In this relationship executive officials work so closely with the Committee that, according to one member of the Committee, "they become *part* of the Committee" (Manley, 1970: 350). Executive officials
are invited to participate, not just to observe, in the meetings of the
Committee at which decisions are made on the details of legislation
that will be reported to the House floor. There is also a great deal of
interaction between executive officials and Committee members outside formal committee hearings and meetings.

Ways and Means members participate in the details of policymaking
(although before 1975 only a few members dominated the detailed
work of the committee; since then there has been broader participation
—see Rudder, 1977). They can, collectively, hold up the endorsement
of some major executive branch initiatives. The members of the Committee do not, however, engage in broad-gauged oversight of the agencies and major programs within their jurisdiction. They make changes
and additions in programs but without ever seeking or obtaining much
evidence on the results of their past handiwork and the agencies' interpretations of that handiwork in the implementation process (see
Pincus, 1974).

In general, it seems fair to say that the desire for stability is also a dominant motivation in the interactions between bureaucrats involved in programs within the jurisdiction of the Ways and Means Committee and the members of that Committee. Major changes are typically generated from the White House (Medicare, health insurance, tax reform, tax increases or decreases, new trade policy, new Social Security benefits). Thus the system of interactions is less stable than in appropriations, and the intervention of the White House and the President personally is more frequent.

Bureaucrats and congressional staff

Civil servants who are experts on subjects that are often complex and their counterparts on congressional staffs usually work together very closely (see Fox and Hammond, 1977: Chapter 7 and p. 197 on frequency of communications between the two groups). In general, the congressional staff members need the information that the civil servants can provide and usually it is forthcoming. This is true even when the executive branch and Congress are controlled by different political parties. In such cases the federal political executives and the majority of various standing committees may have major policy disagreements. Nevertheless, the cooperative relationships between the committee staffs and the bureau staffs continue. For example, in the 80th Congress (1947–1948) when the Democrats still controlled the presidency but the Republicans had won control of Congress, close staff cooperation still marked the relations between the Treasury Department and the Joint Committee on Internal Revenue Taxation even though tax bills were the subject of major public fights between the President and Congress (Kofmehl, 1977: 157). Regardless of party control there are also instances in which the executive branch and the congressional committee are clearly in disagreement on some policy but close technical cooperation between staff members continues unimpaired. Sometimes a staff member for an interest group will also become involved in these staff interactions and will serve to transmit the technical expertise of an executive branch hostile to a specific initiative to congressional supporters of different positions. This happened, for example, as the first federal air pollution legislation to contain federal abatement powers (which became the Clean Air Act of 1963) was developed in late 1962 and early 1963 (Ripley, 1969b).

In the area of tax policy a particularly close relationship between committee staff and Treasury Department staff has grown up (Manley, 1970: 342–346). In this case staff members from the Ways and Means Committee, from the Joint Committee on Taxation, and from the Treasury regularly meet and discuss a whole range of technical details. They even form "staff subcommittees" to pursue various topics. The importance of this close relationship is summarized by John Manley (1970: 344):

> First, the meetings ensure that by the time the Treasury Department sends its tax message the Joint Committee staff is well-versed in the complexities of the proposals and is therefore equipped to explain them to the members. Second, the predictions of Committee response made by the Joint Committee staff have been relayed to the top officials of the Treasury Department and become one more element in their calculation of what they should propose to Congress. Third, having worked closely together throughout the process the two staffs are better able to draft the necessary language after the Committee makes a decision and to present the issues during the Committee's deliberations on the bill.

Relations between members of appropriations subcommittee staffs in the House and Senate and civil servant technicians are also close. Wildavsky (1974: 55–56) summarizes the nature of this relationship and the reasons for it:

> Many agencies choose to keep subcommittee staff informed months and sometimes years ahead on new developments. This expedient enables the staff to have ready explanations if and when Congressmen make inquiries. . . .
> Although it appears that agency personnel are more dependent on committee staff than vice versa, the relationship is by no means a one-way proposition. The staff man knows that he can do a more effective job if he has the cooperation of the budget officer. For much of the staff's work is dependent on securing information from the agency about current programs and the possible effects of various changes. The staff may be blamed for not informing Congressmen of changes in agency plans and expenditures. And when complex problems arise, the agency may actually do the work for the staff. Mutual dependence is the order of the day and both sides generally regard their contacts as prerequisites to doing their best work.

In short, technicians working for both Congress and executive branch agencies have a large stake in maintaining good relations. This means that neither side should spring policy "surprises" on the other side without adequate warning and full discussion ahead of time.

Executive branch congressional liaison officials and members of Congress

Liaison officials throughout the executive branch have a particularly big stake in promoting and maintaining good relations with Congress (see Holtzman, 1970). Their job is to sell the policy positions favored by the executive branch and to promote a sense of congressional confidence in whatever part of the executive branch they are representing. There are many liaison actors in the executive branch—White House office liaison officials work directly for the President and his legislative priorities; departmental legislative liaison personnel (usually Assistant Secretary-level officials) are presidential appointees and promote the President's priorities, but they are also responsive to their department's legislative priorities; liaison officials within the specific agencies and bureaus of a department are concerned primarily with their agency's priorities. All of these liaison officials try to persuade Congress to adopt or not tamper with legislation to fulfill presidential, departmental, agency (and personal) priorities. Their congressional targets include party leaders, committee and subcommittee chairpersons, individual members, and congressional staff members.

There is, of course, considerable potential for tension when liaison officials face committees and individual members who have different predispositions from those of the executive branch. There is also considerable room for tension (and confusion) within the executive branch liaison operation itself—promoting the policy priorities of the President, the departments, and the agencies in an integrated and coordinated fashion is a mammoth challenge. Although in principle the President's priorities are supposed to be supported by the rest of the executive branch, in fact departments and agencies have their own legislative priorities, and these may or may not be compatible with the President's.

There is a natural tendency for liaison personnel from individual agencies to compromise with committee members and staff members in Congress, whereas the liaison personnel working directly for the White House have a stronger tendency to resist compromise. These natural tendencies contribute to tension within the executive branch liaison operation. (This tension reached its height in the Nixon administration. The President and Congress were ideologically at odds on a whole range of domestic issues, and the White House staff felt that the liaison officials for various agencies were too quick to abandon presidential principles. Therefore, the White House attempted unsuccessfully to centralize the entire executive branch liaison operation even more than it had been previously by making the chief liaison official in each agency and department directly responsible to the White House rather than to the agency head or department secretary.)

In contrast to the centralization of President Nixon's liaison activities, the liaison efforts during the first 18 months of the Carter administration were marked by chaos. White House liaison activities were uncoordinated and repeatedly offended key members of Congress. (See Bonafede, 1979; Elder, 1978; and Light, 1979, for details on liaison with Congress during the Carter administration.)

Carter's problems with legislative lobbying stemmed from a variety of personal, political, and institutional factors. Many of the personnel appointed to White House and department liaison jobs had limited experience with lobbying, with Congress, and with the political process in general. The nature of Congress had changed from the early 1960s —congressional reforms distributed power among more members, and members were displaying a greater sense of independence from congressional leaders and the President than they had done in the past. Part of Carter's problems were the result of his righteous, "above politics" attitude, and an unwillingness to engage in political horsetrading.

The Carter liaison staff recognized the severe problems they had in dealing with the 95th Congress and acted to correct them. They made a number of important changes to help focus the Administration's lobbying efforts in the late 95th and the 96th (1979–1980) Congresses. The changes showed they had learned from previous mistakes and illustrate the importance of smoothly functioning, coordinated relationships between executive liaison personnel and Congress. Some of the features of their "new" legislative lobbying effort included:

Expansion of White House liaison staff.

Clearly defining, ranking, and limiting in number the President's legislative priorities. (The 95th Congress had been swamped with "priority" proposals.)

Establishing formal issue-oriented task forces to steer the President's priorities through Congress by coordinating supporters in Congress, the public, and the press. (The task force approach had helped produce presidential victories on the B-1 bomber and the Panama Canal Treaty during the 95th Congress.)

Consulting more with members of Congress in the development of legislative proposals (rather than developing proposals in secret and springing them on Congress).

Coordinating and enlisting the services of constituent groups to promote Administration priorities in Congress.

Increasing personal contact of a continuous nature between White House and department liaison officials and members of Congress, and maintaining personal ties as a matter of course, not just when seeking a vote.

Increasing coordination with departmental lobbyists and placing departmental legislative proposals in second place to presidential priorities.

As the executive branch liaison staff became more experienced and as the revised legislative lobbying effort was implemented, congressional criticism and grievances diminished, at least for the time being.

The institutional presidency, Congress, and bureaucrats

The institutional presidency represents, or at least purports to represent, the President in dealing with the rest of the executive branch and Congress. The heart of the institutional presidency is in the White House, whose members are all political appointees, and in the Office of Management and Budget (known as the Bureau of the Budget until 1970), whose members are a mix of a few political appointees and a much larger number of career civil servants.

The principal role orientation of these officials as they interact with Congress is to create and/or maintain good relations with that body, simply because any President must have good relations in order to get desired legislation through Congress. At times, however, the programmatic or ideological integrity of policy positions may be viewed as more important by the President and his White House and OMB staff than smooth relations. When this occurs, tension characterizes the relationship. The degree of tension is heightened if different political parties control the presidency and Congress, and also if both sides are strongly committed to major ideological differences. In the Nixon administration, for example, tension in the relationship between Congress and the executive branch was very great, and Congress reacted by attempting to decrease the size of staff and the salary schedules for personnel in the White House and OMB. In 1974 Congress did make future directors and deputy directors of OMB subject to Senate confirmation.

In the triangular relationship among members of the presidency, the bureaucracy, and Congress, the President often confronts a preexisting, entrenched relationship between bureaus and congressional committees and subcommittees. If the President's policy preferences differ from those held by members of the entrenched relationship, and if he feels intensely enough about his preferences to want to pursue them and impose them, then it is inevitable that the White House and OMB officials, acting under his direction, are going to be viewed as disturbing influences by members of the entrenched relationship—committee and subcommittee members in Congress, their staff, and officials of the affected agency. When presidentially appointed departmental secretaries seek to control the bureaus within their departments (usually under presidential directive), they also are viewed by bureau chiefs (most of whom are civil servants) as disruptions to the normal ways of doing business with their congressional committees and subcommittees.

Even without presidential involvement, the institutional presidency is not viewed sympathetically by most of the bureaucracy, especially those at the operating level. By definition the White House and OMB staff play a centralizing role in the legislative process (see Neustadt, 1954, 1955); also by definition this tendency poses a threat to the stable relations and the stable policy preferences centered around agency-committee nexuses.

Bureau chiefs and agency heads complain that the centralizing forces in the executive branch don't understand the political realities that they must face on a day-to-day basis. Comments by two different civil servants are illustrative:

> Sticky problems arise because of the political isolation of the Bureau of the Budget. The Bureau does not have good comprehension of what is in the minds of key congressional committee chairmen and members we have to deal with. They find incomprehensible the political problems we try to explain to them. They see us as being more responsive to Congress than to the President. There may be an element of truth here but they don't understand Congress (Davis and Ripley, 1967: 762–763).

> *   *   *   *   *

> We have to tread a pretty thin line and we're always caught in a cross fire between the Budget Bureau and Congress. I just wish those people over there [in the Budget Bureau] had to carry those requests out—just once. They'd learn what the problems were. . . . The budget is made up over there, but we have to carry the ball. . . . They have no understanding of the climate up there, of the pressures, of the personalities (Fenno, 1966: 308).

In general, bureaucrats at the operating level see themselves as caught between unrealistic demands and pressures from their executive branch superiors and the pressures and demands—with which they may have more sympathy—emanating from members of the subcommittees that are essential to the existence and prosperity of their agencies. Agency officials often talk about this sense of being in the middle. Three statements from such officials serve to illustrate the general theme (Fenno, 1966: 308–309):

> Sometimes you wonder just who you are working for. I haven't been in too many embarrassing situations. With my relations with the Congress as they are, I may tell them that, frankly, I don't think I ought to tell them—that I have to maintain my loyalty to the department. Sometimes I go against the department.

> *   *   *   *   *

> Sometimes I'll go over to the Committee and talk about something with them. The first time I went, they told me it was confidential. And I said, "When I came through that door, I started working for the Committee. Whatever goes on in here just didn't happen as far as I'm concerned when I leave here." And I tell them that every time. Some-

times, I'm over here and the Secretary or someone will try to worm it out of me what's going on. But they know I won't tell them.

* * * * *

I've gone out and tried to develop contacts with congressmen, because that's the way the game is played. But I don't like it. You shouldn't have to lobby for your program. But politics being what it is, I've done a little more of that. . . . Some people higher up in the department object to our having any informal contacts with congressmen, but we'll just have to get around that, I guess.

Summary

The five general congressional-bureaucratic interactions discussed above are important ones that occur across all substantive issue areas. Although the individual actors involved may change depending on the issue area under consideration, the general patterns of interaction do not change very much. For example, House Appropriations Committee members maintain a fairly stable outlook in dealing with agency officials, regardless of the issue area or the personalities involved. The Committee members have close ties with many agency representatives and they work together cooperatively, but the Committee members look at agency requests with an eye toward cutting and trimming, and this can promote conflict. The preceding sections have highlighted some of the implications that different institutional outlooks have for cooperation and conflict, and the analytical material in Chapters 4 through 7 will continue to develop this notion.

Congressional-bureaucratic

interaction: Occasions and resources

INTERACTION BETWEEN congressional and bureaucratic actors is continuous and occurs in a variety of settings and for a variety of reasons. The most basic reason is, of course, the constitutionally based governmental feature of separate institutions sharing powers. This feature necessitates that the two branches interact in order to produce, implement, and assess governmental policy. In this chapter we discuss congressional-bureaucratic interactions during the production of policy in terms of the motivations of the actors, the resources they have to trade or withhold, the settings for their interaction, and the techniques that actors may use.

Much attention has been directed by scholars to congressional-bureaucratic interaction, particularly in the form of congressional oversight of bureaucratic activities (see for example, Harris, 1964; Keefe and Ogul, 1977; Olezsek, 1978: Chapter 9). The term *oversight* has been bandied about so much that its use may generate confusion. *Oversight* is used here as an aggregate term describing many congressional activities that are designed to keep tabs on what the bureaucracy is doing. A very specific kind of legislative oversight involves systematic and rational review and evaluation of programs. This activity is referred to here as program oversight. As the following pages will describe, program oversight does not occur as often as other kinds of oversight activities because the rewards for congressmen are not as enticing as the rewards for other activities.

MOTIVATIONS AND RESOURCES FOR INTERACTION

Motivations

Some interactions between bureaucrats and congressmen are simply necessitated by the structure of government within which these individuals work. The constitutional allocation of responsibilities discussed in Chapter 1 in effect mandates a considerable amount of interaction. In addition, the history of governmental and programmatic development for almost 200 years has overlaid the rudimentary constitutional necessities with a number of interactions decreed by statutes, other written documents, and custom. This overlay in a sense summarizes the motivations of the parties to the interactions. But to sort out the strata in the fashion of a political paleontologist would require a separate volume at a minimum. Thus the following brief discussion of motivation focuses on the present.

Both bureaucrats and members of Congress have a variety of motivations for becoming involved in specific ways in policy-related interactions between the two branches. Downs (1967: 88) presents a suggestive fivefold typology of the variety of motives that move bureaucrats. The first two categories are what he calls "purely self-interested officials" who "are motivated almost entirely by goals that benefit themselves rather than their bureaus or society as a whole." The last three categories are "mixed-motive officials" who "have goals that combine self-interest and altruistic loyalty to larger values."

> Climbers consider power, income, and prestige as nearly all-important in their value structures.
>
> Conservers consider convenience and security as nearly all-important. In contrast to climbers, conservers seek merely to retain the amount of power, income, and prestige they already have rather than to maximize them. . . .
>
> Zealots are loyal to relatively narrow policies or concepts, such as the development of nuclear submarines. They seek power both for its own sake and to effect the policies to which they are loyal. . . .
>
> Advocates are loyal to a broader set of functions or to a broader organization than zealots. They also seek power because they want to have a significant influence upon policies and actions concerning those functions or organizations.
>
> Statesmen are loyal to society as a whole, and they desire to obtain the power necessary to have a significant influence upon national policies and actions. They are altruistic to an important degree because their loyalty is to the "general welfare" as they see it.

In interacting with Congress, the bureaucrat's paramount concern is for the health and welfare of his agency. He seeks either to expand his agency's resources and influence or to maintain a low-profile status quo or to fight encroachments against the agency's resources and influence. However, in the case of at least one agency in recent years, the Office of Economic Opportunity, an agency head was given the responsibility of deliberately dismantling the agency by the President. Such occasions are rare, and the bureaucrat's general stance vis-a-vis Congress is to promote the longevity and welfare of the agency.

Congressmen are motivated by two general desires—to survive and/or advance politically and to pursue policy interests. Political survival and advancement are tied to constituency service and local interests, which in turn are tied to a member's reelection—survival in its most basic sense. Choice of policy interests may also be tied to political advantage: members may be most interested in policies that they feel will help them win reelection or advance to other desirable posts. These two factors influence all congressional activity (see Mayhew, 1974) including interactions with the bureaucracy, and they are particularly important in explaining congressional exercise of program oversight (Ogul, 1973). Because members' schedules are always full and there is insufficient time to do all the things worthy of doing, they use these twin desires to help them make choices and set priorities among their activities. Thus the utility of a particular interaction with some part of the bureaucracy may be assessed in terms of explicit calculations, such as "How will this help me with the folks back home?" or "How does this mesh with my personal policy preferences?" in addition to assessment of personal resources, status, and time available for the activity.

Resources

Both members of Congress and bureaucrats possess a range of formal and informal resources upon which they can draw as they seek to pursue their mixes of personal, organizational, and programmatic goals. These resources can be selectively granted and withheld by actors in both branches and thus derive their potency.

From the congressional perspective the formal powers of Congress provide a number of resources upon which individual members can draw if they are in a position to influence their use. These formal powers include, first, the decision about the existence or nonexistence of agencies. Second, Congress provides the jurisdictional and programmatic scope to specific agencies and the limits on that scope both through statutory authority and through money. Third, Congress provides personnel for the executive branch in several senses—through the giving or withholding of statutory authority, personnel money, and confirmation of key appointments. Fourth, Congress influences the specific structure of both programs and agencies through positive statutory action and through action on reorganization plans submitted by the executive branch.

In addition to possessing these formal powers as resources that can be drawn on in interactions with the executive branch, members of Congress also possess more intangible resources, such as the ability to provide or withhold good information on the intentions of other individuals in a policy subsystem or area, the ability to praise or criticize publicly individual bureaucrats, and the ability to build a favorable image of the agency as a whole for a variety of other actors in higher levels of the executive branch, interest groups, and the House and Senate, as well as for potential or aspiring bureaucratic competitors.

From the bureaucratic perspective the formal powers also provide a number of important potential resources. The bureaucracy makes a wide variety of specific decisions that are important to members of the House and Senate. These include formal powers over regulations determining how a program will be implemented; critical personnel decisions involving hiring, promotion, and location both geographically and hierarchically; geographic and programmatic patterns of spending; the timing of spending and other programmatic decisions; decisions about location of facilities; and the disposition of individual "cases" of persons seeking a specific agency ruling.

Bureaucrats also possess less formal resources. Two stand out: first, the ability of bureaucrats to enhance the personal standing and reputation of Senators and Representatives through a variety of forms of deference; and second, the provision of timely and accurate information about both substantive matters and the intentions of other actors in the policy subsystem.

The tie between motivation and resources

Given the time pressures facing members of Congress and higher level bureaucrats, specific individual activity is most likely to occur when both motivation for the activity and resources related to some hope of success are present concurrently. When motivation and resources do not reinforce each other, individual activity by a member or bureaucrat is much less likely. Thus a freshman Representative on the District of Columbia Committee may be highly motivated to criticize the Defense Department for allegedly sabotaging disarmament talks with the Soviet Union but there is little he can do about it; resources are absent and so activity—at least of a meaningful sort—is not likely to take place. However, if the same member becomes concerned about an alleged monopoly on parking in the District of Columbia and resulting exorbitant fees he may be in a position to do something about it if he can convince the chairman of the Committee to hold a hearing or make a few phone calls to the District of Columbia government.

Similarly, a bureau chief may devoutly wish for a large increase in the budget for his agency. However, if he cannot point to specific services to the districts of the senior members of the House Appropriations Subcommittee responsible for his agency he is unlikely to request more than a modest increase in the budget.

Resources can also be present when motivation for action is absent. A senior member of the Senate Armed Services Committee would certainly have the resources to inquire in a serious and perhaps influential way into alleged Defense Department footdragging on disarmament. But if that same Senator is a firm supporter of the defense establishment and simply does not trust disarmament agreements with communist nations then he is not going to use those resources. To take another example, if a bureau chief has two major programs and can point to great service to important Senators and Representatives from both programs he possesses at least some resources to pursue substantial budgetary increases in both programs simultaneously. However, it may be that he believes that program A will soon get into political hot water for reasons he cannot control and so he may choose to pursue increases only in program B, which he believes will be the backbone of agency success for many years to come.

A nice case of the tie between resources and motivation and the organizational and programmatic consequences of that tie is provided in the policy area of soil conservation (see Morgan, 1965, for a book-length treatment of many of the matters summarized in the following few paragraphs).

From the time that soil conservation districts began to be organized in 1936 a rivalry grew up between the Soil Conservation Service, representing centralized authority over the program in Washington, and land-grant agricultural colleges and their extension services, which wished to decentralize the program and gain control of it. Some members of the House and Senate with influence in agricultural matters sided with the SCS and a centralized program. Others sided with the extension service and land-grant colleges (backed strongly by the American Farm Bureau Federation). Morgan provides an analysis of the motivations of the key members on both sides of the question (which was finally settled in favor of the SCS and centralization during the Truman administration).

Constituency interests and interest group patterns seemed more important in shaping the alliances than party lines. For example, a key House Republican supporting the Farm Bureau-Extension Service position was formerly an employee of the Extension Service in his home state. An important House Democrat taking the same position came from a state that was a Farm Bureau stronghold. Two of the leading House supporters of the SCS position—one from each party—came from areas of the country that could be expected to benefit heavily from the small watershed program being put together by the SCS. In addition, the Republican came from a district in which the Farmers Union (a competing group to the Farm Bureau and in conflict with them on this issue) was strong. All of these individuals, on both sides, were relatively senior members of the House Agriculture Committee. Other interested parties in the House were on both the Agriculture Committee and the Agriculture Subcommittee of the Appropriations Committee. Critical individuals in the Senate held parallel positions and their positions and level of intensity also were related to factors such as the relative strength of the Farm Bureau or Farmers Union in their districts or states and the relative benefits provided their constituents by the SCS (including its proposed small watershed program) and by the Extension Service.

OCCASIONS AND TECHNIQUES FOR INTERACTION

Custom and law suggest many subjects that require interaction between Congress and the bureaucracy. These include budgeting; agency organization or reorganization; creation, amendment, or dissolution of a program or agency; personnel matters; evaluation of program performance; and location of projects. In interacting in these areas formal routines may be used—such as a formal hearing before a committee or subcommittee—and there may be formal outcomes, such as statutes, votes on reorganization plans, confirmation decisions, and committee and agency reports. Equally important, all subjects are also likely to be treated in a great number of informal interactions—phone calls, impromptu visits, lunches, cocktail parties. During these occasions a constant two-way flow of information and views on substance, procedure, individuals, and organizations is sustained.

No single listing of the occasions and techniques used by the participants in these interactions is likely to be complete. And, as is the case with any list, reality is not likely to be so neatly organized and categorized as the list may imply. Nevertheless it seems useful to identify and discuss the major occasions and techniques used both by individuals from the Hill and individuals in the bureacracy because, by inventorying the segments of reality, one has a better understanding of the parts and the whole to which they contribute. Naturally, different actors may be involved in different kinds of interactions, and actors may use several techniques during a particular interaction. Their decisions about when to get involved and what techniques to use also vary, but in general each actor makes decisions that he thinks will maximize his personal, organizational, and programmatic goals. The case presented in Chapters 4 through 7 will offer a fuller illustration of techniques and occasions for interaction.

Occasions for interaction

Budgeting. Budgeting is the most regularly recurring occasion for interaction between the bureaucracy and Congress. Budgeting, of course, involves the allocation of dollars among competing agencies and programs. The federal budget process is lengthy and complex and is divided into two major parts—first, the President's preparation of a budget document for the entire federal government, which essentially constitutes a request to Congress for funds to run the government; and second, the congressional budget process, which is essentially a response to the President's budget. The preparation of the President's budget involves widespread interactions internal to the various parts of the executive branch. The Congressional budget process—which includes the appropriations process—is the scene of extensive interaction between parts of the bureaucracy and parts of Congress.

In 1974 Congress passed the Congressional Budget and Impoundment Control Act, a statute designed to rationalize the entire congressional budget process. Prior to the passage of the budget reform act, congressional budget decisions were made individually and in a disaggregated, piecemeal fashion. The traditional locations for major congressional spending decisions were the Appropriations committees in the two houses; the sources of major revenue decisions were the House Ways and Means Committee and the Senate Finance Committee. There was no opportunity or incentive for comprehensive or integrated assessment of the individual congressional budget decisions.

The present congressional budget process, summarized in Table 3–1, differs from the previous one by creating two new budget committees with the mandate to integrate the separate budget decisions in a single comprehensive budget resolution that specifies the total amount (a "ceiling") of congressionally authorized spending and enumerates spending priorities within the ceiling, *prior to* passage of any appropriations bills.

The new budget process in Congress has the potential for sharpening debate over spending priorities and for decreasing the fragmentation of congressional budget decisions, but in the first three years in which the process was fully operational (1976, 1977, 1978), the new budget committees proceeded cautiously. The members of the new committees were intent on surviving as committees and in establishing and preserving the new process. Thus they did not aggressively challenge the traditional budget authorities for fear of generating a hostile coalition

Table 3–1: Congressional budget timetable

Action to be completed	On or before
President submits current services budget to Congress	November 10
President submits annual budget message to Congress	15 days after each session of Congress convenes in January
Congressional committees make recommendations to budget committees	March 15
Congressional Budget Office reports to budget committees	April 1
Budget committees report first budget resolution	April 15
Congress passes first budget resolution	May 15
Legislative committees complete reporting of authorizing legislation	May 15
Congress passes all spending bills	Seven days after Labor Day
Congress passes second budget resolution	September 15
Congress passes budget reconciliation bill	September 25
Fiscal year begins	October 1

Source: Lance T. LeLoup, *Budgetary Politics* (Brunswick, Ohio: King's Court, 1977): 130.

that would re-reform the new budget process out of existence. In shaping the first budget resolution, they sought primarily to anticipate the spending and revenue actions of the other congressional decision making bodies, thus avoiding direct confrontations. This meant that the second budget resolution was generally a ratification of budget decisions made during the summer in compliance with the relatively generous first resolution.

The new budget process has not produced substantive policy outcomes significantly different from pre-reform years, but the new process has succeeded in providing a more informed decision making process for congressional budgeting. (For an excellent summary of the experiences of the first several years of the new process, see Havemann, 1978.) The relations between individual parts of the bureaucracy and individual committees and subcommittees (particularly Appropriations subcommittees) have not been altered in any important way by the new congressional budget process. These interactions still determine the great proportion of the policy and budgetary outcomes affecting agencies and programs.

Agency organization and reorganization. Proposals to create programs and, much less frequently, to dismantle them also stimulate interaction between Congress and the bureaucracy. Such proposals may originate either in the bureaucracy or within Congress, but the decision to implement a new program eventually requires consultation with the other branch at least to secure statutory authority and funding, if not for good political relations with the other branch. Statutory authorization comes after the appropriate legislative committee has held hearings on the proposal. These hearings include testimony from interested parties including those parts of the bureaucracy that feel they may be best suited to administer the new program. The decision to terminate a program generally occurs when a program has clearly fulfilled its purpose or has had a poor record of performance.

Congress and the bureaucracy also interact on the matter of the agency's organization and reorganization proposals. Congress does not get involved in every change that is made in a bureau's structure, but it does usually get involved in changes made at the department level (often put forth as presidential reorganization plans) or within the independent regulatory commissions, which are technically arms of Congress.

In 1978 President Carter proposed creating a separate Department of Education, which would remove a number of agencies and programs from the present Department of Health, Education, and Welfare. Immediately after the proposal was made, affected parties in and out of government registered objections, seeking to exempt their programs from inclusion in the new department. The proposal for a separate education department died in the 95th Congress (1977–78), but not before the Senate Governmental Affairs Committee yielded rather quickly on exempting the Head Start program (a program to help prepare preschool children from disadvantaged families for entering school) from inclusion in the new department. The proposal for a separate Department of Education will continue to be considered, and special exemptions and exceptions will no doubt characterize any decision to create a Department that emerges.

Program evaluation. The evaluation of program performance (program oversight) is an important form of interaction between the bureaucracy and Congress that occurs when congressional committees examine the performance of programs they have authorized and funded. Responsibility for program oversight is shared—the Government Operations committees perform special investigative inquiries, the Appropriations committees are responsible for fiscal oversight, and the legislative committees are responsible for monitoring and overseeing the programs for which they authorize appropriations. Oversight activities may take several forms—special hearings to investigate a program; routine hearings, such as appropriations or authorizations; or program monitoring and analyses. Overall, Congress has not performed oversight extensively. Much of the oversight that has occurred has been in the context of appropriations hearings, but the focus there is understandably more on narrow expenditure concerns than on substantive evaluation. Several scholars (Bibby, 1966; Davis, 1970; Huitt,

1966; Ogul, 1973; Scher, 1963) have studied oversight and the conditions that contribute to it; their findings indicate that the personal and political payoffs of oversight activities are not as rewarding as other kinds of behavior to members of Congress, and hence they are not engaged in as frequently. We will address the issue of Congress' exercise of program oversight in Chapter 8.

Personnel matters. A variety of personnel matters also provides occasion for interaction between the two branches. The Senate must confirm a number of presidential appointments, including agency heads. Congress is involved in setting the pay scales for government employees, and any change in the compensation schedules will generate formal and informal lobbying from bureaucrats. The total amount of money that an agency head has available to pay the salaries and expenses of his employees is also determined by Congress, and it may not (deliberately or not) be enough to allow him to bring the agency up to its authorized personnel strength. Congress also gets involved in the creation of special positions within the agency and in limiting the total size of the agency or specific grades within the agency. Finally, individual members of Congress are sometimes in a position to see to it that friends and associates get particularly good jobs in the executive branch. Controversy over a friend of Speaker Thomas P. O'Neill's in the General Services Administration in 1978 was but one instance of this practice.

Other occasions. Decisions about the location of federal projects also stimulate interaction between Congress and the bureaucracy. Because such projects usually entail employment, money, and other benefits for the area, congressmen are interested in having them visible in their home districts. Bureaucrats are responsible for making the decisions about locations. The interaction on this subject occurs in both formal and informal settings. Occasionally, a project may have unpleasant or undesirable elements, and the interaction may occur over where not to put the project. For example, there is resistance in some areas to having nuclear reactor plants located nearby.

Congress and the bureaucracy also are brought together because of "casework," which involves a constituent's problems with an agency that the Representative or Senator feels obliged to help resolve. Casework occurs on an individual and piecemeal basis, usually at congressional initiative, and is usually resolved through informal means between agency and congressional staff.

Congressional techniques

Personal visits and phone calls. Members of Congress and staff members seek information and desired actions from bureaucrats by keeping in touch with them both in person and on the phone. This kind of personal attention is often sufficient to get the attention of a key bureaucrat and sometimes it alone is sufficient to obtain an intended result.

The use of third parties. Members often seek to mobilize supporters of their position to reinforce the messages they are delivering in other ways to bureaucrats. Thus a member may seek, for example, to have interest group representatives, reporters, or prestigious "clients" of a bureau approach executive branch officials with the same point of view favored by the member.

Release of written materials. Individual members of the House or Senate or individual committees and subcommittees can seek to influence bureaucratic decisions by releasing materials such as committee reports, staff studies, and press releases at the most propitious times.

Hearings. Executive branch officials are constantly appearing before congressional committees and subcommittees simply as a matter of course as both new authorizations and appropriations become necessary. These hearings afford members of the House and Senate recurring opportunities to elicit information about programs and to make their own views known.

An excellent example of a routine appropriations hearing being used to underscore a congressional attitude is provided by a former Manpower Administrator, Stanley Ruttenberg (Ruttenberg and Gutchess, 1970: 77–78). When he became Manpower Administrator in 1965 the Department of Labor was pushing a reorganization of the Manpower Administration that would have given line authority to regional manpower administrators over all of the operating bureaus, including the Bureau of Employment Security and the Bureau of Apprenticeship and Training, whose directors were both opposed to the reorganization because it decreased their relative autonomy. The pressure generated by the opponents of the proposal, who included several key congressional figures, was strong enough to prevent its implementation. An interchange between Ruttenberg and John Fogarty, then Chairman of the House Appropriations Subcommittee responsible for the Department of Labor's budget (among other things), during the March, 1965, hearings on the DOL budget shows Fogarty stating the congressional view forcefully:

> *Mr. Fogarty:* I assume you know the feeling of this committee on the proposed reorganization? If you do not, we will spell it out for you later on. . . . I am not going to belabor the point. As far as I am concerned, my mind is made up on the question of this reorganization of your department. Mr. Goodwin (the Director of the Bureau of Employment Security) has been here through several administrations and four or five Secretaries of Labor. The Secretaries of Labor come and go, but Mr. Goodwin stays on. I think Mr. Murphy (the Director of the Bureau

of Apprenticeship and Training) will stay on regardless of who is Secretary tomorrow or next year, or five years from now.

Mr. *Ruttenberg:* I think that is unquestionably true.

Mr. *Fogarty:* The Congress has always supported these two agencies and there is no doubt in my mind as to how the Congress will respond to this proposal. I thought I made it clear yesterday, but I am trying to make it clearer right now. Is that clear?

Mr. *Ruttenberg:* Mr. Chairman, it was quite clear to me yesterday.

In addition to routine hearings, congressional committees also hold a variety of special investigations to procure additional information. They may be conducted by standing committees or subcommittees, select committees, special committees, or joint committees. At the hearings the main congressional-bureaucratic interaction occurs in the preliminary preparation stages between congressional staff and agency members.

A good example of the kinds of impact that a congressional investigation can have even when dealing with a seemingly minor topic is provided by the activities of the Senate Small Business Committee in the early 1950s in relation to the controversy over an additive designed to prolong battery life (Lawrence, 1965). The case was a complicated one, involving conflicting philosophies over regulation of private enterprise, an aggressive marketer of the product, scientists from a range of public and private institutions, three government agencies (the Commerce Department's National Bureau of Standards, the Federal Trade Commission, and the Post Office), and the Senate Small Business Committee. Near the end of the controversy the Eisenhower administration was trying to fire the head of the National Bureau of Standards, and this action precipitated hearings by the Small Business Committee. As the hearings began there was still pending a regulatory action initiated by the Post Office against the producer of the additive. The Committee was decidedly on the side of the additive manufacturer and against government intervention. By bending to the wishes of the Committee, the Post Office removed itself from the controversy. As Lawrence (1965: 70) writes: "The Post Office Department weathered the storm with little or no damage. Senator Thye (Chairman of the Small Business Committee) had said at the conclusion of his Small Business Committee's hearing on AD-X2 (the name of the additive), 'Only . . . if the Postmaster General feels the mail fraud order should not be set aside, would it be necessary to find out why the order was ever issued.' " Thus the Post Office gave in to the Committee's preferences in order to avoid being investigated.

Requests for studies by outside sources. Senators and Representatives have a number of sources to which they can turn for independent (or at least seemingly independent) studies of problems that can presumably be used to bolster their point of view in a policy controversy. These sources include the General Accounting Office, the Congressional Research Service of the Library of Congress, the Office of Technology Assessment, the Congressional Budget Office, the Government Operations committees in the House and Senate, and respected outsiders (for example, universities or independent research organizations such as the Brookings Institution).

The General Accounting Office is an arm of Congress that in part conducts audits of the expenditure of funds. The GAO also conducts much broader studies, however, and its activity of that sort has been growing in recent years. The reports stemming from these studies can be used by congressmen agreeing with the conclusions to help make the case that their policy views should prevail. For example, a GAO report on the proposed Cheyenne helicopter was negative and the House Appropriations Committee used the report to help it make its case for terminating the project.

The Congressional Research Service is a nonpartisan agency but can be asked for information on programs and agencies that can then be used by proponents of specific views to buttress their case.

The Office of Technology Assessment was created by statute in 1972 and began operations in 1974. Its primary function, in the language of the statute, is "to provide early indications of the probably beneficial and adverse impacts of the applications of technology and to develop other coordinate information which may assist the Congress." Subjects for OTA staff work are decided by requests from congressional committees or by requests from the Technology Assessment Board (six Senators, six Representatives, and the OTA Director) or by the Director after consulting with the Board.

The Congressional Budget Office was created in 1974 as part of the general congressional budget reform of that year. The professional staff of the CBO, numbering about 200, reports to Congress on the short-term and long-term (five-year) economic consequences of legislation that is proposed and enacted. It develops an annual report on alternative budget courses for Congress to consider, with emphasis on fiscal policy and spending priorities. The CBO also responds to requests from the fiscal committees in both houses for economic and policy studies.

The Government Operations committees of both houses were empowered by the Legislative Reorganization Act of 1946 to conduct investigations into the operations of government activities at all levels to determine whether programs were being administered efficiently and economically. These committees work closely with the GAO in conducting their investigations.

Statutory changes. Congress can by statute create or dissolve agencies and programs, alter the jurisdiction of agencies, prescribe organizational structure, and intercede in personnel matters such as limits on total number of slots available, number of slots available for specific grades, and compensation.

Naturally, major statutory activities are relatively visible. But there are also more quiet and subtle uses of statutory power by Congress to achieve desired ends. For example, Congress can maximize the responsiveness of agencies to it through several statutory devices designed to weaken the control of an agency head over the agency. The illustration involving the Manpower Administration cited earlier is an example—in that case the field structure was kept decentralized and more responsive to the decentralized structure of congressional influence rather than allowing a more centralized field structure responsible to the Manpower Administrator. Similarly, some agencies (usually called commissions) have been given multiple executives (called commissioners) by Congress, in order to diffuse the decision making source and make the agency more responsive to Congress. The Atomic Energy Commission and all of the independent regulatory agencies provide illustrations of this technique's use. Congress has often opted to keep the staff assigned to a Secretary relatively small as a way of preventing control over individual bureaus from being centralized in the hands of the Secretary. (On these matters see Seidman, 1975.)

In a few cases Congress can specify that its members be directly involved in what might otherwise be considered strictly executive branch decision making. Two members of each house were included by statute on the negotiating teams implementing the tariff reduction provisions of the Trade Expansion Act of 1962, for example.

Although appropriations statutes are generally thought of only for their fiscal contents, they also may have a policy impact beyond the dollars they allocate to agencies and programs. This impact occurs when the statute contains specific provisions detailing how the money in the bill is to be used or not used. As Horn (1970: 181, 183) notes, these limitations are usually negative in character ("thou shalt not . . . etc.") and are directed at administrative rather than programmatic expenditures, such as travel, subscriptions, number of personnel hired, consulting fees, and entertainment. But more substantive matters are also addressed. For example, a provision inserted in the appropriations statute for the Department of Agriculture in the mid-1950s required that cotton sold abroad be sold competitively, even though the Administration thought this would have a detrimental effect on foreign policy (Kirst, 1969: 5). As another example, the Defense Appropriations Act (an annual bill) contains the provisions "that no funds herein appropriated shall be used for the payment of a price differential on contracts hereafter made for the purpose of relieving economic dislocations . . . so far as practicable, all contracts shall be awarded on a formally advertised competitive bid basis to the lowest responsible bidder" (Horn, 1970: 184). That language has "maintained the preeminence of California in defense procurement against large-scale attempts to distribute defense contracts according to the level of unemployment in an area" (Horn, 1970: 184).

Language in reports. In the technical sense only statutes have the force of law. However, Congress has also made its will felt in programmatic terms through language contained in committee reports. And the executive branch often treats this language as binding.

A good example of report language having the effect of law is provided by a 1960 reorganization of the Public Health Service (Carper, 1965). The Department of Health, Education, and Welfare decision to reorganize the Public Health Service was in direct response to language contained in the 1959 report of the Health Subcommittee of the House Appropriations Committee. And a decision not to divorce the clinical training programs of the National Institute of Mental Health from that organization was directly responsive to language contained in a Senate Appropriations Committee report in 1960.

All committees have the technique of report language at their disposal. The appropriations committees seem particularly active in using this technique. For example, in 1965 alone the Senate Appropriations Committee issued 150 directives and suggestions in its reports. Ninety-three of these directives dealt with programmatic matters, 39 dealt with budget procedure, and 18 dealt with management (Horn, 1970: 188). Not all bureaucrats will conform precisely to all such directives, but they will certainly weigh the costs of not conforming before they decide what to do.

Legislative veto. The essence of the so-called legislative veto is that statutory provision is made for congressional review of executive action before that action becomes binding. The legislative veto can take many forms. Statutory provisions in an increasing number of cases contain one of the following kinds of requirements:

1. That an agency must report proposed administrative actions in advance to a congressional committee.
2. That an agency must "come into agreement" with a committee before a given action is taken.
3. That an executive branch proposal must lie before Congress for a fixed period of time before it can be implemented. If Congress, or a part of it (the exact provisions vary), disapproves of the proposal then the agency cannot act.
4. That Congress, or a part of it, must take positive action to approve an action before an agency can proceed with it.

Whatever the form of the legislative veto, the normal period during which congressional action must occur is 30 to 90 days. The legislative veto provision has been especially heavily used on matters of executive agency reorganization, but its use has spread into a number of other substantive areas as well. Congress has been much more aggressive recently in inserting legislative veto provisions. In 1967–69 it added such provisions less than five times a year on the average. In 1970–73 this average increased to almost 11 times a year. From 1974 through 1977 the average was over 23 times a year (Oleszek, 1978: 204).

Reporting requirements. Congress may require that parts of the bureaucracy make certain information available to it through reporting requirements in statutes. These requirements vary considerably in their form and content. Some are highly visible because they are contained in major statutes and focus on reports from the President. For example, the Congressional Budget and Impoundment Control Act of 1974 requires that the President report annually on the amount of impounded funds and the amount of tax expenditures (that is, the amount of revenue lost through various tax "loopholes"). The War Powers Act of 1973 requires the President to report to Congress on American troop commitments.

Other reporting requirements are directed at bureaucrats lower in the executive hierarchy and are less visible. The kind of information requested can range from details about programs to rationales about decisions. The point of the reporting requirements is the same, however: to increase the amount of information that Congress has, and to increase the consultation between congressional committees and bureaucrats.

The Joint Committee on Atomic Energy offers a good example of how a committee can use the reporting technique to extend its influence over an agency. The JCAE exercised dominant influence over the Atomic Energy Commission during its existence, buttressing its influence with a large variety of reporting procedures, legislative veto provisions, and statutory rights to virtually all information held by the agency (Green and Rosenthal, 1963).

A recent analysis of all congressional reporting requirements (Johannes, 1976) shows that since World War II the number of reports required has risen from around 300 to over 1,000. These requirements fall into three major categories. First, various parts of the executive branch are often required to submit "policymaking" reports such as evaluations of existing programs and recommendations for future action. Second, "post facto" reports are often required simply recounting actions taken. Third, there are "advance notification" reports. These reports must be filed for a specific period of time before an action is taken. This gives members of Congress or of a specific committee a chance to object, propose changes, or react in other ways.

In the 92nd Congress (1971–72) 261 new reporting requirements were included in statutes. Of these, 50 percent were of the post facto variety, 40 percent were of the policymaking variety, and 10 percent were of the advance notification variety. Data using the same categories since 1945 suggest that policymaking reporting requirements have become an increasingly important congressional technique.

The sources of the reports and the routing of them also vary a great deal. In 1974 only 18 percent of all reports to be made (about 1,050) were to come either directly from the President or through the President. Forty-eight percent came from cabinet-level departments directly to Congress and 16 percent came from independent agencies directly to Congress. Others came from such sources as federally chartered private corporations and a variety of boards and commissions.

Budget decisions. By virtue of its powers to levy taxes and appropriate funds, Congress inevitably is the focus of attention from bureaucrats requesting and defending their agencies' budgets, and budget decisions are an important congressional technique for influencing programmatic performance in the executive branch. However, budget decisions are not centralized within Congress—many committees have the power to make these kinds of decisions.

By far the most visible and familiar budget deciders are the appropriations committees. A steady flow of information is traded between committee members and staff and agency personnel during the fiscal year, capped by the appearance of the agency head and other agency representatives at the annual appropriations hearings. The committees have some latitude in setting the amount of money that goes to an agency, and they also can specify limitations on how the money is spent. Even after appropriations are made, the committees have at least potential control over the uses of the money. For example, agency reprogramming of funds (that is, shifting money from one expenditure category to another) often must have at least informal committee approval (Fisher, 1974; Horn, 1970: 192–195).

Before the appropriations committees can appropriate funds, however, authorizing legislation for the agency or program in question must have been considered by the appropriate legislative committee and passed by both houses. Authorizing legislation gives congressional approval to an activity and generally sets a ceiling on the amount of funds that can be made available for that activity. Authorization hearings necessarily encompass more than just this budget figure, but the decision about an authorization limit is an important part of the proceedings, especially from the perspective of the administrator of the activity.

Legislative committees are also involved in budget decisions that have collectively been tagged as "backdoor spending." The central feature of the numerous techniques of backdoor spending is that a funding pattern is established for some activity by a legislative committee, and funds are made available without any input from the Appropriations Committee and without much program oversight once the pattern is set. Once an appropriations-avoiding device is in place it becomes part of the accepted machinery of government and is very hard for Congress to dislodge or modify.

For example, a committee may legislate monetary payments (called entitlements) to certain segments of society and require that money be made available for this purpose in a special trust fund. Social Security payments to the retired and disabled are automatically financed in this manner. Sometimes payments to a group like veterans are tied to the cost of living; increases in the benefits must be met by the appropriations committees—they have no choice. A legislative committee may allow an agency to conduct its business through contract obligations, as the Corps of Engineers does. It can write contracts for services without having the money in hand to perform them—the appropriations committees must provide the money at a later date when the bills come. Yet another device allows agencies to borrow money from the Treasury to finance their activities without requiring a specific authorization. Legislative committees use all of these techniques to finance agency activities, partially because they are under pressure from the agency representatives and their clients, and partially because of jurisdictional rivalries with the appropriations committees.

The recently formed budget committees offer another locus for interaction on budget decisions. As already indicated, the budget committees have not played a dramatically independent role in shaping policy or budgets. In effect, they have tried to predict what others in the budgetary decision process would do, and have for the most part adjusted their budget resolutions to those realities. However, the deliberations and resolutions of the budget committees have at least created yet another forum for considering congressional-bureaucratic budget interactions.

A final setting for budget decisions concerns the source of revenue rather than its allocation. Congress, and especially the House Ways and Means Committee, has responsibility for legislating the government's tax code, which sets the rates of taxation on personal income, corporate income, and excise taxes, and which also specifies an incredible array of tax "breaks" for various groups. A great deal of interaction occurs between the committee staffs that prepare tax legislation and the agencies that administer it, especially Department of Treasury officials.

Good relations between members of Congress who sit on the committees that make budget decisions and bureaucrats whose agencies and programs depend on the committees' decisions are very important from the bureaucrat's point of view. The appropriations process is the most visible and regular budget-deciding forum, and members of appropriations subcommittees have particularly high standing with agency administrators, as Fenno (1966) and Wildavsky (1974) have documented so well. If a senior member of a subcommittee expresses a policy view in the course of appropriations hearings this view is likely to be taken very seriously by the bureaucrats as they make subsequent policy decisions. Even a casual reading of published appropriations hearings shows instances of such statements of policy preferences on virtually every page. A good example is provided from the antitrust field a few years ago by an interchange between the chairman of the House subcommittee responsible for Justice Department appropriations (Mr. Rooney) and an official from the Antitrust Division of the Department (Mr. Orrick) (quoted from Anderson, 1970: 231–232):

> Mr. Rooney: What are they [the 294 lawyers in the Division] doing?
> Mr. Orrick: They are preparing cases, going to libraries, conducting grand juries, conducting investigations, and doing research, and I think the taxpayers' money is very well spent, indeed, on this activity. I might say with the continuing high-level investigations this is important.
> Mr. Rooney: You have been in government three years?
> Mr. Orrick: Yes sir.
> Mr. Rooney: And this is your third time up here?
> Mr. Orrick: Yes sir.
> Mr. Rooney: You should know that these gratuitous statements do not convince us at all. We would like to have some meat to digest. If you were to sit across there and tell us you had produced a case like the Philadelphia electric cases, then you would have something.
> Mr. Orrick: We are looking for those all the time, Mr. Chairman.
> Mr. Rooney: And you have not found any?
> Mr. Orrick: I have not found any since I have been there; no, but we are looking.
> Mr. Rooney: It is pretty hard to understand that with the appropriation . . . of approximately $5 million in 1961 there were 35 criminal cases won compared with 12 in 1962, and 18 in 1963.

Decisions on individual executive branch officials. The Senate possesses the formal power of confirmation over some critical executive branch officials, such as departmental secretaries and assistant secretaries, the Director of the Office of Management and Budget; the heads of independent agencies, such as the Federal Power Commission and the Environmental Protection Agency; and the heads of numerous departmental agencies such as the Census Bureau and the FBI. Hearings on these nominations can be used to transmit policy preferences of members and committees of the House and the Senate in a very forceful way to the nominees. Occasionally a presidential nomination will be rejected or defeat will look so likely that a nomination will be withdrawn.

Even if a nomination is eventually confirmed it may be that the fight over the nomination will convince the President to alter the nature of subsequent nominations. For example, early in the Eisenhower administration a nominee to the National Labor Relations Board won confirmation by only three votes in the Senate. The individual in question had had a career in business management and the Senate Democrats thought this an inappropriate background for an NLRB member. Subsequent Eisenhower nominations to the NLRB did not again draw on this source. Thus, although the Democrats lost the immediate fight they made their larger point and the President responded (Anderson, 1970: 373–376).

Occasionally Congress will also try to extend the confirmation power to new positions. In 1973 there was a battle between Congress and the President over the proposal to make the Director and Deputy Director of the Office of Management and Budget subject to Senate confirmation. The President successfully vetoed one such bill because it required confirmation of the incumbents (who had been particularly obnoxious in the eyes of many congressional Democrats). A bill exempting the incumbents was signed by the President in early 1974. Similarly, but with no particular controversy, a provision of the 1968 Omnibus Crime Control and Safe Streets Act required that all future directors of the FBI be subject to Senate confirmation.

Congress can make its influence felt even if formal confirmation is not required. A good case is provided in the consumer affairs field (Nadel, 1971: 53–55). During the Johnson administration Betty Furness had held the post of Special Assistant to the President for Consumer Affairs and had been a visible advocate of consumer interests within the administration. Early in 1969 President Nixon announced the appointment of a part-time consultant on consumer affairs and chose the director of the Good Housekeeping Institute. Although confirmation was not required, this choice was immediately attacked in Congress on two grounds. First, the Good Housekeeping Institute itself had been severely criticized by consumer advocates in and out of Congress as a sham operation. Second, the demotion of the presidential adviser from a special assistant to a part-time consultant signalled to concerned members of Congress that the new President planned to downgrade programs of consumer protection. The outcry from Congress was so strong that the President withdrew his nomination and a few months later appointed another individual as a special assistant for consumer affairs. This person's background and credentials were considerably more legitimate in the eyes of congressional supporters of the consumer movement.

Congressional influence on appointments is felt even after an agency head has been confirmed. For example, Congress can exert sufficient pressure against an incumbent that, in effect, forces firing or resignation. This occurred in 1974 when the administrator of the Veterans Administration was so severely criticized for his handling of the organization and its programs by both veterans' groups and by key House and Senate members who were handling bills affecting the VA that the administration had virtually no choice but to request his resignation.

Bureaucratic techniques

The above discussion may make it appear that the bureaucracy can easily be overwhelmed by the rich variety of congressional techniques. This is not the case, however, for two basic reasons. First, the bureaucracy is so vast in terms of individual employees, organizational units, and programs that even a very aggressive set of Senators, Representatives, and staff members can influence only a relatively small part of the bureaucracy at any given time. Second, the bureaucracy itself also possesses techniques that allow it to influence congressional attitudes and behavior. These techniques are not as numerous as those in the hands of Congress but they may, nevertheless, be very effective in achieving the ends desired by the bureaucrats.

As in the case of Congress a number of the techniques can be used simultaneously, thus increasing their impact.

Substance of decisions. Bureaucrats make numerous decisions in the course of administering their programs that are important to members of Congress. This decision making constitutes the bureaucrat's most important technique in interacting with Congress. These decisions cover a wide range of topics and occur in a variety of settings. For example, when a new program is authorized or an old one amended, bureaucrats are required to publish proposed regulations in the *Federal Register* that detail all aspects of program operation. A draft of the regulations is circulated for public comment and changes before becoming final. Congressional views during this review and comment period are an important input to the decision making that shapes the final regulations.

Usually bureaucratic decisions don't get written and circulated as the regulations do, but they show up in the way a program is implemented. For example, a statute may contain ambiguity about eligible recipients of a social welfare program. Some members of Congress are likely to favor a broad interpretation of the eligibility requirements in order to broaden the coverage of the program while others will probably favor a more restrictive interpretation. The bureaucrats making the decision can calculate the costs and benefits of pleasing one group of congressmen and perhaps offending another group.

Bureaucrats also maintain a good deal of control over the use of the monies available to them. At one extreme they may not spend all of the money for any given object—in fact, they may be formally prohibited from doing so by presidential impoundment of funds, although such presidential action was limited by the budget act in 1974. More likely, they retain considerable latitude in terms of shifting emphases among expenditures. Again, some programmatic emphases are going to be particularly attractive to some members of the House and Senate, and different emphases will be more attractive to others.

The power that bureaucrats possess to determine where major expenditures will take place and where facilities will be located is important to members of Congress and can be used skillfully by bureaucrats to build support on a range of issues, because in addition to the broad policy concerns that most members of Congress have, they also have narrower concerns about the welfare of their own particular geographical constituencies. Thus decisions about contracts, expansion of facilities like bases, field offices, and laboratories, or the closing of such facilities are usually very salient to at least some Senators and Representatives.

A classic case involving closing of field offices and bureaucratic calculation designed to minimize subsequent loss of congressional support is provided by the Department of Commerce in 1948 (Arnow, 1954). Because of appropriations cuts by the House Appropriations Committee, the Department had to close 4 of its 46 field offices across the country. Efficiency indicators were developed to measure the workload of each office, the cost of processing the workload, and the population of the city in which the office was located. The 14 lowest ranking offices were judged to be candidates for closing. The decision about which four were to be closed during the Democratic administration was made on the basis of explicitly political determinations, as Table 3–2 indicates. As this case illustrates, bureaucrats cannot exercise the power they have over expenditures, location of facilities, or expansion or reduction of services without regard to the political repercussions such exercise of power has in Congress. It is not unusual to see Representatives from districts afflicted with a proposed field office or air base shutdown or a decrease in rail or air or postal service work vigorously to alter the negative proposal. Successful bureaucrats learn how to balance good administrative judgment along with good political judgment.

Table 3–2: Department of Commerce field office closings: Decision factors and outcomes

Location	Outcome	Type of office	Locale	Political features
			Decision factors	
Juneau, Ala.	Closed	Uneconomic office	Large territory	No representation in Congress (Alaska not yet a state)
Fargo, N.Dak.	Closed	Uneconomic office	Small city	State represented exclusively by Republicans in both House and Senate
Cheyenne, Wyo.	Not closed	Uneconomic office	Small city	State represented by a senior, important Democrat in the Senate
Charleston, W.Va.	Closed		Medium city	Democratic Senator opposed field office manager; Republican Senator supported the manager
Butte, Mont.	Not closed	Uneconomic office	Small city	State represented by two senior Democrats, one of whom was up for reelection in 1948
Omaha, Nebr.	Not closed		Largest city in the state	State represented by an important Republican who sat on the House Appropriations Committee
Providence, R.I.	Not closed		Large city containing most of the state population; highly commercial area	Democratic representation in both houses

City	Closed status	Office strength	City characteristic	Notes
Salt Lake City, Utah	Not closed		Principal city in state	State represented by a senior Democratic Senator very loyal to the administration
Reno, Nev.	Not closed	Weak office		Senior Democratic Senator nominated office manager; helped restore appropriations cut earlier in year
Albuquerque, N.Mex.	Not closed	Moderately weak office		State represented by two Democratic Senators, both friendly with the Secretary of Commerce
Mobile, Ala.	Not closed	Moderately weak office	Important seaport	
Hartford, Conn.	Not closed	Moderately weak office	Heavily commercial area	
Charlotte, N.C.	Closed	Moderately weak office	Heavily commercial area	State always elected Democrats, who were usually unfriendly to the administration
Phoenix, Ariz.	Closed, then opened		Large city	Pressure from elected officials, including the senior Democratic Senator from Arizona, forced reversal of decision

Source: Adapted from information in Kathryn S. Arnow (1954) *The Department of Commerce Field Service*. Indianapolis: Bobbs-Merrill. ICP Case #21, pp. 17–27.

Timing of decisions. Not only do bureaucrats possess consider-able flexibility in determining the substance of decisions but they also possess even more flexibility in determining when those decisions are implemented. Thus, decisions can be timed to give a helpful boost to friendly members in reelection contests. They can also be timed so as to magnify the public credit a Senator or Representative gets for pro-moting a given policy development. For instance, the Department of Labor's Employment and Training Administration has instructed its field offices to refrain from announcing budget allocations for programs to grantees until members of Congress have had a chance to make an announcement about the federal money coming into their home state or district. This seemingly minor decision by ETA bureaucrats (a pat-tern followed by virtually all federal agencies) helps build the con-gressmen's public image, and it curries congressional favor and credit for the agency.

Use of information. Bureaucrats possess a great deal of detailed information, and very rarely is information a neutral commodity. Thus the release of critical information in a timely fashion by agencies is often used as a persuasive technique. For example, the Department of Commerce opposed cuts that it was ordered to make in some of its field offices even before the 1948 decisions discussed above. It released a list of the offices to be closed in an effort to get congressional support in overturning or modifying the closings. At least 39 Representatives and 68 Senators from affected districts and states could be presumed to be interested in the list. Enough money was added in the congres-sional appropriations bill to save 8 of the 39 offices slated for closing.

In general, agencies that are managed skillfully will select both the content and the timing of the release of various reports and staff studies to maximize the amount of support they generate in Congress for the ends they wish to pursue. Agencies may also be more selective in the release of information and provide it privately only to a few key Sen-ators or Representatives who can make some use of it in a manner that will redound both to the credit of the member and the advantage of the agency. Agency personnel often help congressional staff members write speeches for their principals in which information is used that puts the agency in a favorable light and puts the member in a favorable light because he appears highly knowledgeable.

Personal visits and phone calls. Top administrative officials are in constant informal contact with key members of relevant congressional committees and subcommittees. In these relationships their central job is to establish personal rapport and trust. The establishment of such a relationship does not mean that all policy and program initiatives will gain congressional approval but the chances of favorable congressional response are certainly enhanced.

A good example of the elaborate round of personal contacts needed to make a bureaucratic decision is provided by Ruttenberg (Ruttenberg and Gutchess, 1970: 80–81) in discussing his tenure as head of the Manpower Administration (later renamed the Employment and Training Administration). In pursuing the notion that there should be regional manpower administrators (after Representative Fogarty's death had made such a change at least possible) he had to establish good working relationships with the new chairman of the House Appropriations Subcommittee dealing with the Department of Labor's budget, with the other members of the House Appropriations Committee, including the senior Republicans, and with the chairman and key members of the House Ways and Means Committee, which had jurisdiction over one of the programs that would come under the purview of the new regional manpower administrators.

At one point I thought we had worked out a compromise with the appropriate committees of the Congress, but when that fell through, the round of conversations and negotiations began anew. Finally, agreement was reached with all parties. We were permitted to establish regional administrators, but on the understanding that they would be staff, not line positions, that their duties would be limited to coordination and would not include direct supervision of other bureau field staff, and that each regional administrator would have under his direct supervision only a secretary and perhaps a deputy. It was also understood, however, that the regional manpower administrators would have complete authority for the development and operation of the *new* programs that crossed bureau lines . . . (Ruttenberg and Gutchess, 1970: 81).

The use of third parties. Like members of Congress, executive branch officials can also use supportive third parties to intervene with members of Congress by arguing their case or reinforcing their point of view. These individuals can include the President or other high-ranking executive officials, newspaper reporters, interest group representatives, and prestigious constituents who also happen to be agency clients in one way or another. Like Congress, agencies can also commission studies and surveys by outsiders (presumably respected) that can be widely disseminated if their conclusions are favorable to the agency and quietly suppressed if the conclusions are not flattering or supportive.

Agency heads must be wary of tapping too often at the doors of higher-ups in the executive branch to bolster their positions before congressional committees. While important issues no doubt warrant the agency's use of heavy artillery, excessive reliance on the President or Secretary has disadvantages. For one thing, as Freeman (1965: 73) noted, "many committee members do not appreciate bureaucratic attempts to exploit the halo which sometimes attends presidential leadership, especially when the bureau spokesman infers that Congress can be pushed around by a strong President." In addition, reliance on high-ranking executive branch officials may encourage agency dependence on them and increase the difficulty of obtaining a favorable response from Congress in the absence of personal support from the President or the Secretary.

Interest group representatives are most frequently mobilized by agency bureaucrats. Horn (1970: 197–198) describes an instance in 1965 when Secretary of Defense McNamara successfully used representatives of the domestic aircraft industry to obtain approval from the Senate Appropriations Committee to allow British suppliers to bid on planned ship construction projects by the U.S. Navy:

> . . . most members of the Defense Subcommittee were opposed to the Pentagon position. In a short period before the markup, McNamara personally contacted almost all committee members. Representatives of the aircraft industry, coordinating their efforts with McNamara's staff, also made known their interest. Potential subcontractor suppliers of various parts were enlisted in the cause. When the showdown came in the full committee, McNamara's personal effort, combined with his skilled use of a rival segment of the private economy, paid off.

In addition to mobilizing the support of interested third parties for a specific cause, agency bureaucrats maintain a steady public relations effort to keep Congress and the public informed about the good they and their programs are doing through newsletters, press releases, and other publications. Agencies also urge their clientele to communicate satisfaction with a program to relevant members of Congress, because in the absence of such feedback, Congress may assume that no one other than the agency cares about a program and its appropriations may be cut as a result. (See Wildavsky, 1974: 65–74, for an interesting overview of agency-clientele relations.)

~ **4** ~

Distributive policy

IN THE FIRST three chapters we have made a number of generalizations about the relationship between Congress and the bureaucracy.
We have portrayed the relationship in broad strokes in Chapter 1 by
talking about its place in the general institutional framework through
which national public policy gets made in the United States. In Chapter 2 we focused more concretely on the individuals involved in the
relationship and on some illustrative examples of the relationship in
concrete institutional settings. In Chapter 3 we discussed the resources
of individuals both on Capitol Hill and in the bureaucracy and the techniques at their disposal for pursuing their various goals—both substantive and institutional—as they conduct their respective parts of the
relationship.

Now we want to get more specific and focus on how Congress and
the bureaucracy interact as policy is made in different areas. We are
going to focus particularly on the presence and importance of subgovernments within the congressional-bureaucratic relationship. We expect to observe differences in the relationship depending on which of
the six policy areas—distributive, protective regulatory, redistributive,
structural, strategic, and crisis—is involved. A number of questions
are both substantively interesting and important to a systematic analysis of the relationship between Congress and the bureaucracy. For example, how important overall is the operation of a subgovernment in
the policy area? With what range of issues does it deal? Do its deci-

sions stand as final, or are they altered before a final decision emerges from the policy process? Is the relationship between congressional and bureaucratic actors in a policy area characterized chiefly by conflict or by cooperation? If conflict occurs, what kind of patterns describe its resolution by congressional and bureaucratic actors? Do the policy positions of one branch seem to emerge dominant over the views of the other branch in the resolution of conflict? In this chapter and the ones that follow, we will present empirical case material to illustrate and explore these questions in different policy areas, and in each chapter we will summarize the findings that emerge.

We begin this analysis with some expectations about how the congressional-bureaucratic relationship will look, and these expectations are summarized in Table 4–1. This table can serve as a guide to the empirical chapters. Our intent is to elaborate our expectations about the shape of the congressional-bureaucratic relationship at the beginning of each empirical chapter, discuss the case materials in terms of the analytical questions, and then summarize the results, making corrections to the entries in Table 4–1 if the empirical evidence suggests that adjustments and modifications need to be made.

THE NATURE OF DISTRIBUTIVE POLICY

The essence of distributive policy is its decentralized distribution of the federal largesse to a seemingly unlimited number of recipients —individuals, groups, and corporations. The mechanics of the subsidy arrangement vary—in some issue areas there may be numerous individual laws that each specify a few beneficiaries, or there may be a general law that allows numerous similar beneficiaries to collect a subsidy. The duration of the subsidy can also vary, as can its material nature. The reward may take the form of a price support payment; a procurement, construction, or service contract; a tax loophole; or a special indemnity payment.

The recipients of these subsidies usually do not compete directly with each other for the subsidies, but rather they each seek a high level of support for themselves without being particularly aware of the other recipients and their subsidies. The petitioners typically seek direct access to the bureaus in the executive branch and the subcommittees in the House and Senate that are primarily responsible for setting their level of subsidy. Once the level of subsidy is set, the implementation of that subsidy is also delegated back down to the bureau level of the executive branch—often with close involvement of personnel from the relevant subcommittees.

The interactions of the members of the subgovernment that emerges once a subsidy pattern has been established are characterized by a low level of public visibility and by a high degree of mutually rewarding cooperation (logrolling) that facilitates both perpetuation of the subsidies within the subsystem and its continued low visibility. Cooperation and logrolling also mark the relationship between legislative members of the subgovernment and the rest of the House and Senate. Eventually most members of Congress want to set up a subsidy for groups they support and need cooperation to do so.

In any given year the structure of interests, bureaus, and subcommittees within a subgovernment looks only marginally different from the preceding year. Substantive change is gradual and the cast of characters—both individual and institutional—varies only a little bit from year to year.

THE CONGRESSIONAL-BUREAUCRATIC RELATIONSHIP IN DISTRIBUTIVE POLICY

Expectations about the relationship

We expect the relationship between bureaucrats (at the bureau level) and individuals on Capitol Hill (both members and staff members at the subcommittee level) to be critically important in distributive policy. As indicated in Chapter 1 it is in this policy area that subgovernments typically hold sway, and the bureau-subcommittee relationship is at the heart of subgovernments. The relationship is important in the sense that the actors deal with the full range of issues in the area from the broadest items of general policy to the most detailed items involving a single subsidy for a single client. It is also important in that the actors usually make what amounts to final decisions on the full range of issues. Only occasionally does a subgovernment lose control of part of its policy area and get overruled by some other authorities such as the full House or Senate, a conference committee, the Office of Management and Budget, the office of the secretary of an executive department, or the White House.

Ordinarily the relationship between the congressional actors and the bureaucratic actors is marked by a high degree of cooperation. All actors have a major stake in supporting and pleasing the interests of their clients because it is, in part, client satisfaction that can produce critical political support for both the bureau and the subcommittee as they seek to enhance their positions in their respective institutional settings.

When there are issues on which there are differences of opinion they are usually resolved by straightforward face-to-face negotiations between the individuals directly involved in the relationship. There is usually no need to appeal to higher authority because agreement is

Table 4-1: Expectations about the congressional-bureaucratic relationship during policy formation in different areas

Policy area	Importance of subgovernment in policy area	Range of issues decided by subgovernment	Importance of subgovernment in determining final policy actions	Degree of conflict or cooperation between congress and bureaucracy	Mode and normal locus of conflict resolution	Substance of conflict resolution	Dominant institution when conflict persists
Distributive	High (subgovernment is major decisional locus)	Broad	High	High degree of cooperation —both have primary interest in pleasing clients	Face-to-face negotiations; resolution within the subgovernment	Compromise between initial specific positions	Congress (typically at the subcommittee level)
Protective Regulatory	Low (major new decisions are made by Congress)	Narrow	Moderately low on new decisions; moderately high in existing areas of regulation	Potentially high conflict when congressmen seek exceptions to general policies	Face-to-face negotiations within the subgovernment or transfer to a higher level	Compromise between initial specific positions; nonresolution; broader compromise at a higher level	Usually Congress at the collective level
Redistributive	Very low (major decisions are made by executive branch interacting with peak associations)	Very narrow	Low	Potentially high conflict based on partisan and ideological differences; possible cooperation in redefining issue as distributive	No resolution within subgovernment; resolution is transferred to a higher level	Broader compromise at a higher level; redefinition of issues in distributive terms; nonresolution	Depends on relative partisan and ideological strength in Congress

Structural	High (subgovernment is major decisional locus)	Broad	High	High degree of cooperation—both have primary interest in pleasing clients	Face-to-face negotiations; resolution within the relationship	Compromise between initial specific positions	Congress (typically at the subcommittee level)
Strategic	Low (major decisions are made in executive branch)	Narrow	Low	Some chance for conflict if Congress gets involved	Subgovernment not involved in resolution; resolution occurs at a higher level	Compromise or nonresolution	Executive branch
Crisis	Very low (major decisions are presidential)	Very narrow	Very low	Little chance for either cooperation or conflict to develop during decision making; conflict may develop after event	No subgovernment involvement; post hoc legitimation (congressional resolutions, executive orders)	Sham compromise or imposed solution	Executive branch (President)

usually relatively easy to reach. In fact, both parties have a stake in resolving conflict without involving other parties. If higher authority is invoked then other matters on which there is agreement at the subgovernment level might also be called into question and long-standing policies and programs might be changed in ways unsatisfactory to both the bureaucratic and congressional members of the subgovernment.

The normal resolution of disagreement within a subgovernment is a straightforward compromise somewhere roughly in the middle of the two initial contending positions. This compromise is generally satisfying to both the bureaucratic and congressional parties, although it would be reasonable to expect that over time congressional interests and positions are likely to be more closely approximated than bureaucratic interests and positions.

Although the distributive arena in general follows the above pattern in terms of the importance of the congressional-bureaucratic relationship and in terms of conflict, cooperation, and conflict resolution, some further distinctions between different instances of subgovernment involvement can be drawn and used to organize examples of policymaking in this area. As suggested in Chapter 1, subgovernments are not always immune to scrutiny from outsiders. The subgovernments' operations can be opened up by a number of factors—disagreement among members that cannot be resolved within the subgovernment; intrusion into subgovernment affairs by outsiders, such as an aggressive President trying to control policy implementation; the introduction of a new issue into the subgovernment's jurisdiction; or the redefinition of a distributive issue into nondistributive terms. All of these factors have the effect of increasing the visibility of the subgovernment and of its functioning, and of thereby broadening the number of participants who get involved.

There are four major variations in the congressional bureaucratic relationships within the distributive policy arena. The most common is *subgovernment dominance*. Two important but less frequent variations are *major subgovernment adaptation* and *competing subgovernments*. *Subgovernment disintegration* is the fourth variation, but it is very rare.

Subgovernment dominance is, in many senses, the "normal" situation in cases of distributive policy. Much of the time subgovernments proceed to make decisions affecting substantive matters within their purview basically without challenge from or involvement of anyone outside the subgovernment except in terms of formal ratification of subgovernment decisions. The subgovernments operate at a low level of visibility and at a high level of effectiveness from the point of view of the interests they champion. In those instances in which challenges are made to the subgovernment it prevails with relative ease, thus retaining its dominance.

In a situation of subgovernment dominance both short-run and long-run policy outcomes favor the interests of those in the subgovernment. No major redefinition of the policy positions by the members of the subgovernment is necessary because challenges can be met without such concessions. The domain in the subgovernment's fief is stable in content or, in the case of particularly strong subgovernments, may expand. Challenges are relatively infrequent and sporadic, and do not pose much threat to the interests of the subgovernment.

Major subgovernment adaptation is required when challenges to a subgovernment become more persistent and powerful. If defeats begin to become frequent and if the subgovernment is being defeated on issues that are central to its interests, then often that subgovernment will undertake some adaptations to adjust itself to new reality. If successful, the subgovernment will reestablish itself as dominant, although on the basis of a new definition of interests, issues, and positions. If either unsuccessful at adaptation or unwilling to make an adaptive effort, the subgovernment may disintegrate or may be supplanted by a competing set of interests represented in another subgovernment.

When a subgovernment undergoes major adaptation, short-run policy outcomes are likely to be a mix of favorable and unfavorable. But, if the adaptation is successful, long-run policy outcomes will be favorable. Obviously, policy positions will be redefined by the members of the subgovernment during the process of adaptation. During this process the domain under subgovernment dominance is also likely to change. Before and during the process, challenges to the subgovernment will be at least moderately strong and relatively frequent.

Competing subgovernments can develop when an issue area is lodged in the governmental decision making apparatus in such a way that allows or even promotes the development of institutionalized competition for dominance. The competition may result in the eventual redefinition of jurisdictions so that one subgovernment becomes dominant, or it may result in the competing subgovernments being replaced by some other mode of decision making, or it may simply result in continued sharing of the issue area space, with sufficient adjustments to mute conflict and allow decisions to be made.

In a situation of competing subgovernments both short-run and long-run policy outcomes typically are mixed from the point of view of either subgovernment. Each of the competitors prevails some of the time. If one of the competitors begins to prevail an overwhelming proportion of the time the element of competition will evaporate. In most competitive situations members of the competing groups do little redefining of their policy positions. Stability of the domain influenced by each of the competitors is relatively low to moderate because competition will ordinarily breed changing patterns of dominance. Challenges to the dominance of any one subgovernment are, by definition, relatively strong and frequent.

Subgovernment disintegration occurs only rarely, but that it occurs at all suggests that change—both procedural and substantive—is at least possible in national policymaking in the United States. Disintegration may occur because the subgovernment loses jurisdiction over its issues (either because of a reshuffling of congressional or bureaucratic boundaries or because of a redefinition of the issue as nondistributive), or because it has been weakened by repeated losses on a series of individually minor challenges, or because it has collapsed in the face of a major challenge.

As a subgovernment approaches disintegration both short-run and long-run policy outcomes became unfavorable. The subgovernment is not likely to redefine its policy positions (if it would do so it might be able to adapt to changed circumstances and survive). The domain in the purview of the subgovernment shrinks until it finally vanishes. Challenges are strong and frequent and, ultimately, fatal.

Table 4–2 summarizes the four major variations in the situations or contexts in which subgovernments find themselves as they participate in distributive policymaking.

Subgovernment dominance

Agricultural policy. Farm policy has long been synonymous with the presence and dominance of subgovernments (Lowi, 1973a; Talbot and Hadwiger, 1968). This is not to say that the policies are not controversial; they often are and victories of agriculture subgovernments are, for example, often ratified by narrow votes on the floor of Congress. Furthermore, it is often necessary for those dominating the agricultural policy area to trade their support to others for other issues in return for building majority coalitions for their own favored farm policies.

Agricultural policy is, of course, complex and made up of many pieces, and subgovernments typically form around each of the separate pieces. Although on some occasions members of these separate subgovernments may form temporary alliances to promote a broader policy, ordinarily they work independently of one another, and focus on narrower policy concerns. A few examples will demonstrate how strong subgovernments work. First, we will look at two broad areas in which success has been fairly consistent over long periods of time: price supports and soil conservation. Then we will look at an agriculture subgovernment absorbing a minor defeat in relation to sick chickens. Finally, we will observe a subgovernment, in effect, expanding its

Table 4–2: Four major subgovernment situations in distributive policymaking

Major attributes of situation	Overall subgovernment position			
	Dominance	Major adaptation	Competing subgovernments	Disintegration
Short-run policy outcomes	Favorable	Mixed	Mixed	Unfavorable
Long-run policy outcomes	Favorable	Favorable	Mixed	Unfavorable
Degree of redefinition of policy positions by subgovernment	Low	Moderate to high	Low	Low
Stability of subgovernment domain	High; may expand	Low	Low to moderate	Low; then vanishes
Strength and frequency of challenges	Low; sporadic	Moderate to high; frequent	Moderate to high; frequent	High; frequent (ultimately fatal)

domain by opening the federal treasury in a major way to new "disaster" claims by farmers.

Price supports. The price support program is a highly complex set of laws administered at the national level by the Agricultural Stabilization and Conservation Service and at the state and local levels by delegated state, county, and local committees. The price support program is designed to protect the incomes of growers and producers of commodities through a combination of acreage allotments (crop quotas), target prices on commodities, government loans and payments to growers, and government purchases of crops.

The price support subgovernments are several, and there is a variant for each major crop or supported item. The basic participants are relevant specialists in the Agricultural Stabilization and Conservation Service (in the Department of Agriculture), the members of the various commodity subcommittees of the House Agriculture Committee, and representatives of the interest groups for the various crops and commodities (such as the National Association of Wheat Growers, the National Wool Growers Association, the Soybean Council of America, and the National Milk Producers Federation). Table 4–3 illustrates some of the commodity subgovernments by giving a partial listing of the institutional locations of some of the members.

Basically, each commodity subgovernment works to obtain the most favorable support possible for the producers of the commodity, both in terms of acreage allotments and target prices set for crops. In general these subgovernments operate without successful challenge in setting the levels of commodity supports, which are ratified by Congress and announced by the Secretary of Agriculture.

The implementation of the price support program illustrates the extent of decentralization that is present in much agricultural policy. Congressional decisions about allotments and supports are apportioned to the states by the ASCS, where in turn they are apportioned among approximately 2800 agricultural counties. The farmer-elected Stabilization and Conservation committees at the county level receive the allotment figures. Then as Lowi (1973a: 187) describes:

> (these committees) . . . make new allotments, work out adjustments and review complaints regarding allotments, determine whether quotas have been complied with, inspect and approve storage facilities, and perform as the court of original jurisdiction on violations of price-support rules and on eligibility for parity payments. The committees are also vitally important in the campaigns for the two-thirds vote required to fix high price supports. Congress determines the general level of supports, and the Secretary of Agriculture proclaims the national acreage quotas for adjusting the supply to the guaranteed price. But the locally elected committees stand between the farmer and Washington.

Table 4–3: Composition of commodity subgovernments

Commodity	Institutional location of subgovernment members		
	Congress	*Bureaucracy*	*Interest groups*
Cotton	House Cotton Subcommittee	Agricultural Stabilization and Conservation Service (ASCS) cotton program	National Cotton Council
Oilseeds and rice	House Oilseeds and Rice Subcommittee	ASCS programs for peanuts, rice, tungnuts, flaxseed, soybeans, dry edible beans, and crude pinegum	Soybean Council of America
Tobacco	House Tobacco Subcommittee	ASCS tobacco program	Tobacco Institute
Dairy and poultry products	House Dairy and Poultry Subcommittee	ASCS milk program	National Milk Producers Federation; National Broiler Council
Livestock and grains	House Livestock and Grains Subcommittee	ASCS programs for wheat, corn, barley, oats, grain sorghum, rye, wool, and mohair	National Association of Wheat Growers; National Wool Growers Association

Thus, although the heart of the subgovernment remains in Washington in the nexus of the subcommittee and the ASCS bureau, the operation of the program evinces a strong flavor of federalism.

Soil conservation. The basic program (or "mission") of the Soil Conservation Service is development of a national soil and water conservation program (although the SCS has never had the only program in this area). This responsibility takes the form of building small dams to help conserve soil, prevent floods, and increase recreational opportunities in rural areas. In addition, the SCS provides a variety of technical assistance to land owners, land users, and land developers located in approximately 3000 soil conservation districts to assist in carrying out locally adopted soil and water conservation programs.

The local districts have a good deal of muscle and are directly involved in the operations of the soil conservation subgovernment. For example, the watershed projects of the SCS are the result of requests made at the local level, usually by the conservation districts, to the SCS. The SCS then obtains the necessary authorizations and appropriations from Congress to carry out the requests. The subgovernment that emerges from this process includes SCS watershed bureau officials, members of the House and Senate Agriculture committees (who must make the authorizations), and members of the House Appropriations Subcommittee on Agriculture. Relevant nongovernmental participants include representatives of the National Association of Soil Conservation Districts and the Izaak Walton League of America. The decisions of this subgovernment are quiet and continuous.

Sick chickens: A minor setback. Usually, relatively small matters of subsidy slide through a subgovernment unnoticed by almost anyone except the members of the subgovernment. Once in a while someone —a disgruntled Senator or Representative or an alert newspaper reporter—will attempt to blow the whistle on a subsidy that appears illegitimate even when measured against the very loose standards for legitimacy used in the distributive policy area. When such whistle-blowing is attempted—regardless of its ultimate result—it offers a good chance to observe the components and processes of a subgovernment because they have momentarily been exposed to a more public view than is normal. The case of the sick chickens related below illustrates an instance where a subgovernment lost to a challenge. (See Hines, 1974a; 1974b; *Congressional Quarterly Weekly Report*, April 27, 1974, p. 1063, and May 25, 1974, p. 1341.)

In March 1974 the Agriculture Department ordered millions of chickens grown in Mississippi destroyed because they contained too much (as defined by the Environmental Protection Agency) of a cancer-producing pesticide that had contaminated their feed. Almost immediately the senior Senator from Mississippi (James Eastland) and the Mississippi delegation in the House introduced legislation in their respective houses to reimburse the poultry growers, processors, and their employees for the losses they had incurred because of the USDA order. The total estimated cost of the reimbursement was between $8 and $10 million, and in the original version of the bill the firms were allowed almost four years (until the end of 1977) to file their claims.

In the Senate the southern-dominated agriculture subgovernment (oriented toward protecting dominant southern crops and agricultural products such as cotton, tobacco, peanuts, rice, and broilers) worked swiftly and successfully to pass the bill. Senator Eastland introduced the bill in late March. A number of other Senators—mostly southern- ers—joined Eastland in sponsoring the bill. The Agriculture Commit- tee—chaired by a Georgian—approved the bill in a few days without public hearings. A few technical amendments were added in commit- tee, but the impact of the bill would have been the same—to give a special subsidy to Mississippi chicken processors.

On the floor of the Senate, a slight disruption occurred when a fresh- man Senator (a Democrat from Iowa) objected to the bill as a bad precedent on several grounds and the press noted his objections. He tried to have the bill returned to the Agriculture Committee for hear- ings, and failing that, he sought to restrict its scope through amend- ments. The Senate did cut the time limit back to the end of 1974 and did specifically direct the Secretary of Agriculture to seek to recover the cost of the indemnity from those responsible for the contamina- tion. With these changes the bill passed 55 to 31 barely a month after its introduction, and the Mississippi chicken processors appeared to be heading for a windfall sponsored by the subgovernment and rushed through quickly, if not completely quietly.

However, opponents of the measure apparently could generate more strength in the House where the southern agricultural interests are both less numerous and less dominant than in the Senate. The bill started off well by being routinely assigned to the Dairy and Poultry Subcommittee of the Agriculture Committee, a subcommittee chaired by one of the co-sponsors of the bill. However, he felt obliged to hold a one-day hearing at which several congressional and industry spokes- men supported the bill, and one representative of the USDA took a lonely stand against its wisdom. Even his objections might not have been raised except for the amount of publicity already accorded the bill. The full Agriculture Committee reported out the bill (after includ- ing a provision to help out some turkey growers in California who were in similar straits), but six Committee members, all Republicans, filed a minority report, objecting strenuously to the bill. Publicity about the reimbursement had reached such a level that the bill's supporters in the House decided to withdraw it from floor consideration because they feared an outright defeat if it came to a vote.

This incident would hardly have affected the future of the Repub-

lic, regardless of the outcome. It represents an unusual occurrence in
that the normal dominance of the subgovernment was stymied on a
single and relatively unimportant issue. It seems reasonable to assume
that many such initiatives succeed quietly for every one that is successfully challenged. This incident was surely no more than a "blip"
in the normal course of agricultural subgovernment dominance.

Crop disasters and the Small Business Administration: Subgovern-
ment expansion. In 1977 farmers in Georgia and other southeastern
states suffered crop losses because of a drought. This triggered events
that have, thus far, cost the treasury of the United States several billion dollars more than it expected to spend. As of the end of 1978 the
future of the program is in doubt but, nevertheless, it offers an instance
of a subgovernment, in effect, expanding its domain (see Havemann,
1977; and Meisol, 1978, for many details).

The crop problems in Georgia triggered action by Sam Nunn, one of
the Senators from that state and a member of the Senate Select Committee on Small Business, to take the lead in pointing out to both farmers and the Small Business Administration (SBA) that a little-noted
provision of a 1975 statute affecting the SBA had made farmers eligible
for SBA disaster loans. That amendment had been offered by two senior Senators, one of them from a rural state (and chairman of the Senate Small Business Committee).

Once Nunn had pushed the SBA into admitting that it could not exclude farmers from disaster loans, the chairman of the House Small
Business Committee, Neal Smith, an Iowan (Iowa farmers had also suffered crop problems in 1977), joined in urging farmers to apply and the
SBA to respond favorably.

The results were bank-breaking. In Fiscal Year 1976 SBA allowed no
disaster loans to farmers. In Fiscal Year 1977 the SBA made only 798
loans to farmers (4 percent of all of its disaster loans) for a total of
about $40 million. All of these came late in the year as Nunn and Smith
pried open the public coffers for the benefit of their constituents and
other farmers. In the first three quarters of Fiscal 1978 disaster loans
to farmers increased to $1.7 billion—44 percent of the number of SBA
disaster loans and over 75 percent of the total money in the program.

Even though the usual members of agriculture subgovernments had
not instituted this action they now rallied to the cause of preserving
this gain, despite the existence of a parallel program in the Farmers
Home Administration. (Because the parallel program had tighter eligibility requirements and a higher interest rate, the SBA loans looked
particularly attractive.)

Challenges came from two locations: the White House and the Senate Budget Committee. The challenge from within Congress was to no
avail as Congress passed an SBA authorization bill extending the di-

saster loan program, keeping it open to farmers, and putting no dollar limit on expenditures ("such sums as are necessary" were authorized). White House opposition was only partially effective and perhaps would remain so for only a short time. After Congress had left town in October, 1978 (and therefore could not vote on overriding a veto), President Carter vetoed the bill for a number of reasons, including the budget connotations of the treatment of disaster loans for farmers. He objected to the duplication of the program with the Farmers Home Administration loan program, the very low interest rate (3 percent), and the lack of a limit on the amount spent. This veto had the effect of raising the interest rate (to 6.625 percent) but, because of earlier legislation, still left the treasury unguarded throughout Fiscal Year 1979 (which would not end until September 30, 1979). The new interest rate was still low by commercial standards and it is reasonable to project additional expenditures of several billion dollars on farm disasters by SBA during 1979. The future of the program is still in doubt, but those supportive of agricultural subgovernment interests were clearly moving to preserve this gain.

Water resources. Water resources, like agriculture, involve a complicated set of policies and programs. This section first considers the traditionally most important subgovernment (it is not the only one) in the water resources area—the Army Corps of Engineers and its beneficiaries both in Congress and in localities all over the country. Second, we describe President Carter's intrusion into the decision making for funding specific water projects in 1977 and 1978.

The Corps of Engineers-Congress-beneficiary subgovernment. Rivers and harbors projects have been a traditional form of subsidy throughout our national history, and the principal agency involved in rivers and harbors projects has been the Corps of Engineers (see Drew, 1970; Maass, 1950). The Corps' responsibility for developing the nation's water resources is greater than that of potentially competing agencies like the Bureau of Reclamation, the Tennessee Valley Authority, and the Soil Conservation Service. The Corps' projects, which have been described by some as a federal giveaway to local communities, include building of dams, levees, and reservoirs; straightening and otherwise rearranging rivers; and building harbors and canals. The purposes served by Corps' projects include flood prevention, creation and improvement of waterways, and provision of hydroelectric power, water supplies, and recreation opportunities.

The Corps' water resource programs operate through a well-established network of ties between individual congressmen seeking projects for their districts, congressional committees (the House and Senate Public Works committees and the House Public Works Appropriations Subcommittee), officials of the Corps of Engineers, and representatives of affected local interests and national lobbying organizations (such as the National Rivers and Harbors Congress, the Florida Waterways Association, and the Mississippi Valley Association). A description of how a project becomes a reality may help illustrate the ties within the subgovernment (see Drew, 1970).

A project originates at the local level, when representatives of concerns that can see profit in a Corps' project (industrialists, real estate developers, barge companies) get together with the Corps' District Engineer and draw up a proposal for a dam, canal, reservoir, or other project. They then proceed to enlist the aid of their Senators and Representative(s) to sponsor legislation to authorize a study by the Corps of the feasibility of the proposed project. Naturally many proposals never advance beyond this stage, but this is a cheap favor for congressmen to do for their local constituents.

The proposals are referred to the House and Senate Public Works committees. These committees make decisions about which of the projects receive feasibility studies by the Corps, and also about which of the projects that have received the Corps' approval will be authorized for funding and construction. The Appropriations committees provide the funds for the feasibility studies and for the construction of authorized projects. Once a proposal has received authorization for a feasibility study, the Corps' engineers in the district conduct the study (this may entail many years and volumes of technical reports) and report back their recommendations for or against a proposal based on determinations of whether the economic benefits to be derived from the project would be equal to or greater than the costs of the project. (At congressional insistence, the criteria used to evaluate the economic benefits are extremely flexible.) Every two years, in an authorization bill, the Public Works committees identify the projects authorized for feasibility studies and those authorized for construction.

The process of making decisions about whose projects in which districts receive funding is characterized by political negotiation, bargaining, and compromise by the committee members, with a large dose of interest-group lobbying to influence the outcomes. In general the projects are distributed to all parts of the country, but the South, West, and Southwest have the largest proportion of water projects. Former Senator Paul Douglas (Dem., Ill.) offered an assessment of the pork-barrel flavor of the decision making that characterizes water resources decision making (quoted in Drew, 1970: 55): "The [Public Works] bill is built up out of a whole system of mutual accommodations, in which the favors are widely distributed, with the implicit promise that no one will kick over the applecart; that if senators do not object to the bill as a whole, they will 'get theirs.' It is a process, if I may use an inelegant expression, of mutual backscratching and mutual logrolling."

By and large, the subgovernment operates quietly and diplomatically, with the Corps supervising the construction of projects that benefit congressmen's local interests, and Congress authorizing and funding projects that continue the Corps' dominance in water resource development. Occasionally there have been disruptions in the smooth relationship. For example, in 1960 the Corps introduced a stricter set of standards for evaluating the economic benefits to be derived from proposed projects. Immediate resistance from Congress forced dilution of these standards; the Chairman of the Senate Public Works Committee (a senior Senator from a southern state) led the drive against tough standards. He successfully included an amendment in the bill creating a Department of Transportation in 1966 that forced the Corps to revert to its former (1960) evaluation criteria—criteria that maximized the number of projects that could be approved for construction. The language of the amendment was drafted by representatives of the waterways and barge line lobbies (see Haveman and Stephan, 1968).

Although environmental groups have long criticized the Corps' projects, neither they nor other outsiders have been able to change water resource policy significantly or to weaken the influence of the Corps of Engineers in determining that policy. The dominant position of this water resources subgovernment, in which the Corps is the most powerful institutional member, is secure enough to weather temporary tempests such as negative publicity about the use of misleading data to estimate the benefits derived from some projects (see King, 1978, for one example).[1]

Presidential challenge, 1977–1978. In 1977 and 1978 President Jimmy Carter behaved atypically for a president by trying to substitute presidential priorities in water project decisions that customarily are made by water resources subgovernments. In this example Carter was injecting himself into the domain of the subgovernments of both the Corps of Engineers and the Bureau of Reclamation in the Interior Department. The principal reaction in Congress to the perceived intrusion and usurpation of congressional prerogatives and priorities was, predictably, one of outrage. The outcome in the short run was compromise, and for the long run, uncertainty. But to proclaim a new era for the making of water resources policy on the basis of the combat in these two years would clearly be premature.

---

[1] A cheering note for partisans of the Corps: Even if its fortunes decline in the United States (and that is a very large "if") its expertise in the water resources development area is apparently welcome and ready to be used in such countries as China, South Korea, the Philippines, Indonesia, Saudi Arabia, Oman, Qatar, Nigeria, Gabon, and Brazil (see Wilson, 1978). When the Yangtze River has been rechanneled to look like the Ohio River then relations between the United States and the People's Republic of China will, indeed, be "normalized."

In early 1977 President Carter announced that he wanted to defund a number of water projects that were already under construction or in operation. Thirty-five projects were listed, but the President quickly had to drop three from the "hit list" in a concession to political realities. By the time the dust had settled, the President had achieved only a small part of what he wanted. Of the 32 projects identified for deletion, only 9 were actually defunded. Fourteen were completely exempted from deletion, and nine more were modified but allowed to remain in operation. Many of the projects that were exempted or only modified were the largest and most expensive of the 32. They were also the ones with strongest support from important members of Congress and interest groups.

In 1978 he moved his attention to the area of initiating new projects as well as continuing to be concerned about ongoing projects. He initiated 26 projects. Congress also initiated 26 additional projects. When Congress passed a public works appropriations bill containing all of the projects initiated both presidentially and congressionally, Carter reacted with a veto, which was then sustained largely on the basis of Republican votes and first- and second-term Democratic votes in the House. In a few weeks Congress arrived at a compromise that the President signed. It kept 25 of the new presidentially initiated projects and 16 of the congressionally initiated projects. It also dropped funding for six projects that had been deleted in 1977 but restored in the first 1978 bill. It did not do Carter's bidding in the accounting area, however. He had asked that the full cost of projects be provided for in one bill rather than spread out over a number of years and thus masked. Congress responded to this request by promising to hold hearings in 1979, but made no substantive promises. On balance, by virtue of a sustained veto, the President did better with his water initiatives in 1978 than he did in 1977 with his attempts to defund water projects, but it would be hasty to compose an obituary for the subgovernment focused primarily around the Corps of Engineers. Congressional leaders of the fight against Carter in 1978 conceded that the timing of the action (in the closing days of the session) and the sustained veto necessitated a compromise in 1978 but they vowed to renew the fight for congressional (and, by extension, subgovernment) prerogatives in 1979.

Tobacco and smoking. Before 1964 the tobacco industry in the United States—including growers and manufacturers of cigarettes—was protected by an effective subgovernment that subsidized the growers and let the manufacturers alone to advertise their product as they saw fit (see Fritschler, 1975, for a full discussion of this area; see also Friedman, 1975). Fritschler (1975: 4–5) summarizes the composition of the subgovernment and its quiet functioning in the normal pre-1964 situation:

The tobacco subsystem included the paid representatives of to- bacco growers, marketing organizations, and cigarette manufactur- ers; congressmen representing tobacco constituencies; the leading members of four subcommittees in Congress—two appropriations subcommittees and two substantive legislative committees in each house—that handle tobacco legislation and related appropriations; and certain officials within the Department of Agriculture who were involved with the various tobacco programs of that department. This was a small group of people well-known to each other and knowl- edgeable about all aspects of the tobacco industry and its relationship with the government.

As long as no one objected too loudly, the important and complex tobacco programs, like price supports and export promotion, were conducted without interference from those not included in this sub- system.

But there were objections to the tobacco subgovernment from out- siders, specifically the "health lobby" and the Federal Trade Commis- sion. Scientific evidence linking smoking and human diseases had been accumulating at least since 1857, accompanied by a very gradual in- crease in public awareness of the dangers of smoking; this culminated in the United States with the publication of the 1964 report of the U.S. Surgeon General (head of the Public Health Service) that placed an official government seal of approval on assertions about dangers of smoking. Aware of the accumulating body of scientific evidence on smoking, the Federal Trade Commission (FTC) had been engaged in trying to discourage advertising and sales of cigarettes, but without much effect. The tobacco subgovernment would have preferred to leave the whole issue of governmental treatment of tobacco and ciga- rettes as a distributive matter. But the challengers—the "health lobby" and the Federal Trade Commission rulemakers—obviously wished to shift the issue into the regulatory arena.

The objections of the outsiders got loud enough to be disruptive to the subgovernment when the FTC, following the Surgeon General's report on smoking and health, published proposed rules in the *Federal Register* that would have severely restricted advertising for smoking and would have required strict health warnings for cigarettes. These regulations were viewed as very detrimental by the tobacco growers and manufacturers, and the reaction from Congress, led by the strong tobacco subgovernment, was swift. The immediate upshot was the Cigarette Labelling and Advertising Act of 1965, which represented a greater victory for tobacco than for health interests. The bill had two main features. First, the tobacco interests realized that public aware- ness about the dangers of smoking had reached a sufficient level that some government regulation would probably be inevitable. Allied with advertisers and broadcasters, they lobbied for the weakest regulation possible and succeeded in including a very weak labelling requirement in the law (the warning was limited to packages—after the sales had been made—and was not required in advertising). Second, the tobacco interests were also successful in cutting the hamstrings of the outsider that had caused the disruption in the first place—the FTC. The 1965 legislation placed a four-year ban on FTC rule-making activity in the cigarette advertising field, and it also foreclosed other regulatory agencies, as well as state and local agencies, from taking action in the field. The tobacco interests had beaten back the challenge, at least for the time being.

In 1970 Congress passed a law that extended the ban on FTC activities for two more years, weakened the wording of the health warning, and required that the FTC give Congress six months' notice of any future rule-making proposals, thus ensuring that the subgovernment would have ample time to rally its forces.

Subsequently, more government restrictions on advertising for smoking have emerged—a ban on radio and television advertising of cigarettes (contained in a new statute and effective in 1971), a ban on radio and TV advertising of little cigars, and the inclusion of a health warning in advertising as well as on packages. But these additions have come over a period of a number of years, and their implementation has always been gradual and milder than it could have been (for example, the labelling requirement does not mention specific diseases but only mentions "health" in general). It seems plausible to suggest that although some regulation has occurred, the changes forced on the subgovernment have been largely symbolic. The challenge from the FTC and the health lobby has failed to produce anything resembling a full-scale government attack on smoking.

In 1978 the Secretary of Health, Education, and Welfare tried to instigate a major campaign against smoking but without any particular support from the rest of the government and without any noticeable impact.

In fact, as the 1980s begin the tobacco industry can feel that it is still quite secure politically. It has developed lobbying institutions (such as the Tobacco Institute and the Tobacco Tax Council), personnel, and skills that are potent both in Washington and throughout the United States (see Jensen, 1978). An opponent of smoking and chairman of a Senate subcommittee on health, Senator Edward Kennedy of Massachusetts, said that "Hour for hour, and dollar for dollar, they're probably the most effective lobby on Capitol Hill." Tobacco still receives generous federal price supports as an agricultural commodity. Tobacco manufacturing production, sales, and profits all continue to rise, while the amount of the federal excise tax on cigarettes remains stable. This political security is, of course, buttressed by the habits and tastes of millions of Americans, who seem disposed to smoke various forms of tobacco no matter what detrimental health effects result.

Veterans' benefits. Over many decades the veterans' subgovernment has become quite powerful, tapping the public purse for enormous benefits (Scott, 1977). The natural appeal of helping those who have served their country, sometimes in combat, has produced the third largest bureaucracy in the government—the Veterans' Administration, with 220,000 employees, is surpassed in size only by the Defense Department and the Postal Service. The budget of the VA in the late 1970s averaged about $19 billion, making the VA one of the largest spenders in the entire federal establishment as well as one of the largest employers. The VA's budget purchases a range of benefits and programs for veterans (and their dependents and survivors) that include:

The largest single hospital and medical care system in the country (about $5 billion annually).

Educational assistance (over $5 billion annually).

Compensation to injured veterans, regardless of their income (almost $6 billion annually).

Pensions for needy veterans, whose needs do *not* stem from their time in service (over $3 billion annually).

A life insurance program covering over 5 million veterans.

Mortgage insurance loans on over 9 million homes.

Both the cost of benefits and the nature of benefits have expanded over time. Naturally, the number of veterans and eligible relatives also helps determine the actual dollar outlay in any given year.

Critical in determining that these benefits continue to grow is a subgovernment involving the VA, veterans' groups such as the American Legion, Veterans of Foreign Wars, Disabled American Veterans, and the Veterans' Affairs committees of both the House and the Senate (the House Committee has been the congressional bulwark of the subgovernment; the Senate Committee was created only in 1970—perhaps in itself a sign of the strength of the rest of the subgovernment).

In 1978 the veterans' subgovernment demonstrated its power by successfully increasing veterans' benefits in three areas. (1) The non-service-connected disability pension program was amended in three major ways: benefits were increased by as much as 50 percent in some cases, a cost-of-living factor was added to keep pensions increasing, and veterans on these pensions were guaranteed what amounted to a minimum annual income; (2) VA housing programs were liberalized in several important ways; and (3) a special employment and training program for veterans was created in the Department of Labor largely as a response to pressure from veterans' groups. Furthermore, an attempt by the Carter administration to eliminate "veterans' preference" points added to civil service examination results in connection with general civil service reform was unceremoniously dumped in both houses of Congress.

In short, the veterans' subgovernment has been very effective, powerful, and successful in securing extensive and expensive benefits (subsidies) for veterans. The subgovernment has operated with relatively low visibility and limited intrusion by outsiders, and it is rarely challenged. The only source of dissatisfaction with the veterans' subgovernment has stemmed from some organizations of younger, mainly Vietnam-era veterans who are not part of the traditional subgovernment and who are not representative of the "main-line" veterans' groups like the American Legion or the Veterans of Foreign Wars.

Merchant shipping. The structure of subgovernments in the merchant shipping policy area is very fluid. This field is even more fragmented than most distributive policy areas. It is itself composed of sub-subgovernments, and disaggregation of subsidies to recipients is virtually complete. The participants and subsidies are numerous, but the supporters of any given subsidy are not concerned with the existence of other subsidies as long as their own subsidy is continued.

Lawrence (1966) estimates that between 50 and 100 federal government components in both the executive branch and Congress are involved in some way with merchant shipping. Given this fragmentation, it is hardly surprising that a single subgovernment has failed to emerge. The resulting fragmented structure has produced a situation in which industry wishes have dominated policy. Subsidy along familiar lines is thoroughly entrenched and there seems to be no locus in which sufficient interest or energy for change can be generated. Congress as a whole shows no interest in supervising the various subcommittees dealing with pieces of maritime policy. Likewise, the upper echelons of the executive branch show virtually no interest in supervising a variety of executive agencies dealing with pieces of the policy. Consequently, each issue tends to develop its own very small subgovernment made up of a very few people from an obscure subcommittee, an obscure executive agency, the subsidized company or companies, and —as appropriate—the subsidized and/or affected labor union or unions.

The companies are given a particularly strong role to play in instances in which there is tension between the relevant portions of Congress and the executive branch. Certainly it has allowed the retention of existing policies, most of which are generally favored by the shippers.

Lawrence's summary (1966: 331–333) describes a classic case of multiple subgovernments that logically should compete but that, in effect, avoid competition by simply increasing the amount of subsidy indiscriminately:

> Because responsibility is diffused and widely dispersed, no single government agency has sufficient power to seize the initiative to overcome the status quo. Operating at the periphery of government, the administrative agencies and congressional subcommittees concerned with maritime affairs have attempted to resolve problems through negotiation rather than referring them to the President or the Congress as a whole. Frequently they have been forced to compromise on the industry's terms. Higher political echelons, when they have become involved, usually have acted as peacemaker between dissident groups. They have often allowed the cost of the government's program to increase rather than risk alienating any immediately affected group. In effect, creeping liberalization of government aids has substituted for hard decisions and real innovation. . . .
>
> Political support of the merchant shipping industry . . . depends on a very narrow base of informed persons. This small core of trade association, executive, and congressional officials who are friends of the industry has been able to use its friendships and position to safeguard the industry's prerogatives, but it has not been strong enough to introduce any real innovations in established programs. This situation immobilizes the political process. Those favored by the subsidy program have reason to avoid any action which will disturb the equilibrium. Those not so favored tend to be so disorganized that they cannot act effectively to win a larger share. Furthermore, the fragmentation of power within the U.S. political system relieves the shipping industry of any sustained external pressure to introduce innovations.

Nothing important has changed in the maritime situation since Lawrence's analysis in the mid-1960s. The variety of subsidies available is incredibly large and complex and makes little economic sense (Jantscher, 1975). No agency checks these subsidies; rather they all are pleased to help give away their share of the roughly half billion dollars that goes in this direction annually to support a number of shipyards and ships (calculated at 21 of the former and 536 of the latter in 1976 by Cohen, 1976c: 1252). Only occasionally does any new subsidy get turned down; this happened in 1977 when a new cargo preference bill looked too much like a direct political payoff from the administration to supporters in the industry for even Congress to stomach. No existing subsidies are rescinded and the whole package is never rationalized.

One analysis by a journalist (Kohlmeier, 1975: 826), after assessing the chances of reform or meaningful regulation in this area, concluded that "The moral of the tale for reformers . . . is that regulatory reformers come and go but merchant marine subsidies go on forever." A member of Congress, Elliott Levitas (D-Ga.), put it even more pungently in 1978 at a hearing on the relationships between the maritime industry and the Maritime Administration: "The symbiotic relationship between private industry and a government agency is spelled out so clearly here. Here you actually had a marriage formalized with documents. Government and business are right in bed together" (quoted in the *Washington Post*, July 21, 1978: A2). The Congressman should have added that many key members of Congress are in that same bed.

Major subgovernment adaptation

Housing and community development. Federal programs for subsidizing housing have elements of both distributive and redistributive policy (see Aaron, 1972, and Wolman, 1971, on housing and housing politics). The policy goals of federally subsidized housing programs are usually stated in redistributive terms—tax revenue is used to transfer resources to improve the housing conditions of economically disadvantaged members of society. But federal housing programs also have important distributive elements. For example, even though there have been substantial federal efforts aimed at creating and maintaining low income housing for the poor, in operation these programs usually have been more important for their subsidy value to construction interests and mortgage bankers than for their social value to the poor. And in addition, many housing programs offer important distributive benefits to other nonpoor persons, particularly middle-class homeowners. For example, the massive guaranteed mortgage subsidies of the Federal Housing Administration and the Veterans' Administration and the Internal Revenue Service's tax deductions to homeowners all operate to distribute benefits to the middle class, often at the expense of the poor. In this chapter, we will focus on the distributive aspects of federal housing policy.

The most aggressive period of federal intervention to create better housing for the poor came in the 1960s, although such efforts dated back to legislation passed in 1937 and 1949. In the 1950s and 1960s it is significant that the liberal Democratic supporters of housing programs developed close ties both with housing officials in the Department of Housing and Urban Development (created in 1965 to succeed the Housing and Home Finance Agency) and with interest groups such as the National Association of Home Builders, the Mortgage Bankers Association of America, the U.S. Savings and Loan League, and the National Association of Mutual Savings Banks, obviously much more interested in profit than in altruistic goals of social welfare. Joined to this subgovernment were groups representing officials administering federal housing programs (for example, the National Association of Housing and Redevelopment officials and the National Housing Conference) and groups representing the cities and their desires to get additional federal dollars to help solve their problems (principally the National League of Cities and the U.S. Conference of Mayors).

During the period of hegemony of this subgovernment (which lasted until early 1969), this subgovernment operated without successful challenge. Federal dollars flowed to the major supporters: builders, mortgage bankers, and cities. Some poor people also got better housing as a result, but the subgovernment proceeded on the pragmatic grounds of spreading subsidies rather than on the more ideological grounds of justice for the poor.

A variety of categorical programs came into existence under the sponsorship of the liberals in Congress and the affected interest groups, the most visible of these being Model Cities, enacted in 1966. The coalition also pushed through federal programs aimed at sustaining a high level of housing and construction sales for middle class persons (programs such as those administered by the Federal Housing Authority and the Veterans Administration). Other programs included public facilities loans (authorized in 1955), open space land programs (authorized in 1961), basic water and sewer facilities (1965), neighborhood facilities (1965), land acquisition (1965), and urban renewal programs dating back to 1949. The liberal subgovernment produced its last major housing bill in 1968, at which time it added a major home ownership assistance program and a major rental assistance program for persons of low income to already existing public housing and rent supplements programs.

As long as the Democrats remained solidly in control of the Congress and the White House this subgovernment was predominant. But an impasse quickly developed after Nixon became president in 1969. The source of the disagreement between the Republican president and the largely Democratic members of the subgovernment in Congress was the President's desire to dismantle low income housing programs for the poor. During Nixon's first term, Congress and the President could agree on little beside extension of most programs, and even in the cases of extension there were conflicts over such matters as appropriate funding levels. Various programmatic and organizational changes were proposed both by the administration and by leading congressional figures in the subgovernment, but nothing substantial resulted. A major bill consolidating a variety of housing programs into a community development special revenue sharing package passed the Senate in 1972 but was killed by the House Rules Committee when the members of the Committee judged the bill to be so loosely drawn that it would fail on the floor of the House.

In early 1973 the Nixon administration decided to take a major initiative on its own: It suspended virtually all of the major federal programs for aiding the poor to obtain better housing. The liberal Democratic supporters (and some Republicans) of the programs in Congress were outraged, as were their interest group supporters, although different interest groups paid selectively more attention to programs benefitting their interest most.

After a year-and-a-half of almost continuous bargaining and maneuvering a major new law finally emerged in August of 1974: the Housing and Community Development Act of 1974, which packaged a variety of categorical housing programs into a revenue sharing block grant to be distributed to the states and localities on the basis of a formula. The liberal Democrats and their interest group supporters lost some major parts of former housing programs in this new law. Further, the continued existence of the categorical programs that were included in the block grant would depend on decisions made at the local level, not at the federal level. However, the Democrats and their necessarily quiet supporters in Housing and Urban Development (HUD) were successful in retaining and adding major features that were attractive to the desires of the subgovernment for subsidy. Thus, for example, the 1974 Act subsidized a leased housing program, more public housing, housing for the elderly, and an expansion of mortgage credit for middle class homeowners. Collectively these subsidies provided some help for the housing construction industry, provided considerable support for the mortgage bankers, and underwrote the jobs of various public housing officials. The block grant community development section of the bill channeled a lot of money (an authorization of $7.9 billion over a period of three fiscal years) and decision-making power to local governments (cities and counties) thus satisfying in part the representatives of these governments and of community development officials in them. The poor got at least some limited attention in the act through a largely symbolic retention of the home ownership and rental assistance programs from the 1968 Act and through provisions presumably requiring "citizen participation" at the local level as the block grant money was parceled out. How many real benefits the disadvantaged will derive from the 1974 Act remains to be seen, although the early signs are not encouraging. But when confronted with a direct and powerful challenge from the administration, the old subgovernment made some major adjustments and compromises to protect its most important interests. It is not surprising that the interests protected were distributive rather than redistributive ones.

Competing subgovernments

Health research and cancer. During the post-World War II period up until the late 1960s the biomedical and health research community created an enviably strong and, from their point of view, productive subgovernment (see Greenberg, 1967; Strickland, 1972). There were tensions in the development of the subgovernment, but for the last decade or more of its dominance (from roughly the mid-1950s to the late 1960s) it routinely could count on virtually all of the funds it could use profitably (usually more than the Bureau of the Budget and the President requested). There were dominant individuals in the subgovernment in particularly critical institutional positions: the director of the National Institutes of Health, Dr. James Shannon; the chairman of the Senate Appropriations Subcommittee responsible for funding in this broad area, Lister Hill; the chairman of the House Appropriations Subcommittee with parallel jurisdiction, John Fogarty; and a persistent and skillful lobbyist for more and more health-related biomedical research, Mary Lasker.

The subgovernment formed in response to perceptions of the need to increase federal support for health and medical research as a means to improve the nation's health. The success of the subgovernment in creating a federal health-related, biomedical research system is clear in the existence of the extensive National Institutes of Health (NIH) structure with its separate research institutes, which "at its peak in 1967–68 [supported] more than 67,000 senior research investigators; it sustains academic science programs and research projects in more than 2,000 universities and medical schools, and helps provide advanced science training in basic science and various clinical specialties for more than 35,000 individuals" (Strickland, 1972: 236).

Support for the programs of this single subgovernment began to lag in the late 1960s in large part because of the economic demands of the Vietnam War during the Johnson and Nixon presidencies, and also because of greater fiscal conservatism during the Nixon and Ford administrations. As one way of resuscitating the flagging fortunes of biomedical research, a new coalition assembled in the early 1970s, stressing the single goal of conquering cancer. Although the new cancer subgovernment drew some of its key members from the broader and older subgovernment, it also challenged the hegemony of that subgovernment and competed for the same resources. Not surprisingly, real issues developed between the two competitors. Specifically, the cancer group sought autonomy from other layers of the bureaucracy and wanted direct access to the President, in addition to a concentration of funds, to spur their research effort. Also, there were warnings from scientists within the older subgovernment that a special emphasis on one disease would lead to diminished attention to other health research programs.

The cancer group's positions were adopted in the Senate, but supporters for the broader biomedical research position prevailed in the

House. When the 1971 Cancer Act emerged in final form both subgovernments got part of what they wanted, and of necessity had to
maintain an uneasy alliance. The government-sponsored drive against
a single disease, cancer (a particular pet of President Nixon's), was
officially endorsed with special organizational and budgetary recognition, but the National Cancer Institute was to remain within the
structure of the NIH.

In the years following the 1971 Act, the broader biomedical subgovernment has seen its fears realized as budgets for the cancer program
have grown while resources for other NIH research programs have
remained stable or shrunk. In an effort to correct the imbalance, the
biomedical subgovernment pushed successfully in 1974 for inclusion
in the bill renewing the Cancer Act of a provision creating a special
presidential panel to monitor and advise on all federal health research
programs. Top level officials in Health, Education, and Welfare (HEW)
opposed the panel (the President had not requested it), but otherwise
the administration supported the bill, which authorized $2.8 billion
for cancer programs over three years. The inclusion of the clause creating the special monitoring panel met no resistance in either the House
or the Senate, where the bill was passed nearly unanimously. Only one
member of the House committee (but not the subcommittee) with jurisdiction over the bill opposed the bill, objecting to special legislation
for separate diseases. Thus the Cancer Act was renewed for three more
years, and the subgovernments were again required to resume their
competing stances. Cancer research continued to be recognized as a
separate, special program, but the special monitoring panel sponsored
by the health subgovernment may help redress the imbalance between
funding levels for cancer and other health research programs. It is
unlikely that either subgovernment will ever overpower the other as
long as some members belong to both groups and as long as each group
has enough clout in Congress to ensure a sufficient level of authorization and funding to contribute their subsidies.

Action in late 1978 by Congress suggests the continued existence of
a competitive situation, however. Congress passed a single bill reauthorizing the programs of both the National Cancer Institute and the
National Heart, Lung and Blood Institute (the two largest institutes) for
two years. The reauthorization was for a total of roughly $4.2 billion,
about half of which went to cancer, about $1.1 billion to heart, lung,
and blood control and research, and the rest to a variety of other purposes. Congress also instructed the Cancer Institute to expand its research beyond looking for single "causes" of cancer (a glamorous
possibility, but one that has produced limited results) to a preventive
focus based on controllable factors: personal habits such as smoking,
occupational exposure to cancer-causing agents such as asbestos, and

environmental exposure to cancer-causing agents such as certain air or water pollutants.

When the budgets for all of the National Institutes of Health are examined the picture of competition also emerges. The Cancer Institute part of the total National Institutes of Health budget was 32 percent in 1977 and was slated to shrink gradually to 30 percent in the next two years. Growth planned for the Cancer budget between 1977 and 1979 was less than that planned for any of the other ten Institutes, although the budget for the Cancer Institute remained much larger than that for any other single Institute.

Patents versus antitrust. An almost invisible and highly technical continuing conflict exists between a distributive subgovernment centered around the Patent and Trademark Office and a subgovernment centered around the Antitrust Division in the Department of Justice that is essentially regulatory (although it has distributive elements, too). Although resolution of the conflict between the two subgovernments has been sought over the past fifteen years, no settlement has emerged. The competition between the two subgovernments has produced a policy stalemate that results in patent policy that favors monopoly but that also has low credibility when challenged in the courts. The detailed technical disputes over the nature of patent policy do not concern us here, but the shape and membership of the competing subgovernments illustrate how two such entities can coexist over a long period of time within the same governmental institutions and produce the erratic and bifurcated policy that characterizes the combination of patent and antitrust policy most of the time.

The patent subgovernment is made up of key individuals from the Patent and Trademark Office, the patent bar (that is, lawyers seeking patents for clients or challenging other patents), corporations seeking and receiving patents, and the Senate Judiciary Committee's Subcommittee on Patents, Trademarks, and Copyrights (see Cohen, 1974). The mission of the Patent and Trademark Office is to promote business growth by granting limited monopolies through patents. It is located in the Commerce Department, which is generally expected to be the administration's supporter of business regardless of which party controls the White House. The lawyers of the patent bar and their clients have an obvious interest in having the Patent and Trademark Office proceed quietly and privately to grant as many patents as possible (although there are, of course, conflicts between companies over specific patents).

The antitrust subgovernment that relates to patent policy is composed of key individuals from the Antitrust Division and members of the Senate Judiciary Committee's Subcommittee on Antitrust. This subgovernment seeks to reform and open up the patent granting subgovernment, and points to the Patent and Trademark Office's poor record in the courts—when its decisions are challenged, they are often overturned by the judges.

Relationships between the two subgovernments are anything but cordial. The Commissioner of Patents from 1971 to 1973 stated a common view among members of the patent subgovernment when he labeled the Antitrust Division as "the enemy" and spoke of mutual hostility between the Patent and Trademark Office and the Antitrust Division. In Congress the chief counsel to the Senate patent subcommittee represented the view of the congressional members of the subgovernment when he criticized a reform proposal made by the Antitrust Division because it had been drafted by people "who have no patent experience" and because "the recommendations of the Commerce Department were not generally accepted" (Cohen, 1974: 480). The chairman of the Senate Patent Subcommittee opposed a bill introduced by the chairman of the Senate Antitrust Subcommittee that would have made the Patent and Trademark Office independent and presumably more visible and more subject to scrutiny by its congressional critics. The Patent chairman favored the existing organizational arrangement, which, of course, kept the Patent and Trademark Office tied to his subcommittee. The Patent and Trademark Office and the administration also favored retention of the existing institutional arrangements.

Despite a presidential commission in 1966 and major legislative activity (but no law) in 1974, the conflict between the patent and antitrust subgovernments continues. Unless major change can be imposed, the patent subgovernment will continue to prevail until it gets to the courts—then, in effect, a number of judges become operative members of the antitrust government. So stalemate continues. Both subgovernments partially check the wishes of the other, but consistent policy that will stand up under judicial review is lost in the process.

Subgovernment disintegration

Occasionally a subgovernment will lose such a major battle that it will distintegrate or at least change character drastically. For example, if the cancer lobby had succeeded in creating a new subgovernment at the expense of the broader biomedical research subgovernment, that might well have been the beginning of the breakup of the broad group into a series of specialized, ailment-specific subgovernments. Biomedical research might have, under such conditions, come to resemble the merchant shipping situation described above.

Another way for a subgovernment to disintegrate is for the issue to be redefined out of the distributive arena into either the regulatory or redistributive arena. This is rare since the natural tendencies for redefinition run in the other direction, but it can happen. For example, the tobacco subgovernment lost at least some hegemony over antismoking activity by the government because the issue was no longer solely one of subsidy but had become one of regulation for public health. Likewise, the rise of ecological concerns in the regulatory arena has caused even such a venerable subgovernment as that focused around the programs of the Army Corps of Engineers to lose an occasional decision. But in neither of these cases was the distributive element— the ability to generate subsidies—seriously impaired, and neither subgovernment appears to be in danger of collapse.

Sugar. A case of temporary collapse followed by what appears to be fairly rapid rehabilitation occurred in one of the most venerable of subgovernments—in fact, the example that Cater (1964) used when he coined the term "subgovernments." In 1974 the world of the sugar subgovernment was turned upside down when the House of Representatives defeated an extension of the Sugar Act by a vote of 209 to 175: The basic structure of a series of subsidies to sugar growers and processors that had been in place since 1934 dissolved.

There were several reasons for the defeat of the Sugar Act in 1974, but the basic reason was that the soaring retail price of sugar in a time of high national inflation made sugar subsidies visible to consumer groups. The visibility was heightened because the timing of the price increases coincided with the renewal of the Act in Congress. Pressure from consumer groups redefined the traditional subsidy issue into one of regulation to protect consumers. The high prices also provoked the opposition of industrial users of sugar (manufacturers of candy, soft drinks, and other refined foods) who felt that the price increases reflected more profit motive than market necessities. An additional element helping to defeat the bill was the inclusion in the House of some pro-labor amendments that diluted the distributive character of the Act by introducing redistributive tones that were jarring to the normal supportive coalition.

The Act had many features, central of which was the detailed division of the U.S. sugar market between domestic and foreign producers. Producers were given a guaranteed market and, in effect, guaranteed profits. An excise tax on the production went to support the income of the growers in the United States. Thus U.S. growers and processors alike worked in a completely managed economy—with set quotas for growers on the amount that could be grown and marketed to processors and with quotas for processors on the amount that could be produced and sold to both industrial and, ultimately, individual users. The payoff was a price usually higher than the world market (despite the availability of less expensive foreign sugar) and profits for growers and producers that were stable, high, and virtually guaranteed for domestic interests and the foreign processors who lobbied frantically for increased shares of the foreign allotment.

The authorization hearings to extend the Sugar Act beyond 1974 began normally. The House Agriculture Committee—a key institution in the subgovernment—held hearings at which leading members of the Committee, representatives from the industry, and officials from the Department of Agriculture praised the bill. The Department did suggest some major modifications that would have moved the sugar price system toward a freer market, but the Secretary assured the Committee of his general support, and the Department was probably not much surprised or dismayed when its modest initiatives were largely rejected by the Committee.

When the bill came to the House floor in June the subgovernment was presumably confident of victory. However, they had not counted on the impact that escalating sugar prices were having on groups such as the National Consumers Congress, the National Consumers League, Consumer Action for Improved Food and Drugs, and the Corporate Accountability Research Group, all of whom lobbied against the bill and found members of the House willing to listen rather than routinely approving the work of the Committee as they had been doing periodically for almost 40 years.

The world economy and, some would assert, the greed of U.S. processors had redefined the political context of sugar, and the subgovernment had not had the foresight to prepare for the redefinition.

The private sector members of the former sugar subgovernment did not suffer economically in 1975 and 1976, although the record prices of late 1974 dropped modestly. However, as world production of sugar increased enormously world prices began to fall substantially—for example, raw sugar had sold for 57.3¢ a pound in November, 1974; in January, 1977, it sold for 11.5¢. Domestic producers of sugar began to lose business and profits because the big users of sugar in the country— soft-drink producers, candymakers, and bakeries—naturally bought cheap foreign sugar. Many of the subsidies, including the high tariffs and quotas for foreign imports, were no longer in place to protect those U.S. concerns with direct economic interests.

Under these conditions the subgovernment began to revive and reassemble itself both in terms of identifying important members and agreeing on programmatic requests to the new Carter administration and to Congress. A complicated set of subsidies won the support of the President and almost came out of Congress in the closing days of the 95th Congress in 1978. However, the smoothness with which the pre-1974 subgovernment had worked had not been fully recaptured; the final conference committee compromise still left enough interests dissatisfied that the conference committee compromise was killed on the House floor.

It was clear, however, that Congress would again consider sugar legislation in the 96th Congress (1979–80). A reasonable guess is that the subgovernment would continue to regroup and polish its technique to insure that success—and subsidies—would be forthcoming, almost surely at the expense of the individual consumer of sugar, an unorganized interest (see King, 1977). Before the 96th Congress convened, Department of Agriculture representatives met with industry representatives to work out a price support bill they could all support. Higher retail sugar prices were predicted.

CONCLUSIONS

The case material presented in this chapter supports two general conclusions: first, that the general picture of the distributive arena drawn at the outset of this chapter is largely accurate, and second, that subgovernments are not completely static (and perhaps not as static as the literature would seem to suggest) but can change and adapt to changing conditions in a number of ways.

The cases of subgovernment dominance lend support to the overview of the distributive arena summarized in the first six columns of Table 4–1. In these cases virtually all aspects of the issues were decided within the confines of the subgovernment: rarely was there intervention by "outsiders." Normally the degree of cooperation was very high, but when there were conflicts they were resolved within the confines of the relationship on the basis of face-to-face negotiations, resulting in a rather straightforward compromise that left everyone reasonably happy.

In the last column of Table 4–1 it is asserted that if conflict persists the congressional position taken by the subcommittee is more likely to prevail than the bureaucratic position (or at least the compromise will be weighted in that direction). In the cases of conflict this generally seems to hold true. When Congress and the Corps of Engineers disagreed over the nature of the proper cost-benefit ratio for the Corps to use, the congressional position prevailed. When Department of Agriculture spokesmen were less than enthusiastic about indemnifying Mississippi broiler processors in 1974, Senator Eastland's position was still accepted by the Committee and the full Senate. Also in 1974 when the Department of Agriculture attempted to modify the sugar bill in the direction of a freer market its suggestions were rejected by the House committee and the committee position was that which went to the floor.

One exception to the generalization appears in the merchant shipping area. Here when Congress and the bureaucracy disagree it appears that the usual resolution is a role larger than normal for industry spokespersons and their position. This seems to be an artifact of the super-fragmented structure of the policy area.

Only rarely do "outsiders" have much impact on the business of a subgovernment, as in the cases of the probably temporary victory for large commercial users of sugar in 1974 and the limited impact of President Carter on the water resources area in 1977–78.

The ways in which subgovernments can change are numerous. A "smart" subgovernment—one intent on preserving its dominance without serious diminution—will adjust to potentially threatening developments ahead of time, perhaps by finding a way of defusing them. Sometimes a challenge that is defeated will provide the cues for the subgovernment about the line of marginal policy change it would be wise to make. Often a challenge that is successful will force marginal adjustments that still preserve the substance of policy and the reality of subgovernment dominance. The ability of the tobacco subgovernment to adjust to the relatively mild antismoking measures that have been adopted is an excellent case of a subgovernment doing well from its own perspective even under a presumably serious attack.

Continuing competition among several subgovernments can also stimulate one or more of them to make adjustments that will preserve their importance and dominant positions. The biomedical lobby has not given in to the challenge of the cancer lobby but has continued successfully to generate support for broad health research.

Only rarely does a subgovernment fold altogether and, as the sugar case demonstrates, a defeated subgovernment may well possess Lazarus-like qualities.

In short, subgovernments are far from unchanging phenomena, even in the distributive arena. They are, however, remarkably persistent and tenacious. Consequently, most distributive policy usually remains under the control of subgovernments. Those policies change—but usually slowly and with a large measure of approval from the subgovernment members. New subgovernments can come into being as new issues emerge and as old issues that have been regulatory or redistributive are redefined as distributive. And old subgovernments can sometimes expand their domains.

～5～

Protective regulatory policy

THE NATURE OF PROTECTIVE REGULATORY POLICY

REGULATION OF private activities for the presumed protection of the general public or major parts of it has been undertaken by the federal government in a major way for nearly a century. The general pattern has been for Congress to legislate broad policy goals and perhaps a few details and then establish a regulatory commission or other agency in the bureaucracy to develop and administer all or most of the details necessary for achieving the goals.

There is considerable variation in the types and operations of regulatory agencies. A few are concerned much of the time with competitive regulation. Thus the Federal Communications Commission (FCC) decides who gets what television channels and what radio frequencies. The Interstate Commerce Commission (ICC) decides what trucking companies, barge lines, pipelines, and railroads get what routes for what goods. And the Civil Aeronautics Board (CAB) decides what airlines get what routes (although the CAB role in this process is being diminished at its own request). But even these agencies have protective duties to perform: the FCC is supposed to make sure that broadcasters serve the public interest by not broadcasting offensive material (either program content or advertisements); the ICC has rules designed to protect the consumer who hires a moving company; and the CAB makes rules designed to protect the lungs of non-smokers from the pollution created by their fire-breathing brothers and sisters on airplanes.

Most regulatory agencies are concerned primarily with protective regulation. Public debate over "de-regulation" often confuses the protective and competitive modes of regulation. Economic and political pros and cons in relation to both kinds of regulatory policy are often debated in a jumble, both by academics and by officials.[1] In this chapter we focus on the politics of protective regulation, paying primary attention to policy formulation and legitimation.

Beginning in the late 19th century a number of agencies were created that were primarily concerned with regulation of the conditions under which different kinds of private activity could and could not take place. At least four major waves of such regulatory activity have been identified, and each wave has left its residue of bureaucracies that have become permanent (Wilson, 1975).

The first wave occurred between 1887 and 1890 and produced the Interstate Commerce Act (aimed at regulating railroads) and the Sherman Antitrust Act (aimed at regulating trusts that had been created to achieve monopolies in the provision of various goods). The second wave came between 1906 and 1915 and produced the Pure Food and Drug Act, the Meat Inspection Act, the Federal Trade Commission Act (aimed at preventing unfair business practices such as deceptive advertising), and the Clayton Act (aimed at strengthening the antitrust law). The third wave came during the 1930s and produced the Food, Drug, and Cosmetic Act; the Public Utility Holding Company Act (aimed at preventing the concentration of economic power in the public utility field); the Securities Exchange Act (aimed at regulating the stock market); the Natural Gas Act; and the National Labor Relations Act (aimed primarily at preventing unfair labor practices by business). The fourth wave began in the late 1960s and was aimed at protecting consumers and the environment. It has produced such legislation as the Water Quality Act, the Clean Air Act, the Truth in Lending Act, the National Traffic and Motor Vehicle Safety Act, amendments to the drug control laws, and the Motor Vehicle Pollution Control Act.

---

[1] Recall that protective regulatory policy is quite different from competitive regulatory policy, as we explained in Chapter 1. Competitive regulatory policy is found almost exclusively at the implementation stage of policymaking; it is rarely formulated at the general level, from scratch, but instead involves application of regulations by the agency to individual participants on a case-by-case basis. The main actors in its implementation are generally members of the agency, representatives of the regulated interests, and individual members of Congress (but not the institution of Congress—the subcommittees, committees, or either house). Protective regulatory policy, on the other hand, is frequently the object of formulation and legitimation, with the actors including representatives from the agency and the regulated interests as well as institutional parts of Congress.

Throughout the 19th century Congress oversaw the activities of regulatory agencies with considerable care, and thus the agencies did not develop a great deal of independent political weight. However, as agencies increased in size and number they began to develop independent political power. At the same time, Congress began to delegate more power to them and to pay less attention to the exercise of that power. Thus the foundations were laid for what has been called "the bureaucratic state" (Wilson, 1975). When government vastly increased its scope of activity in the 1930s, Congress increased the amount of latitude it gave regulatory bureaucracy through rather vague delegations of power, increasing the basis for almost independent bureaucratic influence (Lowi, 1979).

Decisions about protective regulatory policy are characterized by considerable visibility. As policies are debated those entities targeted for regulation are very conscious of what they think is at stake for them. In general, most of those vulnerable to regulation—mining companies, petroleum producers, and pharmaceutical companies, for example—would prefer to avoid government regulation altogether. But where regulation seems inevitable, they pursue options designed to make the regulation as light as possible or to acquire governmentally conferred benefits simultaneously as a form of compensation for being regulated. When new areas of regulatory activity or major changes in existing activity are under debate, however, quiet functioning of subgovernments is not possible. In fact, given shifting interests, subgovernments may not even be a feature of the policy landscape in a given area. When implementation of existing regulation occurs subgovernments may be more likely to form and have an impact.

Coalitions of groups involved in regulatory decisions are unstable, depending on what is at stake. Groups contend for the favor of Congress, but usually at the level of the full House and Senate (and conference committees) rather than only at the level of subcommittee or committee. Subcommittees and committees certainly get involved in decisions but their preferences often get altered by other decision makers. Similarly, in the executive branch, when regulatory policy is implemented, there is more central direction of that implementation and far less autonomy for individual bureaus within a department or other large agency.

THE CONGRESSIONAL-BUREAUCRATIC RELATIONSHIP IN PROTECTIVE REGULATORY POLICY

We expect the relationship between bureaucrats (at the bureau level) and individuals in Congress (members and staff members in Senate and House subcommittees) to be only sporadically critical in protective regulatory policy. Only some of the issues of regulation get full consideration within the confines of the relationship itself. Major decisions on new areas for regulation or on changes in existing regulations typically get made by the full Congress interacting with a high level of bureaucratic actor, such as individuals from the office of a departmental secretary or the White House. Only in the stable regulatory areas does the relationship become important in the sense of allowing the participants to make what amounts to final decisions. And even then the chances of review by higher authorities is greater than in the distributive area.

Conflict is much more frequent in this area than in distributive policy. When conflict occurs at the bureau-subcommittee level it often arises because the congressional actors who are seeking exceptions to regulations for favored constituents or clients meet with resistance from bureaucrats who oppose those exceptions. Less often the congressional actors are pushing the bureaucrats for more rigorous enforcement of regulations. Conflict over regulatory policy also occurs at a higher level than the bureau-subcommittee relationship because participants who are dissatisfied with the decisions made at the subcommittee level can appeal those decisions to the full committee, the House or Senate floor, and the conference committee.

Disagreements between subcommittee members and bureaucrats may get resolved within the relationship, but usually the conflict gets transferred to a higher level, either because the participants themselves appeal to the higher levels, or because higher levels intervene in the conflict on their own initiative.

If resolution of disagreement occurs within the subcommittee-bureau relationship it is likely to be a compromise between initial specific positions. Some disagreements may also go unresolved for some time. Still others may be made part of a broader compromise (not necessarily at some midpoint) reached at a higher level of institutional actor.

In cases of disputes between the two branches, the congressional position probably prevails more often—especially when the full Congress gets involved.

The regulatory arena is not undifferentiated in terms of what is at stake and how the actors behave, however. There are at least three major kinds of situations in which behavior might be expected to vary. Each of these three situations will be investigated by looking at several instances of regulatory action or proposed action in recent years.

The first kind of situation is one in which the focus of debate is over the creation of federal regulatory power that had not previously existed or had existed in only sporadic and scattered form.

The second kind of situation is one in which major alteration of existing federal regulatory power is the focus of debate. These alterations are usually in the direction of more federal power.

The third kind of situation is one in which specific instances of the application of existing federal regulatory power is the focus of debate.

The creation of regulatory power

Strip mining. The strip mining process is an efficient (in a narrow economic sense) means of removing coal from the earth—layers of earth are scraped away to expose veins of coal that lie relatively close to the surface. However the aftermath of this process can be devastating aesthetically and economically debilitating, because unless care is taken in the selection of the site and in the use of reclamation procedures the land can be permanently scarred, eroded, and made barren, and water can be severely polluted. Some 26 states where strip mining occurs have enacted legislation to prevent this negative aftermath, but this legislation varies greatly in restrictiveness and enforcement.

The need for coal, both in the short run and in the long-range future, was dramatically underscored in 1973 by the Arab oil embargo and the "energy crisis." Coal was thrust suddenly into the forefront as a desirable source of energy for the United States both because the deposits are extensive and because the technology of strip mining is present for extracting it. It was assumed that coal would play a major role in helping the United States meet its officially announced goal of energy self-sufficiency, a policy designed to make the country less dependent on foreign sources of fuel, especially oil.

Congress has been involved in the question of whether the federal government should regulate strip mining since 1968, when the Senate first held hearings on specific bills on the subject. In 1971 President Nixon proposed legislation and in 1972 the House passed a bill but the Senate did not act. In 1973 the Senate passed a bill. In 1974 the House passed a bill and went to conference with the Senate on its 1973 bill. After a long conference that almost collapsed at several points Congress passed a bill only to have President Ford pocket veto it, thus preventing an attempt to override the veto. By mid-March 1975, both the Senate and House had again passed bills similar to the vetoed bill, and again the President vetoed the bill. The attempt to override was delayed because of weakening support in the House, and when the attempt was made in July, 1975, it failed by three votes.

In late 1975 attempts were made in the House Interior Committee to revive the bill but they failed, largely because the pro-bill forces calculated that President Ford could again prevent what they wanted by a veto they could not override. Similarly, in 1976, the House Rules Committee forestalled a veto by twice preventing strip mining bills from reaching the House floor. (Also in 1976 the Department of the Interior promulgated regulations that allowed increased strip mining of coal on federal land in the West.)

In 1977 the basic political situation for the proponents of federal strip mining legislation changed dramatically because of the election of Jimmy Carter, who pledged support for a bill in this area. By mid-1977 such a bill became law.

What follows tells two selected parts of the complicated story sketched above. The first part focuses on the debate and decision making in 1974. The second part concentrates on 1977.

1974.   The basic controversy in this area since at least 1971 had been whether there should be a federal law at all and, if so, how strong it should be. The administration bills introduced in both 1971 and 1973 were regarded as weak by the environmentalists and leading Democratic supporters of strong legislation. The coal producers and most of the electric companies that burn vast quantities of coal to generate electricity wanted no bill at all. Their basic contention was that the coal companies were public-spirited about reclamation and that state regulation was sufficient anyway.

The general position of the "anti" coalition (that is, those opposed to any regulation or at least to a strong bill) was that the controls proposed in the legislation would reduce output of coal drastically and would also raise its price. Either result would damage the energy self-sufficiency program endorsed by the administration. The general position of the "pro" coalition (that is, those favoring a strong bill) was that strip mining had to be stringently regulated in order to avoid the risk that the entire country would emerge looking like the worst parts of Appalachia after strip mining. They argued that federal regulation was necessary because the states couldn't or wouldn't act with sufficient force to curb the problem. They disputed the estimates of the opposing coalition that strip mining regulations would cut the output of coal production significantly. Only a few members of the "pro" coalition favored banning strip mining altogether.

A brief chronology of the 1974 process will help to set the background. The Senate had passed a bill in October 1973, by a vote of 82 to 8 (the Senate Interior and Insular Affairs Committee had reported the bill to the full Senate without any dissenting votes). Two subcommittees of the House Interior and Insular Affairs Committee—one on Environment and one on Mines and Mining—considered the bill jointly. The full House Interior Committee reported the bill favorably on May 30, 1974, by a vote of 26 to 15. The House held an unusually long debate on the bill—six days—before passing it with some amendments on July 25 by a vote of 298 to 81. The conference committee met off and on for a total of 87 hours between August 7 and December 3 before finally reaching an agreement. Both houses approved the conference report by voice vote very late in the session, but President Ford refused to sign it and the bill died as a result.

Several features of the 1974 process deserved special mention. First, detailed drafting of the legislation was accomplished in subcommittees, committees, and the conference committee. However, unlike distributive policy, final decisions were not made at the committee level. Whichever interests felt they had "lost" by the decisions made in the various committee stages—particularly in the House—still had a chance to appeal their case to the full House or full Senate by getting a friendly member to introduce an amendment to redress their losses. Thus the same battles tended to be fought before the committee and on the floor because the losers could come forward a second time. The same situation was at least potentially present with respect to the conference committee. The "losers" in conference could always appeal their case again to the full House or full Senate. This route was not fully used because the compromise in conference had taken so long to work out that Congress was very near adjournment, and the majorities of both houses were in a mood to pass the bill quickly and await presidential action.

Organized groups for all of the affected interests—environmentalist groups; coal, steel and electric companies; the U.S. Chamber of Commerce; and the United Mine Workers Union—and a large number of executive officials from the White House Council on Environmental Quality, Environmental Protection Agency, Department of Commerce, Department of the Interior, and the Federal Energy Administration approached both the House subcommittees and committee and the conference committee. Some of the interests—both private and bureaucratic—made some gains at the committee level. As Congressman Morris Udall, Chairman of the House Subcommittee on the Environment, said in speaking of the administration representatives, "We have done all the compromising we are going to do. We accepted a couple of dozen of their amendments in committee, and they just come back for more. The demands are insatiable." (Quoted in the *Washington Post,* July 10, 1974: A–2.)

Second, the coalitions supporting and opposing regulation of strip mining by the federal government were broad-based but unstable. The legislation was complex and contained numerous features that were separable in an analytical sense. Both coalitions included members who were interested only in narrow features of the bill that affected them directly. On other specific issues, these members would be relatively inactive or would even desert the coalition. For example, the United Mine Workers' executive board narrowly endorsed the bill, but their real concern was with an amendment to tax strip mined coal more heavily than deep mined coal. Such an amendment would have encouraged exploitation of coal reserves in the East (most of which are too deep to be strip mined) where most UMW strength exists (a rival union represents the workers engaged in strip mining in the West). (The amendment, offered on the House floor, was defeated.)

Another example is provided by Pennsylvanians who supported the bill but whose real concern was that an amendment be added to exempt Pennsylvania's anthracite coal from the provisions of the bill on the grounds that Pennsylvania was already regulating such mining with sufficient laws and vigor. This amendment passed the House and was included in the final bill.

Yet another example: Once the conference report passed both houses some coal companies broke previously united ranks engineered by the National Coal Association and urged the President to sign the bill as a better alternative than a possibly more restrictive bill in 1975. The same position was taken by the Chairman of the Board of Bethlehem Steel, a major consumer of coal.

Third, the executive branch agencies were badly split in their views of the bill as it progressed through the congressional process, and they kept changing their public stances. There were basically two divisions of opinion among the agencies. The Council of Environmental Quality and the Environmental Protection Agency supported both the legislation in general and the details that emerged from the conference committee. The Federal Energy Office, the Commerce Department, and the White House (with support from OMB and the Treasury Department) supported only relatively weak legislation at most. The Interior Department was caught between the conflicting views and adopted a shifting attitude.

The administration was so divided that key administrators felt safe in making their disagreements public. While the bill was still awaiting floor action in the House, for example, the Administrator of the Environmental Protection Agency publicly supported the bill, thereby contradicting the official administration position at the time that the bill was unacceptable because of its alleged impact on coal production and energy self-sufficiency.

Later in the process, when the head of the Federal Energy Administration said that he had recommended that the President veto the bill, two other officials—one from the Environmental Protection Agency and one from the Interior Department—said that they had urged him to sign it.

The Interior Department constantly changed and modified its position throughout the process. It was thought through the spring of 1974 that the Department supported a reasonably strong bill. But after the House committee had agreed on a bill the Secretary of the Interior attacked it on the grounds of diminished coal production. During the summer of 1974 both the Energy Administration and the Interior Department revised downward their estimates of how much production would be lost, and by the time the bill finally passed, the Interior Department counseled the President to sign it.

The administration was so indecisive at the very end of the process that a somewhat unusual—or perhaps bizarre would be a better word —attempt was made to effect a last-minute compromise that would avoid a veto. While the President was still deciding whether to sign or veto the bill, communications between the Chairman of the Senate Interior Committee and the administration led the administration to think that somehow Congress could pass another strip mining bill in the few days left in its session to be signed along with the original bill. Presumably this additional bill would contain amendments that would make the two put together palatable enough to gain Ford's signature. Congress, of course, can rarely act with such speed short of a genuine national emergency. And the spectacle of a President signing a bill and amendments to weaken it before it had been law for more than a day or two made such a happening unlikely. Nothing emerged, except that the President used the amendments he had requested in late 1974 as the basis for the administration bill sent to Congress in early 1975.

Fourth, the critical decisions on the substance of the legislation were made on the House floor and in conference committee in the form of acceptance or rejection of amendments. Naturally, the House subcommittees and full committee had set the agenda for House floor action— as is the case for virtually every piece of legislation in all policy areas —but a broad range of options was presented, debated, and decided on the House floor. Likewise, enough differences remained between the House version passed in July 1974 and the Senate version passed in October 1973 that a broad range of options also received consideration in the lengthy conference committee proceedings.

In short, the quiet, stable politics of distribution were nowhere to be seen in the maneuvering and decision making that marked this proposal for a major new federal regulatory endeavor. Instability and public proceedings were much more characteristic than were the stability, predictability, and privacy that usually are the hallmarks of a distributive issue. Furthermore, resolution of the conflicts was transferred all the way up to the highest level—the President—where the "compromise," determined by a presidential veto, was a decision to have no regulation at all. This pattern of visibility, conflict, and presidential resolution was repeated again in consideration of the 1975 strip mining bill.

1977. In 1977 the proponents of strong federal legislation had to retreat a bit further than even the 1974 and 1975 bills to get a bill through Congress. Unlike the previous years, however, getting the President's approval was no problem.

The first compromise decision made by the proponents was to limit the bill almost exclusively to coal mining. Earlier bills had covered other kinds of mining, such as for copper, but the possibility of a powerful negative coalition being formed by a number of the interests targetted for regulation led to the focus on only one interest.

As in 1974, issues were not settled quietly and finally in subcommittee and committee. Rather, decisions made in those settings were reexamined, debated, and extensively amended on the floors of both the House and the Senate. And some issues remained to be resolved in the conference committee.

In general terms the House committee produced a moderately strong bill in late April. It passed the House a week later and had been strengthened even more on the House floor. In the Senate a different outcome occurred: The Committee reported a moderately strong bill in early May but a few weeks later the bill was weakened considerably on the Senate floor by expanding the allowable mining in alluvial valley floors in the West, withdrawing the requirement that the owners of the surface approve the mining of federally owned coal under their land, exempting small miners from some of the environmental standards set in the bill, and watering down the provision that the original contours of the land had to be restored at the conclusion of mining.

The conference committee bill, reported in July, was, predictably, somewhere between the two versions presented to it. The principal concessions to the mining interests were in the areas of mining alluvial valley floors, a 24-month exemption from environmental standards for smaller operators, variances allowed in restoring original contours, and permission of mountaintop removal as an acceptable mining method. Both houses passed the bill and the President signed it in early August.

As in 1974, then, the final decisions were made on the floor and in conference and the regulated interests prevailed on some issues. The supporters of federal regulation made an early decision to focus only on coal in order to keep an opposing coalition from forming (copper mine owners and companies could not be expected to weep and work for coal mine owners and companies unless they too were threatened).

The coal companies did not give up their fight with the passage of the Act. In a sequel typical of protective regulatory policy, the regulated interests simply shifted their pressure from Congress to the bureaucracy responsible for implementing the legislation. The Department of the Interior drafted elaborate regulations to spell out the details of the legislation, and in 1978 the coal owners, led by the single largest coal company in the nation, filed suit in Federal District Court to protest a number of regulations that the Interior Department had promulgated. In early 1979 a six-month delay in the imposition of the new strip mining limits was granted. White House economists, Energy Department officials, and the coal industry reportedly forced the Interior Department to grant this delay, despite the displeasure of environmental groups.

Consumer protection. Policymaking for consumer protection might be labelled *ad hoc* policy entrepreneurship, because there is a high degree of opportunity for individual participants—interest representatives, bureaucrats, members of Congress, and presidential appointees—to have important impact on what the government does or doesn't do with specific regulatory activity. It is also an area in which the policies of old-line agencies are particularly susceptible to influence of aggressive members of Congress (see Nadel, 1971). Their intervention may cause creation of new regulatory power or change in existing power, but it also results in piecemeal regulatory policy, not new statements or restatements of coherent policy, not even industry by industry let alone industrial sector by industrial sector. Naturally, too, the aggressive congressmen and subcommittees can also be on several sides of an issue—some can be pushing for new regulatory powers or more stringent use of existing powers; others can be pushing in the opposite direction.

"The consumer" became a salient issue in American public life in the late 1960s and early 1970s, but regulatory agencies with a variety of actual or potential powers to wield in behalf of consumers—the Food and Drug Administration, the Federal Trade Commission, the Federal Power Commission—were slow to act on their own to redefine and broaden their regulatory functions to include advocacy for consumers. They were caught up in the status quo, which often had a lethargic, industry-oriented flavor. The impact of consumer interest groups on these agencies was virtually nonexistent, and so the pro-consumer position had to be represented forcefully to the agencies by interested congressmen and subcommittees if it was to be represented at all. Because Congress as an institution can apply sanctions to agencies (withholding funds, delaying authorizations, not granting desired bills) and because agencies are aware of this potential, they do pay attention to the wishes of individual congressmen. Thus activist members played something of an agenda-setting role in many of the regulatory agencies. Although there have been many contacts between congressional offices and regulatory agencies, however, most of these are of an ad hoc nature, not a lasting relationship.

A great many committees and subcommittees of Congress are involved in aspects of consumer protection. In the 89th and 90th Congresses (1965–68) for example, Congress passed 15 consumer-oriented statutes. In the Senate these came from five different committees (Agriculture, Commerce, Judiciary, Banking and Currency, and Labor and Public Welfare) and in the House they came from four different committees (Agriculture, Interstate and Foreign Commerce, Science and Astronautics, and Banking and Currency). This proliferation of decision loci enhances the opportunities for policy entrepreneurship emerging from Congress. (See Nadel, 1971: 117–118 for a complete listing of acts and committees.)

Thus in the broad range of consumer issues, it appears that subgovernments do not exist but rather coalitions will spring up over individual issues as they arise. In general, the consumer groups do not appear to have established themselves as consistently powerful or influential. Individual congressmen, staff members, and subcommittees have shown the capacity for generating new regulatory power for often unwilling bureaucracies and for generating at least sporadic pro-consumer action by the same bureaucracies on the basis of existing statutory powers.

One of the most recurrent consumer-related issues since 1970 has been the question of whether a new pro-consumer agency should be established within the federal bureaucracy, basically to lobby other federal agencies on behalf of consumers and to represent them in the courts.

The Senate first passed a bill setting up such an agency (the name of the proposed agency has varied over the years) in 1970. The House Rules Committee defeated the House bill later the same year, however. The House then approved bills by large margins in 1971 and 1974 but in both years filibusters on the floor of the Senate prevented that body from reaching a decision.

In 1975 the Senate acted first. This time there was no filibuster, and the Senate passed the bill by a large margin. The House waited a number of months before passing it narrowly. Given the virtual certainty of a veto by President Ford (which almost surely could not have been overriden in the House) the managers of the bill finally decided in late 1976 not even to bother to send the bill to conference because they thought their efforts would be wasted. They also hoped and believed that a Democratic president favorable to the bill would be elected in 1976 and would pave the way for success for a consumer protection agency bill in the 95th Congress (1977–78).

A Democratic president sympathetic to the bill did, indeed, win the 1976 election, but congressional proponents failed to produce a bill for the President to sign. The Senate supporters, more sure of a positive outcome, decided to wait for the House to go first so that they would not waste their time. The House Government Operations Committee reported a bill in May 1977, but with a margin of only one vote. The House Speaker postponed scheduled floor action in November because he thought the bill would fail. When he finally did schedule the bill for floor action in February 1978, it was, in fact, defeated. Supporters of the creation of a federal Office of Consumer Representation (as the agency had come to be called in 1977–78) still had additional persuasive work to do if they ever hoped to realize their desires. Specific aspects of this long history in 1974, 1975–76, and 1977–78 are worth recounting for purposes of observing policy formulation in the protective regulatory arena.

1974. The maneuvering over the Consumer Protection Agency in 1974 had some similarities to that over strip mining in 1974. First, as in the case of strip mining, the administration did not present a consistent and united front. The President's Special Assistant for Consumer Affairs, Virginia Knauer, supported a relatively strong bill. The Director of the Office of Management and Budget, Roy Ash, pressed for a weaker bill than that passed by the House, one that would limit the powers of the new agency considerably. He advised the head of White House congressional liaison that the White House should let it be known that a veto was intended unless major modifications were made in the language of the bill. The head of the Domestic Council staff urged first Nixon and later Ford to veto the bill—at least unless it were much weakened. Neither President had to make a decision, of course, since the filibustering Senators killed the bill before it could get to the White House.

Second, the coalition in favor of a strong bill and the one opposing it were both unstable. In 1974 the AFL–CIO, nominally part of the lobby in favor of the new agency, lost considerable enthusiasm when the Senate Government Operations Committee added an amendment that would allow the new agency to intervene in certain kinds of labor matters. Previously, in 1972, Ralph Nader, one of the guiding lights in the drive for the bill since 1970, had disagreed with the Consumer Federation over how much compromise was allowable in order to try to gain cloture in the Senate in that year.

The coalition opposing the bill passed by the House was not united and stable either. For example, although "peak" associations (large conglomerate associations made up of smaller associations and organizations), such as the National Association of Manufacturers and the U.S. Chamber of Commerce opposed the bill (with differing degrees of rigidity), some individual companies supported the bill, including Motorola, Zenith, Montgomery Ward, J. C. Penney, and Giant Food Stores.

Third, this case illustrates the presence of subgovernment aspects even in a regulatory area. Senator Ervin tried to mobilize a variety of regulatory agencies against the bill by writing them a letter warning them that their own powers would be cut if the bill were adopted and the new agency established. Presumably he was banking on the instincts of the regulatory agencies not to want their arrangements with their various regulated persons, companies, and segments of the economy upset by some new interloper such as a Consumer Protection Agency.

1975–1976. The consumer agency bill was again a live issue in Congress in 1975. Several changes made passage in the Senate possible: the retirement of leading (filibustering) opponents, notably Senator Ervin; the addition of new liberal members; and a new Senate rule that made it easier to obtain cloture (requiring only 60 rather than 67 votes). As passed by the Senate (61–28), the bill would create an Agency for Consumer Advocacy (the name was changed from Consumer Protection Agency because of complaints from certified public accountants that their acronym was being stolen) to represent consumer interests before other agencies and in federal courts. The ACA would not be regulatory in the sense of telling other agencies what to do (in fact, none of the proposed consumer agencies would have regulated in this sense), but it would intervene in the regulatory decisions of other agencies as a consumer ombudsman. While it couldn't issue regulations of its own, it could petition other agencies to do so. The agency's authorized funding was set at $60 million for three years.

Supporters of the bill had learned lessons over the years of debate. This time the initial bill that was introduced was very similar to the weaker bill that was filibustered to death in 1974. The debate in committee and on the floor focused on the issues of special exemptions and on the need for consumer advocacy versus reform of the regulatory system. Representatives for certain agencies and activities had sought and won exemptions in previous consumer agency bills since 1972 with the argument that their activities were not part of the marketplace transactions that the consumer agency was to monitor. The bill introduced in the Senate included two significant exemptions, one for labor-management negotiations, and one for license renewal proceedings of the Federal Communications Commission. These exemptions remained in the bill despite attempts to remove them, and others were added, notably for gun manufacturers, for the Alaska pipeline, and for federal proceedings directly affecting producers of livestock, poultry, and agricultural products (for example, price support or agricultural exports determinations). Overall the bill's supporters in committee and on the floor were able to prevent amendments intended to gut the bill, and they supported most, but not all, of the amendments that were adopted.

In the House the Government Operations Committee reported out a reasonably strong bill—not including all of the exemptions adopted on the Senate floor—by a lopsided margin in July. The bill came to the floor in early November and was passed by only nine votes—a large disappointment for the supporters, given the certainty of a presidential veto. The sponsors of the bill had agreed prior to floor debate to accept four key amendments they believed would widen the appeal of the bill through restricting its impact: a provision transferring consumer programs from other federal agencies (presumably to avoid duplication and save money); an exemption for many Department of Agriculture programs including deliberations on price support levels, loan payments, soil conservation, rural electrification, crop insurance, and Food for Peace; an exemption for small businesses from answering questionnaires distributed by the agency; and a provision that the agency would expire in seven years without congressional action to the contrary. The Senate's exemption for labor-management relations was included in the House Committee bill and was reaffirmed both in Committee and on the House floor.

But the fact that even a weakened bill could barely attract a majority led the sponsors in both the House and Senate to drop their pursuit of final action for the rest of 1975 and all of 1976. They saw no point in getting conference committee agreement only to have an unavoidable and unbeatable veto by President Ford make all of their labors in vain.

House leaders supporting the measure attributed their problems to heavy lobbying from the White House and business interests (that coalition was now coalescing) and to the developing "anti-government" and "anti-bureaucratic" mood that seemed to be gaining much favor both in the country at large and within Congress.

1977–1978. 1977 dawned bright for the consumer agency advocates. Now they had a president committed to the bill and they still had an overwhelmingly Democratic Congress.

The debate developed along familiar lines and processes. Floor action and the role of the President and the influence of lobbies representing the potentially regulated were all important.

Both the Senate committee and the House committee reported the bill in May. And the content of the bill in the two houses was not very different. Many of the by-now familiar exemptions designed to build support were in both bills and a few new ones were added (for example, national security and intelligence); some exemptions were in only one of the bills. However, the mood of the two committees was very different: the Senate Committee routinely and easily passed the bill, but the House committee had heated debate and took roll calls on a number of amendments and finally reported the bill by only one vote.

Between May 1977 and February 1978 the Senate supporters simply waited for the House to act. If favorable action was not forthcoming from that quarter there was no point in the Senate's proceeding. The House supporters and leaders (who were also supporters) had problems. First, the antibureaucratic mood in the country and in Congress had not abated but had, if anything, gotten stronger. Second, it was nice to have the President in support of the bill, but his own antibureaucratic image countered some of his support for this bill. Third, many business lobbies opposed the bill (no matter how many exemptions were made), and these lobbies were well-organized and well-financed and were putting lots of pressure on members of the House at the local level in constituencies as well as in Washington. Fourth, at least some of the pro-consumer lobbying by the Ralph Nader groups was counter-productive because it denounced other supporters publicly with unflattering language: three were labeled "mushy liberals," one was accused of being a "broker for agribusiness raids on the treasury," one was called "reactionary," and one was labeled "disgustingly repulsive and a double-crosser." Such undiplomatic language helped fracture the pro-consumer ranks (Russell, 1978). The Speaker of the House estimated that eight votes on the House floor were lost as a result.

The Speaker and his associates counted noses in the House but did not see a winning coalition emerging in 1977. A vote was scheduled for the floor in November but was cancelled by the Speaker because he saw a loss developing, even though supporters had drafted a much weaker substitute bill they intended to offer on the floor instead of the somewhat stronger committee bill.

The situation did not improve for the next few months but the pro-agency forces decided to go ahead with floor action anyway. The bill debated was the weakest version yet to appear on either floor, and on the House floor it became even weaker. Eleven additional amendments were adopted, including one prohibiting the Office of Consumer Representation from establishing regional offices or from testing products tested by other agencies under most circumstances and exempting any matters pertaining to firearms. But the proponents' strategy of trying to absorb the opposition by agreeing to weakening amendments ultimately was still not enough: in February 1978 the bill was defeated 227 to 189. Although the issue of a pro-consumer agency was dead for another Congress, given its persistent position on the congressional agenda it will assuredly be revived in future sessions. The difficulty of achieving a satisfactory outcome in the consumer protection area well illustrates the struggle that accompanies the creation of protective regulatory power.

Land use. The handling of the proposal to create a federal land use policy resembles both the establishment of federal strip mining controls and the creation of a federal consumer agency. The general intent of land use policy would be to aid the states in their efforts to prevent urban sprawl and plan for orderly use of their territory. There would also be incentives for the states to institute regulatory measures on their own.

The closest to success the proponents have come thus far was in 1974. In 1975 the House Interior Committee killed a bill and the issue has not again appeared on the congressional agenda, in part because the sponsors and their committees have been fully occupied by a large range of other legislation.

As in the case of strip mine regulation the two principal congressional proponents and managers of the proposed protective regulatory legislation were Representative Morris Udall and Senator Henry Jackson. Jackson introduced the first bill in 1970. The Senate passed a bill in 1972 but it was killed by the House Rules Committee. The Senate passed another bill in June of 1973 by a vote of 64 to 21. Udall's subcommittee of the Interior Committee completed action on the bill in late summer 1973, but did not report it to the full committee until early 1974. Then the House Rules Committee again held up the bill—but this time only for about three months. The full House, however, killed the bill by voting 211 to 204 to refuse to debate the bill.

A number of the same patterns observed in the discussion of the strip mine regulation and Consumer Protection Agency issues again emerge here. First, once again the administration appeared unable to adopt a consistent stance. This public vacillating was accompanied by private division of opinion among various concerned agencies. The administration had supported a land use bill along the lines favored by Jackson and Udall from 1971 until 1974. In 1973 and early 1974 the administration had publicly labeled land use as its "number one environmental priority," and the Secretary of the Interior had specifically endorsed the Udall bill in late January 1974. However, shortly thereafter a conservative Republican in the House introduced a much weaker bill and the White House threw its support to that bill. The Secretary publicly changed his position to conform to that of the White House in early June 1974, shortly before the House voted not to debate the Udall bill. In early 1975 the administration announced through the Secretary of the Interior that it would support no land use bill at all. This probably contributed to the death of the bill in the House Committee in July 1975.

Behind this public withdrawal of support first for a strong bill and then for any bill was considerable disagreement among a number of executive branch agencies. The strongest spokesmen for a bill like that supported by Jackson and Udall came from the Department of the Interior and the Environmental Protection Agency. The forces within the administration opposed to such a bill included the Federal Energy Administration (which feared slowdowns on energy facility siting decisions), the Department of Housing and Urban Development (which

wanted jurisdiction over land use itself through the comprehensive
planning section of an existing statute), and critical parts of the institutional presidency—the Domestic Council and the Office of Management and Budget. (In early 1975 a former HUD secretary, who had
opposed land use—at least in the hands of Interior—in that capacity,
became the director of OMB.) When the Nixon administration reversed
itself on the bill in the spring of 1974, some Democrats labelled the
move as part of "impeachment politics"—an overall strategy to woo
conservative supporters whose votes might be critical in the impeachment proceedings against President Nixon that seemed inevitable at
the time (the same charge had also been made about Nixon administration shifts with respect to strip mine legislation).

Second, as in the other two cases, broad coalitions of groups formed
to support the two sides of the controversy: the one side favoring a
reasonably strong bill such as that favored by Udall and Jackson and
the other side favoring either a weak bill or no bill at all. However, in
this case the coalitions were relatively stable. The major supporting
groups included all of the environmentalist groups, the AFL–CIO, the
United Auto Workers, the representatives of general purpose state and
local governmental units (the National League of Cities–U.S. Conference of Mayors, the National Governors' Conference, and the National
Association of Counties), and the National Association of Realtors. In
opposition were the home construction industry (both the builders and
the construction unions), rural groups (such as the Farm Bureau Federation and the National Cattlemen's Association), the U.S. Chamber
of Commerce, and ideologically conservative groups fearing increasing
"socialism" (for example, the American Conservative Union and the
Liberty Lobby).

Third, despite the detailed work done both in Udall's House subcommittee and Jackson's Interior Committee in the Senate the critical
decision was made by the whole House when it rejected the rule for
debating the bill. The issue was simply too visible and volatile to be
decided quietly in a subgovernment setting.

Fourth, the process of continuing to grope for a winning compromise did not end with the 1974 defeat. The Interior Department circulated draft legislation to the concerned executive branch agencies in
late 1974 and early 1975, although they did not succeed in getting the
administration committed to supporting a bill. Simultaneously, Udall
made a number of changes in his bill designed to mollify opponents
and win votes. A compromising attitude was not enough, however.
The House Interior Committee's consideration of the land use bill in
1975 was marked by a high degree of visibility and emotional lobbying. Opponents of the bill reported an unusual level of grass roots opposition. On a key Committee vote in July, three previous supporters

defected in the face of the pressure, and the land use bill was killed for 1975. In this case, the opponents were successful in persuading members of the Committee to kill the proposed regulatory measure in Committee, and they did not have to fight the battle again on the floor of the House.

The alteration of existing regulatory power

Antitrust enforcement, 1975–1976. Antitrust legislation has long been on the congressional agenda. Two major landmark statutes were created in 1890 (the Sherman Act) and 1914 (the Clayton Act). In 1975 and 1976 means of improving enforcement of antitrust activities again provided the occasion for decision making in the protective regulatory arena. The debate was, obviously, not over the creation of a brand-new federal effort. Rather it was over the details of how to proceed in an area in which the government had a well-established history of involvement.

Action began in 1975 when the Senate passed a bill aimed in part at providing states financial help for improving their antitrust efforts. A second, broader measure never came out of the Senate Judiciary Committee. In the House one part of that broader bill—authorization for state attorneys general to bring antitrust suits to recover damages on behalf of citizens—was reported by the House Judiciary Committee. But, after intensive business lobbying against the bill, the House Rules Committee refused to send it to the floor.

The bill that emerged in 1976 had three principal provisions. First, it expanded the power of the Antitrust Division of the Justice Department to investigate possible violations. Second, it required that the Antitrust Division and the Federal Trade Commission, the two key enforcement agencies in the antitrust field, be notified 30 days in advance of proposed mergers to give the agencies time to consider proposed court action to stop the mergers. Third, it granted authority to state attorneys general to sue for damages on behalf of classes of consumers injured by price-fixing.

The fight over the bill—especially the second and third provisions—was intense (see Cohen, 1976a, 1976b, and 1976d). And the fight involved argument over both substance and procedures. As expected in a regulatory case, the debate and decision making spread well beyond the relative quietness of subcommittees and committees to the floors of both the House and the Senate.

The administration wavered in its positions. Basically it started endorsing fairly strong positions in the bill but then backed down in some areas, presumably at the urging of business lobbyists for both individual companies and for large "peak associations" in the business realm (the U.S. Chamber of Commerce, the National Association of Manufacturers, and the Business Roundtable). Some Justice Department lawyers were reportedly upset by this "backsliding" in the White House.

Business lobbyists got some of what they wanted because the authorization for state attorneys general was narrowed in two ways—by restricting it effectively to only price-fixing violations and excluding more subtle forms of prohibited collusion and by prohibiting states from hiring outside attorneys to help conduct the suits. They also limited the pre-merger notification provision by getting the Senate to drop a provision that would have allowed temporary restraining orders issued during the 30-day-notice period to block the mergers until a court could have ruled on their legality. (It is worth noting that the most vigorous opposition to the 30-day pre-merger provision came from investment banking firms that make a good deal of money by arranging mergers.)

A coalition also emerged to support the legislation although it was less active and effective on details than the business lobby. The supportive lobby included consumer groups, public interest groups, and the National Association of State Attorneys General.

The contest was hard-fought on procedural grounds, too. There were two cloture votes in the Senate, both followed by additional delaying tactics that wrung some weakening concessions out of the bill's supporters. Instead of a formal conference committee, the report of which would be subject again to filibustering in the Senate and delays in both houses that would have made final passage before Congress adjourned problematical, a substitute mutually agreeable to the most important members of both the House and Senate Committees was worked out informally; that substitute was then introduced in both houses and passed (one of the two cloture votes was needed in the Senate at this point). The procedural battle was the most fierce in the Senate, where both sides pushed technicalities to the limit. At one key point the House supporters and leaders had to get the Parliamentarian to rule that they were within the House rules in avoiding the House Rules Committee, which they feared might well kill the bill.

Two other features of this complicated debate are worth underscoring. First, the administration's position kept shifting in large part because of the anti-bill position taken by the Secretary of the Treasury (himself an investment banker) and his forcefulness in fighting with the Justice Department for the ear of the White House. Second, given the complicated nature of the legislation, the business groups had trouble getting their coalition together and getting individual companies very interested, although their coalition was more effective than were the lobbyists in support of the bill. In short, this struggle over altering a long-existing set of powers resembles the struggles over creation of protective regulatory power that we have already outlined.

Deregulation of natural gas prices, 1977–1978. In April 1977, President Carter declared the struggle with energy problems facing the United States to be "the moral equivalent of war" and he sent an extensive set of proposals to Congress dealing with many facets of the problems. Congress—after 18 months of intense political debate—responded to the President's overall energy program by producing a bill that made numerous major changes in what had been requested. Despite the changes, the President signed the bill into law in 1978.

One area of change involved pricing for natural gas, an important source of energy. The President had proposed to continue the price controls on natural gas, but to provide a higher ceiling on those controls. The law Congress passed had only the vaguest resemblance to the President's proposal in this area. Congress scheduled a phaseout of those controls (this is what the term "deregulation" means) by 1985 and set interim prices higher than the ceiling requested by the President. Natural gas producers did not get everything they wanted but they certainly had reason to feel satisfied with that section of the energy package. In addition, large industry users of natural gas had reason to feel content with this alteration of protective regulatory power. The President had wanted the bill to favor homeowners and businesses at the expense of large industry in terms of dividing the shrinking reserves of natural gas in the United States. The final bill was much more generous to industrial users and much stingier with residential and commercial users. (For details on the process and outcome involving natural gas pricing see Corrigan, 1977a, 1977b, 1978; Corrigan and Kirschten, 1978; Greider, 1978; Pelham, 1978a, 1978b; and Rankin, 1977.)

Table 5–1 summarizes the chronological development of the natural gas section of the energy bill in 1977–78. The story is much too long and complicated to be told in detail here but a few parts of the story illustrate an alteration of protective regulatory policy that, in this case, resulted in less regulation rather than in more regulation.

After the President's proposals were made to Congress in April 1977, the Speaker of the House moved quickly to take charge of the procedure for considering them—thus giving him and other staunch supporters of the President the whip hand in generating the substantive results. After different parts of the total program, including natural gas pricing, had gone to five individual committees those committees were given a mid-July deadline for reporting. Then the five separate reports would be coordinated by a House Ad Hoc Select Committee

Table 5–1: Chronology on natural gas pricing, 1977–1978

1977

April 20—President Carter appears before joint session of Congress to outline energy proposals, including continued price regulation for natural gas.

April 29—President sends draft legislation to Congress.

June 20—at conclusion of hearings and reports by five different House Committees, the House Ad Hoc Select Committee on Energy reassembles the total package.

August 3—House rejects natural gas price deregulation on floor.

August 5—House passes entire bill, including continued regulation of natural gas prices.

October 4—full Senate adopts a gas deregulation plan after stopping a filibuster against it.

December 22—conferees dealing with natural gas pricing give up for the year because they cannot reach agreement.

1978

March 22—conferees on natural gas pricing hold their first formal session of the year after working in private during the preceding weeks.

April 21—Senate and House conferees announce an agreement in principle on natural gas pricing.

May 24—both sets of conferees vote narrowly to approve the deregulation plan—still "in principle."

August 18—a bare majority of both sets of conferees (13 of 25 from the House and 9 of 17 from the Senate) sign conference report on natural gas pricing.

September 27—the Senate narrowly approves the conference report on natural gas.

October 13—the House agrees by one vote to consider all conference reports on energy (including natural gas) in a single yes or no vote.

October 15—the entire energy package, including natural gas price deregulation, is passed by the House.

November 9—President signs bill into law.

Source: Adapted from National Journal, November 4, 1978: 1762.

on Energy, an invention of the Speaker's to allow him to keep track of decisions and to make sure the final product came as close to what the President wanted as possible.

In the natural gas area Carter asked that "old" gas (that coming from wells already in production) be priced according to existing regulations, that "new" gas (that from new wells) be sold at controlled prices —higher than existing prices but not dramatically so. The "old" gas (cheaper) would be allocated to residential and commercial users. The "new" gas (more expensive) would be allocated to industrial users. Regulation of prices would continue for the indefinite future.

The President's natural gas request got rough treatment in the subcommittee of the House Interstate and Foreign Commerce Committee to which it had been referred. This subcommittee voted narrowly to deregulate all natural gas prices. However, the full Commerce Committee narrowly reversed this decision and stayed with the President's proposal. The Ad Hoc Energy Committee made one concession to the producer interests by expanding the definition of "new" gas to allow more to be priced at the higher level. That compromise was concession enough to help get the House as a whole to defeat a proposal for complete deregulation on the floor by a vote of 199 to 227.

The outcome in the Senate in 1977 was quite different. Here there was no forceful central leadership allied with the President. Instead all of the energy issues were, in effect, up for grabs with the strongest temporary coalitions (which were constantly shifting as the specific issues changed) winning. A House staff member, commenting on the seemingly chaotic and random Senate performance, said, "I'll never try to interpret what the Senate is doing. For my own mental health, I'll never try to do that." (Corrigan, 1977a: 1489.)

The natural gas issue was involved in the Senate chaos. The Committee on Energy and Natural Resources could not reach a decision. A vote deregulating all natural gas pricing in five years resulted in a tie that could not be broken. Thus the question was passed onto the Senate floor unresolved. There, after a filibuster and other delaying tactics by the opponents of deregulation (who were supporting the President's original position, although the administration had abandoned that position at this critical point in the debate), a compromise form of deregulation passed 50 to 46.

The rest of 1977 and much of 1978 were taken up by the efforts of conferees from the House and Senate to reach agreements on a whole range of issues involved in the energy package. Lobbying was intense on these issues, including, of course, many aspects of natural gas pricing—whether to regulate prices or not, the maximum rates allowable, the differences between old and new gas, the treatment of gas sold in the same state in which it was produced, and the allocation of different-priced gas to different kinds of users. No stable coalitions on this complex welter of specifics emerged; rather each lobbyist for each organization or company had his or her own self-interest to serve and defined it slightly differently than anyone else's.

By mid-1978 the administration, in the interests of getting an energy package before Congress adjourned in October, indicated its willingness to go along with phased deregulation. The Carter administration also flip-flopped its original priorities for minimizing costs to consumers by promoting lower prices for industrial users and passing the higher prices along to individual residential users and commercial establishments such as stores. The opponents of deregulation in the Senate again fought these moves but were finally defeated, after considerable delay, in late September by a vote of 52 to 47. White House representatives in effect pressured lobbyists from a vast variety of other organizations to join them in their position that the deregulation of natural gas was an acceptable and necessary price to pay compared to the alternative of sacrificing the entire energy package. Thus a temporary and fleeting coalition of unlikely elements was put together, at least on paper, and confronted the Senators. The outcome in the Senate was widely hailed as a presidential victory, although it is not overly cynical to point out that the President's people wound up working hardest for provisions that 17 months earlier they had flatly opposed. The symbol of victory had become more important than the content of the legislation.

When the House considered natural gas pricing for the last time, in October 1978, it agreed by only one vote to keep the natural gas pricing part of the package in that package (rather than being broken out for separate consideration). The Rules Committee had at first, on a tie vote, been unable to keep the package together. But White House pressure apparently got a change of vote out of one Democrat on the Committee retiring from Congress at the end of the session (literally in a few days) and the Rules Committee endorsed keeping the whole package together. The package, despite gas provisions unsatisfactory to many and quite different from what the House had passed in 1977, passed with relative ease, 231 to 168.

The final gas package that emerged from all of the foregoing activity (and our discussion covers only a few of the details) allowed the price of new gas to rise about 10 percent a year until 1985, when all price controls were scheduled to end. The allocations would make industrial users pay higher costs in earlier years but the burden would gradually be shifted to residential and commercial consumers. The pressures coming from numerous (although not tightly coalesced) lobbyists and the gradual adoption by the White House of a "we must have a bill at any cost and no matter the content" philosophy helped produce this result.

The application of regulatory power

Three cases illustrate the forces that are loosed when the application of existing regulatory power (that is, enforcement) is at issue.[2] In the

---

[2] We have included discussion of the application of protective regulatory authority, which, strictly speaking, is an implementation activity, although we excluded discussion of competitive regulatory policy, which also involves implementation, for several reasons. (1) Unlike protective regulatory policy, competitive regulatory policy involves implementation activities almost exclusively, rarely activities of formulation and legitimation, which are the focus of this book. (2) Because so much detail is delegated by Congress to regulatory agencies in the protective regulatory field during formulation and legitimation, the application of their authority can be construed as a continuation of the legislative process

first case we want to look at some of the major activities of a relatively new agency with important regulatory powers—the Environmental Protection Agency—in 1974. The next two cases involve specific applications of regulatory power by an old agency, the Food and Drug Administration.

The Environmental Protection Agency in 1974. Bernstein (1955) has argued that new regulatory agencies proceed vigorously in their youth, and this seems to be true of the Environmental Protection Agency in the first few years after its creation in 1970. But, inevitably, the aggressive stance of the EPA has led to attempts by the regulated industries to seek exemptions to the regulations and also to try to weaken the regulatory functions of the EPA.

The natural aggressiveness of a new regulatory agency and its supporters and the natural reluctance of the regulated to submit to such aggressiveness almost surely would have produced a variety of cross-pressures and a continuing debate over EPA powers and performance no matter what else was going on in the world. But, as it turned out, the normal or expected controversy surrounding EPA's efforts was increased by the occurrence of the energy crisis in 1973, which greatly heightened the agency's visibility, political salience, and political vulnerability. It was clearly in the middle of a variety of major disagreements both within and between elements of the executive branch, Congress, and the private sector. A look at a few of the specific disputes in which the EPA became involved illustrates again a pattern of shifting coalitions in a broad regulatory area.

A conflict developed between the need to increase domestic energy supplies and energy self-sufficiency and the need to preserve the environment following the energy crisis of 1973 and subsequent increased national energy-consciousness. The EPA has been intimately involved in this conflict. One instance of EPA involvement occurred in 1974 when the administration was drafting amendments to the 1970 Clean Air Act to make allowances for the energy problems facing the country—particularly the desire to use more coal and less oil. EPA and other executive branch agencies had been working on specific amendments to the basic statute to allow delay in the implementation of the relatively rigorous standards and some of the shorter deadlines contained in the 1970 law. There were, however, major disagreements

(formulation and legitimation) as well as implementation. (3) The politics of implementation of protective regulatory policy closely resembles the politics of formulation and legitimation of protective regulatory policy. Similar relationships are present among the actors in both stages. (4) The politics of implementation of competitive regulatory policy is different from the politics of either the implementation or formulation/legitimation of protective regulatory policy (mainly in the absence of a role for the institutional parts of Congress).

within the executive branch as interested agencies sought agreement on what package to present to Congress.

On the side of making substantial amendments to the law and suspending or delaying many provisions regarding both automobiles and industries (especially those burning coal) were officials in the Federal Energy Office, the Domestic Council, and the White House. The EPA itself was willing to relax the law but did not want to go as far as the other agencies. Two key issues were whether there should be a provision that would allow the deterioration of air quality to the federally prescribed level in those cases in which it began at a better level (this would involve overturning some court decisions interpreting the 1970 statute as preventing such deterioration) and whether "intermittent controls" (that is, the use of periodic shutdowns rather than the installation of expensive devices to remove pollution from industrial smokestacks) should be mandated as a basic control device or used only in rare emergencies. The EPA opposed allowing air quality to deteriorate to the level of the federal standard when it had been better and opposed intermittent controls except in very short-term special situations. The FEO–White House–Domestic Control positions (supported by most industries) were on the other side.

The meetings on the issue within the executive branch were heated, and no compromise could be agreed upon. So a unique solution was reached: two packages of proposals would go to Congress. One would have the blessing of the EPA and the other agencies—these would be proposals on which all could agree. The second would have the support of the White House and Federal Energy Office but would not have the support of the EPA. The idea was tried out on key Republican members of the House and Senate committees that would be handling the legislation, and they approved.

When the proposals did reach Congress the environmentalists generally supported the EPA position as opposed to the White House–FEO position, although they were unhappy about some of the concessions that had to be made in the application of the 1970 standards in the name of responding to energy necessities. A number of industries—led by the coal industry and the electric utilities—supported the administration position in its entirety. The Senate was more disposed to "tougher" controls and the House more willing to relax those controls. In this case the final compromise supported the Senate–EPA position on the critical issues of deterioration of air quality and the use of intermittent controls, although it went further in terms of relaxing standards and deadlines than the Senate (particularly Senator Muskie) would have liked. The 1974 amendments represented a major revision of the basic air pollution legislation.

A separate issue that involved the EPA in debate with the usual range of interested parties concerns the use of "scrubbers"—devices for cleaning sulfur pollutants from coal smoke. (See Noone, 1974, and Phillips, 1975).

EPA has long advocated the use of scrubbers, and in June of 1974 Congress passed legislation (the Energy Supply and Environmental Coordination Act) authorizing the Administrator of the FEA to order power plants to convert to coal as their source of energy and to use scrubbers to reduce emissions if adequate supplies of "clean" coal were not available. Although the Act was designed only as a stopgap measure to help curb domestic consumption of oil, President Ford used it as the backbone of his energy self-sufficiency program, announced in October of 1974. As part of that program, he proposed that oil-powered utilities convert to coal in a magnitude sufficient to save 1 million barrels of oil a day.

The pro-scrubbers—environmentalists, the EPA, Senator Muskie—argued that the cost of the conversion is worth the investment, that the technology is perfected, and that use of scrubbers should be mandatory. Opponents—utilities, the Federal Power Commission, conservative members of Congress, and to a lesser extent coal companies and the FEA—argued that the technology of scrubbers is far from perfect; that the cost of installation is exorbitant (up to one-quarter of the total capital investment in a power plant); that there is an inadequate supply of low sulfur coal and, given present environmental constraints, adequate supplies cannot be obtained; and that the oil savings realized from conversion will not be as substantial as the administration has predicted. The utility companies threatened to sue to overturn FEA conversion orders that required installation of scrubbers, and environmental groups also threatened suit if EPA did not enforce antipollution standards for converting plants vigorously enough.

The FEA and EPA collaborated in drawing up a list of about 80 candidates for conversion to coal. Of the 80, EPA estimated that 27 would require scrubbers. Although originally the FEA was to have issued the conversion orders by June 30, 1975, only nine orders were made by late May, and the agency estimated that no more than 30 (the "easy ones") would be issued by the end of June. The administration requested an amendment to extend the period for conversion orders.

In addition to helping identify candidates for conversion, EPA's role under the Act is to continue to enforce air pollution standards by sending out notices to power companies whose emissions exceed the allowed levels. EPA can also take violators to court, impose fines, or, ultimately, close down offending plants, although it prefers to seek voluntary compliance on the scrubber issue rather than using criminal sanctions.

A good example of the kind of harassment to which a regulatory agency can be subjected by congressional friends of those being regulated is provided by a relatively minor incident in late 1973 and early 1974. One provision of the National Environmental Policy Act of 1969 stated that all federal agencies were to file a statement of environmental impact along with all proposals for legislation and for taking major administrative actions. Although not explicit on the point, the law was widely understood to apply only to potentially harmful proposals and actions, not to actions taken to protect the environment. Thus the EPA had not been filing such statements.

In late 1973, however, the Chairman of the House Appropriations Subcommittee responsible for the EPA budget (Jamie Whitten, a friend of a variety of agricultural interests but not known for his concern over the environment) put language in an appropriations bill requiring EPA to start filing such statements. (Whitten's subcommittee gave up jurisdiction over environmental matters in 1975 at the urging of pro-environmentalists. Their leverage to achieve this stemmed from the newly created power of the House Democratic Caucus to choose Appropriations Subcommittee chairmen by vote.) Friends of a strong EPA contended that if such a requirement were enforced it would inevitably delay EPA actions and thereby dilute EPA's strong posture as a protector of the environment. The provision became part of the appropriations statute. However, in the spring of 1974, Senator Muskie upbraided the EPA Administrator for being willing to go along with Whitten's mandate and engineered the inclusion of a specific exemption for EPA in the 1974 Clean Air Act amendments. Thus only an alert congressional friend of the agency prevented a potentially damaging act in Congress—seemingly minor and relatively invisible.

EPA also clashed with Representative Whitten over dieldrin, a pesticide that had caused cancer in laboratory animals. In this case EPA gave in to Whitten and refused to suspend dieldrin production and marketing (this was the same pesticide that contaminated 7 to 8 million chickens discussed in Chapter 4) in deference to Whitten's wishes. The *Washington Post* summarized the susceptibility of EPA to Whitten on the whole issue of pesticide regulation: "Observers acquainted with EPA's operations attribute the agency's reluctance to order a suspension primarily to its need for an accommodation with Representative Whitten. . . . In recent weeks, EPA also has withdrawn its case against the pesticide 2,4,5–T, stating that its evidence against the chemical was insufficient. In June, Rep. Whitten's subcommittee allowed EPA even more money than it had requested for fiscal year 1975. Much of the surplus is earmarked for research to determine whether DDT, banned for almost all uses in 1972, should be reintroduced." (See *Washington Post*, July 28, 1974, p. 65.) (EPA had already granted an exception for a large-scale use of DDT to fight the tussock moth in some forests in the northwestern part of the country.)

At another point in 1974 EPA also seemed to be under quiet attack from the Office of Management and Budget, which seemed intent on shifting the jurisdiction for fuel economy testing of new automobiles from EPA to the more industry-oriented Transportation or Commerce departments.

EPA's embroilment in controversy is inevitable given the competing demands of energy versus environment, and inevitably, compromise on environmental issues has occurred. Like most new agencies, EPA has had a high turnover of its top people. Eager and aggressive young administrators have sought to have an impact and make a reputation for themselves, but many have moved on to other agencies or back to the private sector. This turnover, along with changing issues and changing pressures from Congress, from parts of the executive branch, and from lobbies on both sides of most issues, has contributed to the pressure to compromise. Indeed, the literature about regulation in general suggests that as the agencies age they will become more mellow and more accommodating to the demands of the regulated and their allies (Bernstein, 1955; Huntington, 1952).

Cranberries in 1959. A few weeks before Thanksgiving of 1959 the Secretary of Health, Education, and Welfare—operating on the basis of findings of the Food and Drug Administration—indicated that some of the cranberries currently on the market had been found to be contaminated with a weed killer that had caused cancer in laboratory rats (see Feingold, 1965). He advised shoppers not to buy cranberries unless they knew them to be uncontaminated, although he indicated there was no practical way to be sure. Thus the cranberry industry, on the eve of the Thanksgiving–Christmas season when 70 percent of all of its sales were usually made, was faced with an economic disaster.

A variety of negotiations took place, after the announcement, between the cranberry growers and their supporters in Congress on the one hand and the HEW and FDA officials on the other hand regarding details of the testing and its publicity. As a result a short-run labeling program was agreed on to help certify uncontaminated berries and thereby, perhaps, salvage some of the lost sales.

However, the cranberry growers and their supporters also argued that many of their losses caused by the contamination simply could not be regained (and they were, no doubt, accurate). Like the sick-chicken processors discussed in Chapter 4 this group now attempted to turn what had begun as a regulatory issue into a distributive issue as they sought indemnification from the government for about $15 to $20 million in losses. Unlike the sick-chicken supplicants, however, the cranberry growers succeeded. A distributive subgovernment in effect intervened in the aftermath of a regulatory decision and obtained about $10 million in payments for losses. The mode of achieving this payment is interesting in itself and suggests the vast range of possibilities open to individuals or groups seeking subsidies, particularly when their claim seems to stem from governmental regulatory action. In this case an obscure section of a 1935 statute intended for other purposes was interpreted by Department of Agriculture lawyers to allow an administrative decision to set up an emergency indemnification program not requiring legislation. The Department of Agriculture checked out the response of key members of the relevant congressional committees (House and Senate Agriculture committees and agricultural appropriations subcommittees) to the idea of setting up the program on the basis of this somewhat questionable interpretation of a statutory section that had not been used for 17 years, and then only for another purpose. The members of Congress agreed, although they were not happy about charging off what they considered to be an HEW–FDA mistake, or at least responsibility, to the Department of Agriculture. Despite their reluctance, however, their desire to support the claims of the growers and the cooperative spirit shown by the Department of Agriculture was stronger, and the indemnification of the cranberry growers proceeded.

In the following year the Secretary of HEW had to help defend FDA from several different attacks on the scope of its statutory regulatory authority over foods. He and the agency were generally successful, but the fact that the attacks were made suggests the price that regulatory agencies may have to pay for their activities and also suggests that the incentives for such agencies may be to "go easy" when faced with choices. Thus this story of the 1959 cranberry scare illustrates some broader themes about regulation by federal government agencies: Regulation always brings the possibility of protest and reprisal, and the regulated can still come out well if they can involve a supportive distributive subgovernment in some way.

Panalba.®   On May 1, 1969, the Commissioner of the Food and Drug Administration issued an order that an antibiotic drug called Panalba was to be decertified and removed from the market. (See Nadel, 1971: 77–79, and Mintz, 1969, on the Panalba case.) Further distribution and sales of the drug by its manufacturer, the Upjohn Company of Kalamazoo, Michigan, would be illegal. The reason for the FDA order was that scientific evidence had shown that Panalba, a combination drug of two antibiotics, was not more efficacious than either of its components used singly, and in addition that it was hazardous to users. The evidence led the FDA to conclude that the benefits from using the drug were outweighed by the accompanying risks.

The Upjohn Company objected vigorously to the decertification of a best-selling drug and demanded an administrative hearing, which the FDA refused to grant because the issue was safety, not simply efficacy. (Upjohn could have continued to market the drug during the hearing proceedings, which could have taken years to complete.) The Congress-man from Kalamazoo also objected to the FDA order, and he arranged a meeting with the Secretary and Under-Secretary of HEW and representatives of the Upjohn Company to work out a compromise. The top level HEW hierarchy was sympathetic to Upjohn's plight and tried to push the drug company's position on the FDA Commissioner. It is highly irregular for a Secretary to try to overrule the decision of the FDA on antibiotic certification when the issue is public safety.

The FDA's original decision remained in place only because a long-time, key congressional supporter of the agency, the chairman of the House subcommittee with FDA jurisdiction, held a hearing following the decertification order, at which time records from FDA files showed that the decision on the decertification of Panalba was being made by the Secretary, not the Commissioner. Although the House subcommittee and its counterpart in the Senate had, in the past, been critical of the FDA and its Commissioner for failing to carry out the assigned tasks of the agency with sufficient vigor, they were more than willing to support the agency when it did enforce aggressively. The threat of copious unfavorable publicity emanating from the subcommittee hearings led the HEW Secretary to withdraw his decision and allowed the Commissioner's original order to stand.

This case, although like the cranberry case not overwhelmingly important in itself, also illustrates larger themes—especially how regulatory decisions are liable to quiet attack and subversion unless there is some counter force outside the agency that is supportive of regulation.

CONCLUSIONS

We can now enrich the very broad picture of the protective regulatory arena presented in the opening pages of this chapter and summarized in Table 4–1. In general the patterns described in those locations are accurate, especially in cases involving the creation of new regulatory powers. But the introduction of the distinction between the creation of regulatory power, the alteration of existing power, and the application of power in specific cases also allows us to make some amendments and refinements to the initial statements. Naturally it should also be noted that creation, alteration, and application of regulatory power are also interrelated. For example, the application of powers may lead to demands for alteration as it did in the case of cranberries (where FDA successfully weathered some demands for restriction of power) and as it did in the case of EPA and clean air (where the energy problems of the nation were used to help generate restrictions and limitations on the ability of EPA to apply its powers in the field). The creation of powers also usually is followed by continuing dispute over proposed alterations of powers both by those who think the initial powers too broad and sweeping and by those who think them too pallid in comparison with the problems they are supposed to address.

In virtually all of the cases discussed in the foregoing pages the lowest organizational units—subcommittees in Congress and bureaus in the executive branch—discussed the full range of issues both internally and with each other. However, when dealing with broad questions such as the creation or alteration of regulatory powers virtually no final decisions were made at these lower levels. Inevitably the issues were escalated to higher organizational levels for continuing discussion and, in some cases, resolution. Only in a few instances—such as the decision of EPA not to suspend dieldrin or the statutory decision to exempt EPA from making environmental impact statements—were final decisions made at lower levels. Even such seemingly minor matters as cranberry contamination and Panalba got escalated to the level of the Secretary of HEW in the executive branch before final decisions were made. It should also be noted that escalation of issues to higher levels does not automatically mean that any final decision will necessarily be reached. Many regulatory issues are debated over and over in much the same terms for many years, as was the case with strip mine regulation, land use regulation, and the creation of a consumer protection agency.

Regulatory issues—whether involving creation, alteration, or application of powers—all contain the seeds of considerable conflict. It should be noted that the conflict does not merely stem from aggressive agencies being challenged by congressmen representing regulated clients. Indeed, in a number of cases discussed here the Senators and Representatives involved were more aggressive in asking for regulatory action than were the agencies themselves. And often the higher reaches of the executive branch seemed to be the most reluctant to pursue aggressive policies. There are certainly members of the House and the Senate who fight regulation. But for every Ervin in the Consumer Protection Agency dispute and for every Whitten trying to limit EPA there are likely to be individuals like Jackson, Udall, and Muskie taking the lead in such areas as strip mine regulation, land use regulation, and pollution control.

The potential for conflict of a multifaceted nature in most regulatory areas also means that often the coalitions that can broadly be labeled as supportive of and opposed to some specific power or its use are not highly unified or stable. Congressmen, executive branch agencies, and interest groups all have been shown to have varying degrees of commitments to general questions depending on what specific, more focused question is at stake. Thus, in a sense, regulatory issues are also separable just as are distributive issues. But the nature of the issues themselves means that instability and volatility will result in the regulatory arena instead of the relative stability and quiet of the distributive arena.

Conflict resolution generally occurs above the level of the bureau-subcommittee interaction when it occurs at all. But often resolution does not occur and the conflict continues. Many important regulatory issues seem to be almost permanently on the agenda of the federal government before solutions are reached. And very few solutions seem permanent but are continually reopened as new conditions and new political forces warrant. Thus, at this writing, land use and the existence of a consumer protection agency have been on the federal agenda for about a decade and no resolution has been reached. In addition, even when legislative solutions are reached, the conflict may continue, and the legislation may be amended later on, as happened with the Clean Air Act. It would be surprising if the natural gas, antitrust enforcement, and details of strip mine regulation issues did not reappear for serious debate in the near future.

One way in which regulatory issues become less volatile is for them to begin to be turned into distributive issues. Arguments have been made in the literature that, over a long period of time, regulatory agencies will become "captured" by the presumably regulated interests. When such capture occurs this means that regulatory issues are treated as distributive—or, at least, that a good deal of the presumed regulation will be left in the hands of the regulated interests themselves (this arrangement might be called self-regulation with governmental blessing). In the cases we have discussed here, distributive subgovernments became involved in the sick-chicken case and cranberry case in the aftermath of regulation.

Over time, if Congress is persistent, it probably will possess the potential to be more important in making all kinds of regulatory decisions than the executive branch. However, the element of persistence is critical—particularly for the friends of regulation. The foes of regulation have an advantage in that they are more likely to have more powerful private interests supporting their position. The private interests supporting regulation (except for competitors) are usually not numerous or at least not very politically sophisticated or powerful.

Redistributive policy

THE NATURE OF REDISTRIBUTIVE POLICY

REDISTRIBUTIVE POLICY is characterized chiefly, in terms of process, by the amount of time required to reach agreement on an issue and by the ideological nature of the debate. In terms of outcome, redistributive policy is best characterized in terms of who wins what at whose expense.

Many groups get involved in the debate over redistributive issues, often whether or not they have a direct stake in the outcome of the issue being debated. Although there may be many different arguments on a redistributive issue, they always reduce to two sides—a pro (liberal) and a con (conservative) position—no matter how many middle positions there may logically be and no matter whether any final outcome in fact represents some sort of middle way. These issues tend to produce similar coalitions of associations on a number of specific matters. "Liberal" and "conservative" may not be highly pleasing labels to political theorists, but to participants in the political process dealing with redistributive issues they have meaning in the sense that the same two coalitions usually emerge for any measure in dispute, whether it be Medicare or aid to the disadvantaged in a variety of forms (war on poverty, Model Cities, aid to education) or civil rights or even procedural issues such as the Senate filibuster with important implications for the handling and resolution of redistributive issues in the future.

The executive branch—particularly at the presidential level—is an important actor in the redistributive arena. The President and his closest advisors and appointees negotiate with representatives of the "peak associations" that get involved in the debate.

Controversy characterizes redistributive policy, because it attempts to reallocate items and symbols of value among different groups in society. The intended beneficiaries also help distinguish redistributive policy from other types of policy—in redistributive policy, less privileged groups are the intended principal beneficiaries, at the perceived expense of more privileged groups. Some programs reallocate items of value from the less well-off to the more well-off, or from minorities to whites and anglos, but such programs and policies are not perceived as redistributive, and do not generate the same kinds of politics. In this chapter we examine the politics of redistributive policy, efforts in which the intended beneficiaries are the relatively disadvantaged in society, and in which the relatively advantaged classes perceive themselves to be in danger of losing something they value.

REDISTRIBUTIVE POLICY AND THE
CONGRESSIONAL-BUREAUCRATIC RELATIONSHIP

We expect the importance of subgovernments (that is, individuals at the bureau and subcommittee level) to be minimal in terms of final decisions made regarding redistributive domestic policy. This is the case both because only parts of some redistributive issues are likely to be considered in the interactions of a subgovernment, and because final decisions are almost always made at levels higher than a subgovernment.

The potential for conflict between various combinations of congressional and bureaucratic actors on redistributive issues is high because there are usually ideological and partisan differences present. If general agreement on these differences can be reached, the conflict potential can be reduced considerably. If these differences are not muted and if redistributive issues are not redefined in some way, then the debate and final decisions may take a long time. Three substantive areas— the "war on poverty," Medicare, and civil rights—illustrate the congressional-bureaucratic relationship in reaching decisions on redistributive policy, and also illustrate the factors that tend to impede and facilitate those decisions.

Even when there is conflict based on partisan and ideological differences, however, the contending parties in the two branches (and within each branch) may be able to reach agreement by casting the issue in distributive terms rather than continuing to debate it in redistributive terms. Four substantive areas—Model Cities, manpower revenue sharing, aid to education, and tax policy—illustrate how redistributive policies can be redefined to emphasize distributive aspects both during the negotiation of the initial decision and afterwards to amend that initial decision.

When conflict exists usually there is no resolution at the bureau-subcommittee level. If resolution is achieved it comes at a higher level, usually in negotiations between the President, his top appointees and advisors, and the full Congress, often represented by the party leaders and relevant full committee chairmen. If conflict is resolved at this higher level it is either in terms of a broad compromise or in terms of a redefinition of issues in distributive terms. Many times, however, resolution of the conflict evades the actors, sometimes for many years. When resolution of conflict does occur, the prevailing view depends largely on the relative strength of competing ideologies in Congress, the ties of those ideologies to the parties in Congress, and the relative strength of the parties and of the major ideological factions of the parties.

It is worth noting that all of the examples of redistributive policy we have chosen for this chapter (except the case on the dismantling of the war on poverty) occurred some years ago. We did not make this selection because we think the dim and distant past more informative than the recent past, however. Rather, we found there have been few contemporary redistributive debates. Following an outburst of redistributive debate and legislation in the mid-1960s, interest and support for redistributive policies among government leaders and the public waned, and few redistributive issues made legislative headway in the 1970s.

Reaching basic decisions about redistributive issues

The war on poverty. The creation, alteration, and eventual dismemberment of the war on poverty between 1964 and 1974 exhibit a number of patterns common to redistributive policy. Individual members of the House and Senate, particularly those in strategic committee positions, were important in helping make decisions, as were individuals scattered throughout the administration and relevant executive branch agencies. However, these individuals could not make binding decisions by themselves: a much broader set of decision makers got involved, including all Senators and Representatives (through floor action), the President and his top advisors, and a large variety of interest groups. Programs avowedly redistributive along class and/or racial lines (in favor of the poorer classes and black citizens), once established, were the center of constant debate and controversy and were gradually surrounded with restraints, both organizational and programmatic. The entire history of the war on poverty is too extensive to tell in compact form (for good discussions of its origins and early years, see Donovan, 1973; Levitan, 1969; Loftus, 1970; and Sundquist, 1968: chapter 4), but a look at a few individual programs and events in that history will illustrate the broader points we wish to make. These episodes include the 1967 Green amendment to the Economic Opportunity Act of 1964, the Job Corps, the Legal Services Corporation, and the end of the Office of Economic Opportunity as a separate organizational entity in the federal government.

The Green Amendment. In 1967 the basic legislation authorizing the OEO and the poverty program was up for renewal after the first three years, and the war on poverty seemed to be in serious trouble (see Loftus, 1970, for a fuller account of what follows). There had been complaints about its administration and about its alleged involvement in stirring up the urban riots that had torn the country apart for the previous three summers. And in the 1966 congressional elections the liberal Democrats suffered badly in races for the House of Representatives. Thus 1967 began with the expectation that the newly revived control of the House by the conservative coalition of Republicans and southern Democrats could kill the entire poverty program, which required a new authorization before the end of the year.

As it turned out the program survived, largely because the House adopted an amendment sponsored by Representative Edith Green, an Oregon Democrat who had been critical of the Office of Economic Opportunity and its programs. The amendment was designed to mollify two groups: conservative southern Democrats and some northern urban Democrats from cities whose mayors had had poor relations with OEO and its community action program. Basically it gave the mayors and other locally elected officials the means to gain substantial control over the community action agencies.

The negotiations that produced the amendment were carried on by Mrs. Green on the one hand and the director and staff of OEO and members of the White House staff on the other hand, through the mediation of five Democratic supporters of OEO who served with Mrs. Green on the House Education and Labor Committee. Green was in the position of not wanting to admit that she was willing to help save the program; the administration was not able to admit that it was willing to pay the price of accepting the Green Amendment in order to save the program as a whole. Therefore, their public stances remained conflictual but through the intermediaries—who both wanted the program and realized the political necessity of acceding to the Green Amendment—they, in effect, negotiated a compromise. These relatively quiet third-person negotiations illustrate that even in the midst of loud public discord over redistributive policy some features of subgovernment activity can appear and have an impact. This was not a consensual "poverty subgovernment" at work but rather a dissensual one in which private negotiations and compromises produced an outcome with which the disagreeing parties could live.

Job Corps. (For a fuller discussion of the Job Corps from 1964 through 1971, see Ripley, 1972: chapter 3. Some of the following discussion is adapted from that chapter.) The Job Corps, one of the initial parts of the war on poverty, was aimed at preparing disadvantaged teenage youths for the labor market by offering them residential training and experience in centers both in cities and in rural areas. The central premise was that individuals from extremely deprived backgrounds needed to be removed from "the culture of poverty" in order to get basic skills (such as adequate reading), job-related skills, and appropriate attitudes about work and job-holding.

Controversy surrounded the Job Corps from the beginning. It received very negative press coverage during its first year of operation. Many incidents that reflected poorly on the program received national attention out of proportion to their importance. In addition, the program was expensive in terms of per enrollee cost. Even with the support of the Democratic Johnson administration the Job Corps had trouble holding its own in Congress. Although the initial goal was for 100,000 enrollees that target was soon revised downward, and the Job Corps leveled off at between 35,000 and 40,000 enrollees with an annual budget of about $280 million.

When the Nixon administration took over the executive branch in 1969, however, the Job Corps was quickly and severely cut. Nixon had promised such action in the 1968 presidential campaign and lost no time keeping his pledge. The Job Corps was taken away from the Office of Economic Opportunity and given to the more traditionally oriented Department of Labor (these two agencies had been competing for Job Corps administration since its beginnings), and the program was cut roughly in half both in terms of enrollees and budget. The residential centers that remained open—all in or near urban areas—drew enrollees from the local labor markets rather than from a more national market.

In short, the Job Corps survived, but only in a form that made it seem relatively nonthreatening and relatively minor in terms of its actual and potential redistributive impact. In this case—unlike the case of the Green Amendment—no private negotiations saved the original concept and location of the Job Corps. It apparently was so vulnerable that continued existence—even under dramatically altered circumstances —was about the best it could hope for. It still retained enough Democratic supporters to be continued as a categorical manpower program in 1973, however, even though most other manpower programs were included under the Comprehensive Employment and Training Act, a form of special revenue sharing enacted by Congress. Its fortunes revived in the Carter administration.

Legal Services Corporation. The final form in which a Legal Services Corporation was permanently established in 1974 again illustrates compromise between individual Senators and Representatives (in this case, mostly the members of a conference committee) and representatives of the administration that resulted in the breaking of a long deadlock (three years) over a program with considerable redistributive potential, at least in the perceptions of those debating its fate, especially the opponents. Like the previous two cases this was a visible dispute in broad terms, with one group committed to the federal government's providing legal services to the poor, arguing that such a program would redistribute the outcomes of the legal system in a more equal way, while the other groups opposed the redistributive program for being disruptive of the social order. As with the Green Amendment, final resolution of the conflict was achieved because some relatively private negotiations took place among the most concerned individuals at the last minute, which avoided the possibility of a direct confrontation with the President, whose veto could not have been overridden. Proponents were also motivated to negotiate by the awareness that OEO was not likely to survive past 1974, and without resolution that year on the legal services issue, executive branch agency support in the future was extremely unlikely.

Congress passed a bill establishing a Legal Services Corporation in 1971, but President Nixon successfully vetoed it, primarily because it did not give him the power of appointing all of the directors of the corporation. In 1972 conferees eliminated an amendment to the bill reauthorizing all OEO programs that would have set up a Legal Services Corporation because they feared its inclusion would have provoked a presidential veto of the entire bill. In 1973 President Nixon sent his own proposal for a Legal Services Corporation to Congress. The House passed a version that was even more conservative and restrictive than what the President asked for in June of 1973. Opponents of any Legal Services Corporation at all, no matter how restricted, filibustered against the bill in the Senate in 1973 and early 1974. The Senate stopped the filibuster on the third cloture vote and passed a bill that was far more liberal (that is, less restrictive on the activities of the corporation and its professional staff) than the House or President's version.

The conference committee reached a series of agreements that both chambers approved in the spring of 1974. One provision of the bill continued to generate trouble, however. Conservatives in the House were opposed to a provision in the bill authorizing the creation of so-called backup centers (corporation-funded poverty law research centers), and they narrowly missed (by seven votes) sending the bill back to the conference with instructions to delete the research centers. Even though the Senate was solidly in support of the research centers, the Senate supporters realized that the President would probably veto a bill allowing them and that the House would certainly sustain such a veto. Therefore, in a series of last minute negotiations that avoided a more visible conference setting, the supporters met privately and agreed to delete the research centers from the bill as the price for having a Legal Services Corporation at all.

Other restrictions put into the bill also indicate the kind of price the liberals had to pay on this redistributive issue. The President was given the power of appointment for all of the directors of the corporation. Attorneys employed by the corporation were severely restricted in terms of their political activities, even on their own time. Legal Services lawsuits aimed at school desegregation or obtaining nontherapeutic abortions were forbidden. And lawyers for the Corporation cannot become involved in draft cases or criminal cases. Given this conservatively oriented bill, President Nixon signed it, although the staunchest opponents of any federally supported legal services for the poor urged him to veto it.

The end of OEO. The flagging fortunes of the Office of Economic Opportunity since 1969 and its eventual dismantling under Republican administrations suggest how critically important presidential support is to the success of redistributive policy, and how devastating presidential opposition to redistributive policy can be. OEO was established in the poverty-conscious political climate of the mid-1960s with President Johnson's strong support. Although its community action program had been amended in 1967, funding support did not begin to diminish until Nixon became President. Nixon had never been enthusiastic about the poverty program, and although he made no mention of OEO during his campaign, his 1969 message to Congress expressed skepticism about the agency and its programs. In 1973 he began a full-scale attempt to kill the agency and cut off federal funding for its community action programs that provided a variety of services to the poor.

OEO had been created as an operating agency at the insistence of its first director, Sargent Shriver. When Nixon came into office, he began to whittle away these programs from OEO and to cut its budget in order to reduce the operating role of OEO. In 1973 Nixon appointed an acting director of OEO (without Senate confirmation) specifically to dismantle the agency and to transfer certain of its programs to other agencies. At the same time, he sent his budget for fiscal year 1974 to Congress. In it no money was requested for OEO as an agency (although it was authorized through June of 1974). The budget proposed placing OEO's legal services in a separate corporation, transferring certain OEO programs to other agencies (HEW, Department of Labor, Department of Commerce), and allowing the community action programs to expire with no request for any funding at all. This executive action sent threatened community action agencies and employee unions to the courts, where a judge ruled that no budget message could overrule a legislative authorization. The actions of the acting director were declared null and void, and he was declared to be illegally appointed.

The court decision forced Nixon to name another acting director, this time with Senate confirmation (the vote was 88–3 because the nominee said he was in favor of continuing OEO; later on Nixon fired him for this very reason), but Nixon continued to move programs out of OEO and into other agencies by administrative action (by declaring that a program was being "delegated" by OEO to another agency for administration, Nixon required no congressional approval). By the end of 1973, there were only three programs left in OEO: legal services, community action, and community economic development. Moving any of these required congressional approval.

Despite Nixon's wish to let the community action programs expire in 1974, there was still strong liberal support in Congress for their continuation. In addition, support came from new quarters—mayors and governors who in earlier years had opposed the poverty programs now came forward as supporters, declaring that loss of those services would place their communities in disastrous situations. The rising national unemployment rate gave sharp emphasis to the need for programs for the poor, and the less enthusiastic supporters in Congress realized that a bill passed in 1974 was bound to be less liberal than one that would emerge from the newly elected, more liberal Congress in 1975.

Given the support in and out of Congress for the community action program and the new President's lack of opposition to the poverty program, a bill emerged in the late days of the 1974 congressional session. Again, as in the case of the Legal Services Corporation, conference committee members negotiating among themselves and presumably in touch with representatives of the Ford administration produced a winning compromise that reduced the redistributive potential of the poverty programs and of the successor agency to OEO but at least kept many of the programs in existence (and even added two small new ones).

The Community Services Act was a victory in that OEO's poverty programs were authorized through fiscal 1977, but the redistributive impact of those programs was considerably reduced. OEO as an agency ceased to exist; its programs were lodged in a new independent agency (the Community Services Administration), but the President had the option of reorganizing this agency and its programs. The overall federal commitment was greatly reduced (Ford requested only $363 million for the CSA for fiscal 1976, a far cry from the $2 billion OEO budget of fiscal 1969), and the share of federal funding for community action programs was cut back to 60 percent over three years.

President Ford did not exercise the option to reorganize or transfer the CSA, but the redistributive impact of the agency and its antipoverty programs was seriously curtailed by the decreased funding level. Although Congress routinely provided much larger appropriations than the President requested between FY 75 and FY 78 (for example, in FY 76, when President Ford requested only $363 million, Congress appropriated $496 million), the size of the appropriations was much lower than in pre-CSA days. The agency stayed alive, and kept pace with inflation, but did not expand.

In 1978 the CSA and other antipoverty programs were reauthorized through 1981. The CSA emerged from the authorization with no deletions from its programs, but with no additions, either. The federal sharing formula was once again altered, with the 60 percent figure increased to 80 percent, while the share that local communities were to provide was decreased from 40 percent to 20 percent to relieve the economic burden they were bearing. However, unless Congress significantly increased the amount of appropriations, the change in the sharing formula would mean less total dollars available at the local level. The mood of Congress as the 1970s ended was one of fiscal conservatism, and dramatic increases in appropriations for CSA or any redistributive program were unlikely.

Medicare. The notion of government sponsored health insurance to assist citizens in meeting the cost of their medical care has been on the national agenda since 1935, as the chronology in Table 6–1 makes clear. But it was not until 1965, after years of debate, that a major piece of health insurance legislation emerged (the Social Security Medicare Program), and even then the scope and redistributive potential of the new program were reduced considerably from the initial proposal for comprehensive national health insurance. Medicare set up a federal medical care program for the aged under the Social Security system.

The central features of the story of Medicare involve the emergence of two ideologically based positions that were used as the focal points by two large coalitions in direct opposition to each other. The debate between the two coalitions in rhetorical terms was largely static: The same arguments were repeated by the same actors year after year. The debate in procedural terms was also static: The opponents of action found the numerous levers in Congress that can be used to stymie action and, with relatively marginal exceptions, were successful in their endeavors for most of the period.

However, the deadlock broke with the emergence of an aggressive political majority in the presidency and in Congress (particularly in

Table 6-1: Chronology on national medical insurance

1935	Roosevelt administration explores compulsory national health insurance as part of the Social Security Act, but no legislation is recommended to Congress.
1943	Three Democratic Senators cosponsor a bill to broaden the Social Security Act to include compulsory national health insurance to be financed with a payroll tax. No legislative action.
1945	President Truman, in his health message, proposes a medical insurance plan for persons of all ages, to be financed through a Social Security tax.
1949	The Truman proposal is considered and hotly contested in congressional hearings; no legislative action results.
1954	President Eisenhower opposes the concept of national health insurance as "socialized medicine." He proposes the alternative of reimbursing private insurance companies for heavy losses on private health insurance claims. No action taken on this proposal.
1957	Representative Forand introduces the "Forand bill," to provide hospital care for needy old age Social Security beneficiaries to be financed through increased Social Security taxes. No action taken by Congress, but heavy AFL–CIO lobbying generates public interest.
1960	The Forand bill was defeated by the House Ways and Means Committee on a decisive vote (17–8). Chairman Mills opposed the bill.
1960	As a substitute for the Forand bill, Congress enacts the Kerr-Mills bill, designed to encourage the states to help older, medically needy persons (those not poor enough to qualify for Old Age Assistance, but too poor to pay their medical bills).
1960	Health care is an issue in the presidential campaign; Kennedy vows support.
1961–1964	President Kennedy's version of the Forand bill is submitted annually in the House and Senate, but the House Ways and Means Committee defeats it.
1962	Senate defeats an amendment to a public welfare bill embodying the Kennedy proposal (52–48).
1964	The Senate passes (49–44) a Medicare plan similar to the administration proposal as an amendment to the Social Security Act. The plan died when House conferees (from the Ways and Means Committee) refused to allow its inclusion.
Jan. 1965	The 1964 elections brought many new Democrats to Congress, and the composition of the Ways and Means Committee is finally changed to have a majority of Medicare supporters.
Jan. 1965	President Johnson makes medical care his number one legislative priority.
July 1965	Medicare bill signed into law after passage in both houses by generous margins.

Source: Adapted from material in Congressional Quarterly Almanac, 1965: 236–247.

the relevant committees) that allowed the passage of Medicare in 1965. Even in 1965 the final decision floor votes in Congress could accurately be interpreted as logical outcomes of 20 years of conflict between a set cast of characters with set attitudes—the difference in 1965 was that the election of 1964 had simply produced more proponents than opponents. But the final success of the proponents was achieved only with considerable bargaining and compromise among members of the House and Senate with differing viewpoints and between members of the House and Senate and members of the administration at high levels. And given the unusual electoral results in 1964 that determined the balance of political forces in Congress in 1965, Congress played a more creative and shaping role in 1965 than might be expected in a redistributive issue.

The intensity of views held by proponents and opponents of medical care insurance remained high throughout the 30-year debate. Two basic positions were taken by the broad coalitions on the general question concerning the federal government's proper role in this area. Proponents (AFL–CIO and other labor unions, a variety of public welfare organizations, the National Medical Association [a group of black physicians], the National Council of Senior Citizens, and northern Democrats) supported full federal sponsorship of medical insurance and believed that private insurance companies could not handle the job of national medical insurance, that their high premiums would place too much burden on the elderly, and that a state charity approach was unsatisfactory because state benefits were inadequate and because only the neediest could qualify.

Opponents of national medical insurance (the American Medical Association, the insurance industry, business groups like the U.S. Chamber of Commerce, Republicans, and southern Democrats) favored only a very narrow federal role, limited to encouraging private and state efforts, and to providing federal health care assistance only to the neediest (state charity) cases. (The Kerr-Mills bill was a response to this line of reasoning.) Opponents greatly feared government interference in private medical practice and warned against the dangers of "socialized medicine."

Marmor (1973: 108–109) reflects on the explicitly redistributive features of the Medicare debate:

... debate (was) ... cast in terms of class conflict. ... The leading adversaries ... brought into the opposing camps a large number of groups whose interests were not directly affected by the Medicare outcome ... ideological charges and counter-charges dominated public discussion, and each side seemed to regard compromise as unacceptable. In the end, the electoral changes of 1965 reallocated power in such a way that the opponents were overruled. Compromise was involved in the detailed features of the Medicare program, but the enactment itself did not constitute a compromise outcome for the adversaries.

As the chronology in Table 6–1 shows, the debate over medical insurance narrowed in 1957 to a focus on assistance for one group, the elderly. The next eight years were spent trying to overcome stalemate on this narrower redistributive program. The lobbying efforts during this period were notable both for their intensity and because they were directed not only at Congress to sway votes, but also at the public to educate and increase consciousness (Is there anyone who has not heard the term "socialized medicine"?). In the end, the static and largely unchanging debate was resolved with a compromise that included considerable conservative and Republican input into the final product to blur some of the redistributive features. Republican contributions included coverage of almost three million people who were not covered by the Old Age and Survivors Insurance provisions of Social Security, the separation of Medicare funds from OASDI funds, the authorization of the use of private nonprofit organizations to deal with hospitals, and the addition of a subsidy to cover surgery and doctors' fees. The latter two features in particular introduced elements of distribution into the program.

The issue of national health insurance for all Americans did not disappear with the passage of Medicare in 1965. As the cost of health care soared in the late 1960s and in the 1970s, some of the stigma of "socialized medicine" was reduced, replaced by a concern with distributing relief to the many middle-class and upper middle-class voters saddled with rising health care costs. Many national health insurance bills have been introduced in Congress during the 1970s with a variety of backers including both Republican presidents, the American Medical Association, the American Hospital Association, the private insurance industry, and Senator Edward Kennedy (Dem., Mass.), the leading congressional proponent of health insurance. The features of the various proposals differ greatly, and divisive debate characteristic of earlier years recurred. The sharpest division of opinion focused on issues of the role of the federal government versus the private sector in the administration of a health insurance program; the degree of voluntary participation versus mandatory participation; and the nature of financing of the program (for example, payroll tax versus income tax credit).

None of the bills introduced in the 1970s met with success. Only in 1974 did compromise on a health insurance program seem possible. The House Ways and Means held lengthy hearings and came close to a compromise, but the Committee was sharply divided on two issues, and lacked strong leadership from the Chairman, who was suffering from personal problems. The Committee failed to report a bill, and since 1974 there has been little congressional activity other than ritualistic introduction of bills.

Jimmy Carter made a campaign pledge in 1976 to produce a comprehensive national health insurance program, but failed to redeem his pledge during his first two years as President. Other legislative priorities took precedence, and he did not propose any such legislation to Congress. The President was expected to continue to hedge on his pledge as the 96th Congress opened (1979–80), proposing only a statement of broad principles or at best a limited health insurance program, much narrower in scope than the kind of program sought by the chief congressional supporter of comprehensive health insurance, Senator Kennedy. Given the state of the economy, the tight-fisted mood of most members of Congress, the vigor of opponents of a broad national health insurance program, and the weak to nonexistent leadership from the President, it is likely that any health insurance legislation that emerges from Congress will be very limited in its redistributive impact.

The Civil Rights Act of 1964. Civil rights for racial and ethnic minorities (understood and debated almost exclusively in terms of blacks from the 1930s through the 1960s) had a long and complex, and often heartbreaking, history from the end of the Civil War up to the passage of the first postreconstruction civil rights legislation of much substance in 1964. This history was both legislative (characterized largely by nonaction) and judicial (characterized by sporadic, faltering, and often negative action until 1954 and then a quickening tempo of positive action after that). Recounting that history would take an entire book (see Kluger, 1976, for a superb summary of civil rights history). In this section we will focus on one important part of civil rights history, the passage of the Civil Rights Act of 1964, to illustrate the kinds of political forces that are generated when considering a redistributive policy measure that deals with questions of racial justice and injustice. As with other redistributive policies there was a combination of highly visible and emotion-filled debate, both in Congress and in other public arenas, and private negotiating of compromises that allowed forward movement at critical points. The public debate was carried on by two large coalitions of groups and individuals that had opposed each other for years. The private negotiations were carried on by key individuals in both the executive branch and Congress (source material for this case is drawn from Lytle, 1966; Sundquist, 1968: chapter 6; Congressional Quarterly, 1965: 1615–1641; and Kluger, 1976).

When John Kennedy became President in 1961 he had raised the hopes of leaders in the civil rights movement that some federal civil rights legislation might be forthcoming if he chose to play a leadership role. Instead, he chose to proceed very cautiously in the area (critics said he was not proceeding at all) primarily to protect other parts of his domestic program from being defeated because of the actions of angry southerners well placed in the House and Senate. However, as the pace of the civil rights movement at the local level increased with a variety of demonstrations, protests, boycotts, and some violence, the Administration at last felt compelled to submit legislative proposals. Thus the President announced in February, 1963, that such proposals would be forthcoming, but in the absence of firm presidential commitment, only some bills of mild and minor character were introduced in May as a somewhat slow follow-up to his announcement. Major action still did not seem imminent.

However, in May and June the attention of the nation was directed to Birmingham, Alabama, where a particularly evil manifestation of officially supported and sanctioned violence in support of blatant racial discrimination was being challenged by dedicated civil rights leaders and large numbers of followers. Additional public drama was created when Governor George Wallace of Alabama took his stand in "the schoolhouse door" to prevent two blacks from registering at the University of Alabama. (He gave up in a few hours when the President put the Alabama National Guard into federal service.) The President, pushed by his own reading of these events, by supporters of civil rights in Congress, and by a host of interest groups and coalitions of groups supporting civil rights, submitted a civil rights bill of moderate strength to Congress in mid-June. More important, he committed his personal prestige to the fight to get the legislation passed. He immediately became involved personally in a number of meetings with groups supporting the legislation to work on strategy. These included a variety of black-led groups (for example, the National Association for the Advancement of Colored People, the National Urban League, the Congress of Racial Equality, and the Southern Christian Leadership Conference), a number of labor unions (particularly the industrial unions from the old Congress of Industrial Organizations), a large number of church groups, and the Leadership Conference on Civil Rights—a "holding company" of groups supporting civil rights, including all of the above plus many more (a total of 79 groups in 1963). The President also began meetings with pro-civil rights Democrats and Republicans from Congress and with officials from the Justice Department (headed by his brother Robert as Attorney General) and the White House.

A subcommittee of the House Judiciary Committee held hearings in the summer of 1963 and moved to strengthen the bill proposed by the President in a number of ways. The White House feared that the bill had been strengthened so much that it would never pass the Senate. The administration calculated that the votes of a number of western Democrats and moderate Republicans were critical to passage, particularly in the Senate, and that only a bill of moderate strength could gain their support. In order to gauge what could pass even the House, Attorney General Kennedy now entered directly into negotiations with two key Republicans—the ranking Republican on the Judiciary Committee and the Minority Leader. When the bill went into full committee the southern Democrats worked to obtain the strongest possible bill because they felt a strong bill was more likely to be defeated on the floor than a bill of moderate strength, which could not be defeated in their view. The administration intervened both publicly and privately to get the majority Democrats to weaken the bill so that it could pass the full House. The Attorney General asked for weakening amendments in full committee hearings and was also active in private negotiations. The administration was successful and the House Judiciary Committee reported a bill most agreed would pass the House relatively easily.

In 1963 in the Senate not a great deal occurred. The Senate Judiciary Committee, chaired by one of the most reactionary of the southern Democrats had, predictably, buried the parts of the bill referred to it. One major part of the package—that guaranteeing nondiscriminatory access to public accommodations such as hotels and restaurants—had gone to the Senate Commerce Committee and had been approved, although not formally reported (for strategic reasons), by the end of the session.

Nineteen sixty-four dawned with a new President, Lyndon Johnson, in office because John Kennedy had been assassinated in November. Johnson quickly made his total commitment to a strong law in the civil rights area quite evident and worked closely with friendly lobbyists and members of Congress and individuals in the White House and Justice Department to develop a strategy and generate compromises that would attract enough moderate votes to pass the package.

Pressured by northern Democratic and Republican support, the House Rules Committee, although chaired by an arch-conservative Virginian, proved to be no major stumbling block for the progress of the bill in early 1964. The full House debated the bill for ten days and passed it by a large margin (290 to 130) on February 10. The bill's managers acquiesced in accepting a few amendments on the floor restricting the scope of the bill but, on the whole, the bill the House passed was very close in nature to the bill that had been hammered out in the multiparty negotiations in the autumn of 1963 in the Judiciary Committee. Two amendments even strengthened the bill a bit.

The first critical action in the Senate occurred when the whole Senate voted simply to place the House-passed bill on its calendar for floor consideration rather than referring it to the Judiciary Committee, where it no doubt would die. The Senate then debated the bill from early March until mid-June, 1964 (one year to the day after President Kennedy had submitted his legislative request). The key figure in the Senate soon turned out to be the Minority Leader, Senator Everett Dirksen of Illinois. If he could be persuaded of the fairness of the bill he would vote for closing off a filibuster the southern opposition had mounted and would also vote for the bill. More important, he would bring along a number of moderate Republicans with him on both votes. The vote on the filibuster would clearly be the most important, since two thirds of those present and voting must vote yea (67 votes were required because all 100 Senators were present—a rare event—for the vote on cloture and also for the vote on final passage of the bill). The Attorney General and the Senate Democrat taking the lead in floor debate, Hubert Humphrey of Minnesota, negotiated extensively over several months with Dirksen. Eventually they reached some compromises that weakened the bill somewhat but brought victory—71 to 29 on cloture and 73 to 27 on the bill itself.

The majority on the House Rules Committee again overrode its chairman to guarantee that the House could vote directly on the Senate-passed bill without sending the bill to a conference committee, where again it might die (the chances for death in Congress are extraordinarily high for any single bill). The House easily approved the Senate bill 289 to 126 on July 2 and later the same day President Johnson signed it into law on national television.

Despite the numerous compromises that had been necessary to get the new law through several sticky points in both houses it was not toothless legislation and, in fact, the contributions of the negotiations and discussions among the White House, Justice Department, supportive interest groups and organizations, and supportive Senators and Representatives had strengthened the bill beyond what President Kennedy had initially requested. It was a broad bill and had titles dealing with voting rights, public accommodations, desegregation of public facilities, desegregation of public education, extending the life of the Civil Rights Commission, nondiscrimination in programs assisted with federal dollars, equal employment opportunity, registration and voting statistics, and the creation of a Community Relations Service in the Commerce Department.

The passage of the 1964 Civil Rights Act was characterized by lengthy debate that was highly emotional and highly visible. There was no quiet subgovernment at work in this policy area. The benefits to be conferred by the legislation—equal treatment under the law—created distinct classes of perceived winners and losers. Successful passage of the legislation required the forceful personal involvement of many key actors, most notably the President, and a willingness of the supporters to compromise. The passage of the Act alone did not guarantee implementation of its provisions, but it was an important step in the country's history of providing simple justice to its citizens.

Redistributive issues redefined as distributive

The redefinition of redistributive issues may occur as the price for allowing any redistribution to emerge at all. Reaching accord is easier if the participants in a redistributive debate choose to emphasize the distributive aspects and mute the redistributive aspects. This approach was used in some of the cases already discussed. The retention of community action programs and the retention of legal services for the poor were bought at the cost of severe limitations on the redistributive potential of these programs—a very small budget in the case of community action and strict limitations on the services that could be provided in the case of legal services. In the case of Medicare, success was achieved in part because subsidies went to hospitals and doctors. Procedural safeguards were added to mute the redistributive potential of the 1964 Civil Rights Act.

The redefinition of redistributive issues may also occur following their passage, as subsequent amendments are made that gradually whittle away the redistributive emphasis. The examples that follow illustrate how distributive aspects of redistributive policy were stressed in order to secure passage. The first three cases also illustrate how continuation of the redistributive policies was achieved by stress on their distributive features.

Model Cities. The history of Model Cities—from its germination in a presidentially appointed Task Force on Urban Problems in 1965 and its initial statutory authorization in 1966 until its replacement by a special revenue sharing program in 1974 and its organizational programmatic termination in 1975—is one characterized by a short initial period of redistributive rhetoric followed by the reality of a program that was basically oriented toward distributing federal dollars to cities (with increasing autonomy on the part of those cities in making decisions about the purposes for which the money was spent) and improving relations between the federal government and cities. (This discussion of Model Cities is based on Ripley, 1972, chapter 5.) The central reason for this important shift lies in the nature of congressional attitudes and reactions to administration initiatives. Both through informal contacts with high-ranking officials in the Model Cities Administration, the Department of Housing and Urban Development, and the White House, and through formal actions taken on authorizing legislation and appropriations, members of the House and Senate helped set the direction that Model Cities took in practice—a direction altered from the early reasons given for the passage of the Act by President Johnson and the liberal Democratic supporters of the program.

The original formulators saw Model Cities as a program that would consciously manipulate social conditions in favor of the poorest residents of city slums. They sold the program to others—especially those in Congress—in two ways: In speaking to liberals they advocated it as a program of social redistribution; but in speaking to conservatives they portrayed it as a program of subsidy for city governments.

Achieving congressional legitimation of the Johnson administration's program of redistribution was a difficult task from the outset. Significant opposition to the program developed in Congress, especially among Republicans, including members on the authorizing committees in both houses. Compromise was required to pass the initial authorizing statute in 1966. These compromises—like those in other programs we have already discussed—muted the redistributive potential of the program. For example, provisions requiring Model Cities to have racial integration as a goal of their plans were dropped. Subsidy to cities and the autonomy of cities were stressed in changes in the administration's proposal that increased the number of eligible cities, dropped the requirement that cities establish a separate agency specifically designed to administer the program, and eliminated a federal coordinator who was to be stationed in each model city.

Under congressional pressure and then by administration preference the stress in Model Cities implementation came to rest more on the process of administration than on outcomes. The shift began in the Johnson administration. The themes stressed in 1967 and 1968 mixed a concern for the subsidizing of increasingly autonomous city enterprises. These themes included emphases on Model Cities as the ultimate federal tool for eradicating urban blight and poverty, on concentrating the planning and implementation efforts on limited areas of selected cities, on citizen participation in the planning and implementation of the program (but not at the expense of the established local government's role), on the centrality of the mayors' role in the program and on the bolstering of local government in general, on improving the "delivery systems" for existing federal programs for the cities, and on according states a place in the program.

In the Nixon administration in 1969 and 1970 the themes became almost exclusively devoted to a concern with creating strength and autonomy in local governments and to creating a distributive rather than a redistributive image for the program. The emphases now changed to making the program more responsive to local needs and less susceptible to federal management; to supporting mayoral authority; to deemphasizing citizen participation in the program, especially in administration; to expanding the scope of the program to include entire cities rather than just target neighborhoods (while cutting total funding); to toning down the promises of social results; and to stressing the need for a more unified interpretation of administrative policies at all levels of administration. From 1971 on, the themes changed even more strongly in this direction as HUD officials announced their desire to give cities almost complete control of mobilizing and coordinating resources, to reduce federal monitoring to simple auditing rather than setting national program standards against which performance would be measured, and to make block grants to cities rather than categorical grants. Beginning in 1971 President Nixon made evident his desire to do away with the Model Cities program in favor of a broader special revenue sharing program for housing and community development. He was stymied for several years by liberals in Congress reluctant to see another "Great Society" program succumb, but in 1974—shortly after Nixon had resigned the presidency—Congress passed the Housing and Community Development Act that spelled the end of Model Cities (and numerous other programs) as a separate entity.

In summary, at its inception the Model Cities program was envisioned by its formulators and most liberal supporters as a vehicle for the manipulation of social conditions and the redistribution of economic rewards. It was to be a demonstration project for a small, limited number of cities that would eradicate blight and create monuments of true urban renewal. But the realities were that the environment in Congress from 1966 onward was not hospitable to such goals, and thus the administrations of both Johnson and Nixon used the program as a device for regulating intergovernmental relations (through strengthening city halls) and intragovernmental relations (through coordinating federal delivery systems) and for creating the appearance of subsidizing a lot of cities (although with severely diminished funds).

Special revenue sharing: The case of employment and training. As mentioned in Chapter 1, special revenue sharing is a means for passing federal funds to states and localities for a particular use (for example, education or transportation) with relatively few federal strings attached. Commonly, the special revenue sharing money comes in the form of a block grant that replaces a variety of federal categorical grant programs in the issue area. Special revenue sharing, long advocated by the Nixon administration, is now an important part of the political landscape in two policy areas, housing and community development, and manpower training.

In general, special revenue sharing programs seem to be replacing programs with considerable redistributive potential (which were perceived as such by the participants) with programs that emphasize distributive potential much more (and which are generally perceived in terms of their distributive features). Now the clients receiving benefits are governmental units—states, cities, counties—rather than a class of persons—the economically disadvantaged. The choices about who gets what at the expense of whom (the essence of a redistributive program) are fuzzed over by the use of a formula to allocate funds and by the stress on local control. To the extent that redistributive questions get discussed directly, that discussion may take place either in the parts of the federal bureaucracy that supervise revenue sharing programs (the Employment and Training Administration in the case of the Comprehensive Employment and Training Act [CETA] and the Department of Housing and Urban Development in the case of the Housing and Community Development Act) or at the local level (presumably through some mandated mechanism for citizen input). But neither the federal bureaucracy nor local government is used to confronting redistributive questions head-on and both are generally inexpert at it. Both are also severely hampered even if the desire is present. The federal bureaucracy is hampered because its role in revenue sharing is limited to only "technical assistance," and the local citizen input mechanism is hampered because it is defined explicitly as being "advisory" only. Given the absence of a national mandate to emphasize redistributive benefits, and the inexperience and/or unwillingness of city and county governments to engage in redistributive activity, special revenue sharing programs will get defined and implemented as distributive programs, and the conflicts that arise will focus on questions of jurisdiction and dollar allocations to geographically defined units rather than on who benefits to what effect in a broader social sense.

The replacement of categorical employment and training programs with a revenue sharing block grant was a lengthy battle. (For an excellent summary, see Davidson, 1972; 1975.) It took five years for the Nixon administration to get a comprehensive manpower bill (the Comprehensive Employment and Training Act of 1973) passed, and the resulting package was less than it had wanted, but more than the supporters of categorical programs had wanted to give. The debate over comprehensive employment and training revenue sharing focused on three major aspects of the Nixon proposal: decategorization, decentralization, and public service employment.

The categorical programs represented a piecemeal approach to redistributive manpower policy. Although they were established for their redistributive potential (training unemployed and disadvantaged workers to improve job skills and standard of living), the categorical grant funding approach emphasized their distributive features, and numerous subgovernments sprang up around each grant program, its congressional committees, and relevant bureaucrats. These groups fought the hardest to resist revenue sharing because they feared it would mean the end of their categorical programs and their subgovernments. The proposals being considered in the 1969 to 1973 period would give discretion to the local governmental units to decide which categorical programs might be continued—none of them (except the Job Corps, as it turned out) had any guarantees about their future. This fact had implications not only for the continuation of the subgovernments, but also for the redistributive potential of their programs themselves, since the prime sponsors (the local elected officials) could shift clientele orientation as they saw fit, and those served would not necessarily be among the most needy.

Decentralization was also an issue, and there was competition among states, cities, and counties with large populations for chief administrative responsibility under the comprehensive bill. Cities especially feared that they and their urban problems (where those most in need of redistributive policies tend to reside) would be slighted if responsibility were lodged with the states, which historically had not been sensitive to urban problems. Likewise, the bulk of the populous counties' population is suburban, and not typically the most needy.

Debate on the consolidation of employment and training programs was complicated by the inclusion of the public employment issue. This issue aroused the historically divisive, ideologically based question of the proper role of the federal government in creating and subsidizing jobs for the unemployed. Liberals were traditionally in favor of a strong federal role, while conservatives have opposed this activity. President Nixon strongly resisted the inclusion of a public employment title in a comprehensive manpower bill (ultimately he was unsuccessful), but public service employment was included in the consolidation debate because its supporters argued that it was pointless for manpower programs to focus only on training workers if there were not enough jobs to go around. The concept of public service employment has been around since the New Deal, and supporters were anxious to have an existing employment program continued.

The essence of the final compromise was that the administration got its basic mandate for decentralization and decategorization and a much diminished federal role in making program choices, and the liberals got the retention of a few categorical programs (notably the Job Corps) and some categorical references in the statute and a sizable permanent public service program (augmented in late 1974 by a large emergency public service program designed to combat the economic problems facing the nation at that time).

The central features of CETA can be summarized very briefly:

1. Basic responsibility for deciding how to spend money for manpower purposes is given to "prime sponsors," which are, with only

a few exceptions, cities or counties with more than 100,000 population, consortia of cities and counties, and states.

2. The great bulk of manpower money is allocated to the prime spon-
sorships by formulas based on various weightings for unemployment, number of low income people, and previous federal manpower spending.

3. Several forms of advisory council are mandated by the statute and
the regulations issued by the Department of Labor. Most important
are the planning councils that are required in each prime sponsorship.

4. The regional offices of the Department of Labor retain a variety of
supervisory duties and responsibilities, although in general they
are to offer primarily "technical assistance" to prime sponsors.

5. In pre-CETA manpower operations the standard model of service
delivery to clients was for the regional or national office of the
Manpower Administration to contract directly with deliverers.
Under CETA the prime sponsors write and monitor the performance of those contracts.

6. The congressional role in CETA is limited to providing appropriations and, if so desired, to basic statutory revisions such as re-
drawing the allocation formulas or setting different standards for
eligibility for prime sponsor status. Given that such decisions are
distributive by nature and given that considerable logrolling—as
might be expected—went into the initial compromises on such details it seems unlikely that Congress will engage in such activity.
The nature of congressional oversight of the performance of CETA
is also unclear. As of mid-1975 the main congressional interest
shown in CETA had been in insisting on spending much more
money on public service jobs (a classic form of direct subsidy to
states and localities with only minimal concern for social impact)
than the Ford administration wanted.

The experience under CETA underscores the generalizations made
earlier about the implications of revenue sharing for redistributive policy impacts. For example, a greater stress on white clients compared to
black clients and other minorities and on near-poor clients compared
to the poorest clients quickly developed. Community action agencies
—presumably among the more redistributively oriented of local institutions—were losing their role as service deliverers in a number of
jurisdictions. "Work experience" for youth—including large numbers
of black youths—was given greater stress under CETA than in pre-
CETA programs. This is a relatively cheap way of "serving" large
numbers of clients who are both black and among the most disadvantaged. This can be used by prime sponsors to offset charges from po-

litically hostile groups that the program is shortchanging such clients. It also seems clear that the advisory councils are not meaningful bodies for representing clients. In some jurisdictions they may be relatively effective in representing officials, service deliverers, or high status individuals, but as representatives of actual and potential clients they are simply not structured to serve as effective access channels.

When CETA was reauthorized in 1978 Congress attempted to insert a bit more redistributive potential into the program by tightening some of the eligibility requirements. But a good deal more effort was spent on considering the public service employment program—both its size and how to prevent abuses. Questions of size primarily have to do with how much subsidy CETA should generate for units of local government—an essentially distributive question.

Aid to education. The history of federal aid to education in the United States since World War II is complex and tangled (see Bendiner, 1964; Eidenberg and Morey, 1969; Munger and Fenno, 1962; Sundquist, 1968; chapter 5). In broad terms it can be asserted that the federal government began to give increasing amounts of special purpose aid to both elementary and secondary education and to higher education during the early parts of the period but that a logjam developed on the question of broad general aid—especially to elementary and secondary schools—and that the logjam was broken only by shifting the form and purpose of general purpose aid. In more analytic terms it can be asserted that aid to education measures that were perceived as providing benefits to many special segments of the population or to specially defined geographic areas (that is, measures that were distributive) were much easier to enact than broad general purpose aid measures that were perceived as shifting benefits from one racial or religious group to another racial or religious group. The final breakthrough on a form of general purpose aid in 1965 was possible only because the redistributive focus was shifted away from race and religion to poverty and because distributive features were emphasized. Redistribution was still perceived to be taking place, but given the heat of the philosophical, racial, and religious controversies that had raged for the preceding 13 years, it was a muted form of redistribution.

Throughout all of the debates, members of the House and Senate and a few individuals in the hierarchy of both the Department of Health, Education, and Welfare and the White House were important in framing initiatives, attempting compromises, and—usually—shifting the grounds of debate until the most threatening aspects of redistribution were removed. Generally these individuals were subcommittee chairmen and ranking members in the House and Senate and individuals in HEW at the level of Assistant Secretary or above. However, given the broad involvement of many groups and interests, agreement at this level was never sufficient to generate policy decisions. Inevitably, large associations and groups such as the National Education Association, civil rights groups, and both Catholic and Protestant religious organizations also got involved. And the highest echelons of the executive branch—usually including the President personally—also got involved. Consequently, most members of the House and Senate felt a personal stake in outcomes even though their own committee assignments might be quite remote from education, and congressional decision making tended to get escalated out of quiet committee settings onto the floors of the two chambers. Perceived redistribution—coupled with philosophical and some partisan differences—increases the likelihood that more participants and participants in higher formal positions will become more important than the normal subgovernment members. The aid to education case certainly illustrates this generalization. Committee members and HEW and Office of Education bureaucrats even up to the level of Assistant Secretary and Commissioner of Education were only moderately important actors rather than dominant actors in reaching final decisions.

The tenor of the federal aid to education provided between 1940 and 1965 is clearly distributive, and that fact alone explains the relative ease of establishing those aid programs. Table 6–2 summarizes the most important of the aid programs. In all cases, except the 1965 Elementary and Secondary Education Act, subsidies for students or institutions (colleges, school districts) are provided in a nonredistributive way.

General aid to school districts foundered throughout the same period because of hostility to federal "control" of a traditionally local function, because of the perception after 1954 that aid would be used as a lever to force public school integration, and because of the issue of whether private schools (especially those run by the Roman Catholic Church) would or would not receive benefits. Various combinations of these issues—with the racial question being explicitly redistributive in nature—repeatedly killed general aid in Congress, although various presidents—especially Eisenhower and Kennedy—were unable or unwilling to find a winning solution. Eidenberg and Morey (1969: 23–24) summarize the history of failure to achieve compromise:

> In searching for school aid stumbling blocks, one is quickly led to the House of Representatives. Starting in 1948 the Senate passed each bill that reached the floor—1948, 1949, 1960, and 1961. On the other hand, in the House three bills were killed on the floor (1956, 1957, and 1961) and another (1960) was passed but subsequently held in the Rules Committee on the way to conference.
>
> From 1943 to 1955 the prime obstacle in the House was the Education and Labor Committee. During this period hearings were held on

Table 6–2: Federal aid to education, 1940–1965

Program	Benefits	Recipients
Higher Education		
1944 ..... G.I. Bill of Rights	Living expenses, books, tuition	World War II veterans (later Korean, cold war, and Vietnam veterans)
1950 ..... National Science Foundation	Support for science research and education	Colleges, universities
1950 ..... Housing Act of 1950	Low interest loans for dormitory construction	Colleges, universities
1958 ..... National Defense Education Act	Loans; training in science, math, languages; equipment purchases	Students; teachers; colleges, universities
1963 ..... Classroom construction	Grants for classroom construction	Public and private colleges
1965 ..... Higher Education Act	Scholarships, library support, construction grants	Colleges, universities
Elementary and Secondary Education		
1940 ..... Lanham Act	Financial aid	School districts impacted by war-related personnel dislocation
1946 ..... National School Lunch Act	Aid for providing school lunches	School districts
1950 ..... Impacted areas aid	Financial aid	School districts impacted with federal personnel
1954 ..... Agricultural Act	Aid for providing school milk	School districts
1958 ..... National Defense Education Act	Matching grants for equipment and classrooms; aid for foreign language training institutes, testing, guidance, counseling	States
1965 ..... Elementary and Secondary Education Act	Aid for equipment, classrooms, staff, construction; aid for library resources; matching aid for supplemental education centers; aid for education research; aid for state departments of education	School districts with concentrations of poor and unemployed persons; state departments of education; local education agencies; colleges, universities, states; state departments of education

Source: Adapted from material in Eidenberg and Morey (1969: 16–18, 247–248).

seven bills, but not one was reported. In 1955 the opposition bloc finally crumbled when 15 non-Southern Democrats aligned with 7 Republicans to approve a bill for the first time in recent history. By 1959 federal aid supporters had a solid majority on the committee. . . .

As the complexion of the Education and Labor Committee changed in the mid-1950s, the antifederal aid bloc in the Rules Committee was solidified. This committee was the principal obstacle to school aid bills in 1955, 1959, 1960, and 1961 through 1964.

The breaking of the logjam in 1965 came for several reasons. One was that liberal Democrats made sweeping gains in the House of Representatives in the 1964 election as a result of President Johnson's landslide victory. But, even more important, the effort to achieve general purpose aid essentially was compromised in favor of a special-purpose approach. As Sundquist (1968: 206) describes it, both proponents and opponents of general purpose aid finally decided that some benefits were better than none.

The sudden turnabout reflects, perhaps most of all, a simple fact: people *do* learn from experience. First, both sides of the religious controversy had learned. The NEA and its public school allies now knew that an all-or-nothing attitude would mean, for the public schools, nothing. Likewise, Catholic leaders now understood that an equal-treatment-or-nothing position would mean, for the Catholic schools, nothing. For each side the question was whether it preferred to maintain the purity of its ideological position or receive some tangible benefits for its schools. The Washington representatives of organizations on both sides were, with a few exceptions, cautiously on the side of accommodation. . . . Accommodation was supported by public opinion polls, which showed that a majority of Americans no longer opposed aid to parochial schools. Second, the tacticians had learned. The National Defense Education Act had shown that special-purpose aid, carefully designed, could be enacted at a time when general-purpose aid could not be.

Basically the breakthrough came because the proponents of a redistributive aid policy packaged their program in a way that emphasized special-purpose, distributive features (which had been succeeding since 1940) and combined it in a bill with other special-purpose aid. The new special purpose was "the education of children of needy families and children living in areas of substantial unemployment." As Sundquist (1968: 210) points out, "Congress had, after all, acknowledged a federal responsibility for assistance to families on welfare and for aid to depressed areas. Assistance to school districts 'impacted' by federal activities was also long-established; would not it be as logical to assist 'poverty-impacted' districts?"

A change in the general political climate was also important in establishing the partially redistributive emphasis on disadvantaged children in the 1965 aid to education bill. The changed climate included the recent rediscovery of poverty by the federal government a few years earlier, a commitment by the liberal portion of the Democratic party to attack poverty in a number of ways, and the dominance of the government by an aggressive liberal Democratic President and large liberal Democratic majorities in the House and Senate.

Income tax revision, 1978. Tax laws are complicated. Seemingly, debates over them would be dry and dusty affairs dominated by economists and accountants and similar dry and dusty people. Nothing, however, could be farther from the truth. Debates over tax laws are often heated and colorful. And a great deal is at stake because tax laws are used to distribute billions of dollars in tangible goodies. The overall impact of a tax system can, at one extreme, redistribute wealth in ways to promote economic equality. At the other extreme a tax system can both cement and increase the privileged position of the already privileged classes. In the United States the overall tax system does some of each. Thus debates over marginal changes in details are often fierce, because at stake is real, material wealth—personal cash—and those stakes emphatically generate classes of winners and losers. Some forces push for greater equalization in favor of less advantaged classes in society by enhancing the redistributive aspects of the tax system. Other forces push for retaining or even expanding existing privileges of the well-off strata.

In his campaign for the presidency in 1976 Jimmy Carter labeled the tax system in the United States a "disgrace." In early 1978, after a year in office, he released his program for changing this situation by proposing a large tax cut and some moderate tax "reforms." The overall size of the cut was to be $24.5 billion, with 94 percent of the total going to taxpayers with incomes under $30,000 annually. He proposed eliminating some itemized deductions (general sales tax, taxes on personal property other than real estate, and state gasoline tax), eliminating or curtailing a number of deductions for business entertainment, and tightening various provisions that apply to "tax shelter" investments used by upper-income persons to reduce their tax burden.

By the time Congress adjourned in October 1978 it had produced a tax bill that contained both a cut and some revisions in treatment of deductions and tax shelters. But the content of that bill bore little resemblance to what the President had requested. He had asked for mild redistribution in favor of the less well-off; he had received a bill that basically cemented most privileges for the well-off, created a few new ones, and aimed the tax cut (smaller in total size) at upper income people as well as at others. This bill, which the President signed anyway, came about both because entrenched supporters of existing privileges were too strong to defeat and because the President and his top administration lieutenants were not very skillful at cooperating with their natural allies in Congress to achieve desired results. Given the critical role of the President if redistribution in general is ever to be achieved, a failure on the part of the President to proceed effectively almost surely will doom redistributive efforts. Here the natural pressure toward treating taxes in a distributive fashion, plus the ineptness of the Carter administration, produced a result that poorly served the less well-off.

In the House the President's position had some allies on the Ways and Means Committee who might have prevailed on some issues had the administration given them timely and effective help. A key presidential assistant and the Secretary of the Treasury became involved in negotiations with the Ways and Means Committee but in a way and at a time that proved of little help to the administration's preferences. Thus the disintegration of the original package in the House was almost complete by the time the bill was passed on August 10, despite a last-minute attempt by the administration to salvage part of what it wanted. The size of the cut was still within bounds (in fact, it was only about two thirds of what the President had requested) but it was no longer directed toward the lower income categories. Furthermore, most hints of meaningful "reform" had vanished.

Matters got even more out of hand in some ways in the Senate and the administration continued to intervene in nonproductive ways. The total of the tax cut now ballooned to over $29 billion, an amount the President found unacceptable, particularly because national economic conditions had deteriorated since his initial request in January. The Senate was not as oriented toward upper-income people as the House although much more so than the President had initially proposed. Carter had asked for 94 percent of the tax cut in personal income taxes to go to those with incomes less than $30,000 a year. The House had targeted about 53 percent for those under $30,000. The Senate had increased that to 65 percent, still a long way from the President's initial request. As in the House, "reform" had all but vanished. Senate passage came on October 10.

The Conference Committee had only a few days left to work (and its members were also besieged with other end-of-session duties). The Carter administration sought to influence the outcome of these tax negotiations and did so in the area of the total size of the tax cut. But in terms of who got the cuts and in terms of "reform" the administration got only a few scraps. The Secretary of the Treasury was, in effect, a participant in some of the deliberations of the Conference Committee. In fact, the Conference Committee met formally very little. The con-

ferees from each House caucused separately and privately. The staff
of the Joint Committee on Taxation served as mediators and messen-
gers between the two caucuses. The President personally met with the
Chairmen of the House Ways and Means Committee and the Senate
Finance Committee—the two most important figures in the Conference
—early in the process.

The distributive (and nonredistributive) flavor of the outcome is
clear although, as with any tax bill, the provisions are extremely complicated, much more so than we care to summarize. The results can be
briefly summarized as follows:

1. The size of the tax cut was 18.7 billion, acceptable to the President
    even under the worsened economic conditions of late 1978.
2. Fifty-six percent of the tax cut was targeted for those with incomes
    of less than $30,000—a figure much closer to the House version
    (53 percent) than to the President's request of 94 percent or even
    the Senate's figure of 65 percent.
3. One Senate addition unacceptable to the President—the addition
    of tuition tax credits for college expenses that would benefit the
    more privileged societal strata—was deleted.
4. Cuts in the tax on capital gains were included in the final bill, de-
    spite the President's opposition. Almost 80 percent of the benefits
    of this provision were expected to go to persons with annual in-
    comes of $50,000 or more, and over 40 percent to individuals with
    annual incomes of $200,000 or more!
5. Several technical provisions reversed "reform" actions included
    in tax law revisions in 1969 and 1976. Conservatives were quite
    vocal in gloating over these specific victories.
6. Of the President's initial proposals for reform little was left: the
    itemized deduction for gasoline taxes was eliminated; unemploy-
    ment compensation benefits for individuals earning more than
    $20,000 would be taxed for the first time; only part of one busi-
    ness deduction was removed from the eligible list; and only a min-
    iscule tightening of one provision with regard to tax shelters was
    approved.

That the President could even prevail on the total amount of the cut
and the elimination of tuition tax credits was because he had threatened a veto if his wishes were not respected on these issues. Congress
—which was set to adjourn in a few days to allow members to campaign for reelection (the election was only a few weeks away)—did not
want to forego the symbol of providing the nation with a tax cut. Tax
cuts are always popular even if their provisions benefit very few and
are understood by few besides tax lawyers, accountants, and wealthy
beneficiaries.

CONCLUSIONS

The general shape of the redistributive arena and the specific characterization of congressional-bureaucratic relations in that arena outlined at the beginning of this chapter and in Table 4–1 are generally confirmed by the case material at which we have looked. However, several important additions to that general picture can now be made.

First, it seems clear that initiative for redistributive policy can come from within Congress and, occasionally, from the higher levels of the career bureaucracy. But more often the initiative comes from the White House, and presidential participation in an active way is helpful and usually essential for those wanting to achieve redistribution—at least on behalf of the poorer segments of society.

To the extent that the President is either opposed to the proposed redistribution or active only verbally or only sporadically or unenthusiastically or ineffectively the chances increase that either nothing will happen and a long-standing stalemate will persist or that the issue will be redefined, at least in part, as distributive. There are always strong natural tendencies in Congress to seek compromise through such redefinition.

Another recurring pattern also gives a particularly important role to Congress. At those critical moments in the history of debate over a redistributive proposal when the political situation seems to allow movement rather than repetition of previous positions resulting in continued stalemate, important congressional figures—often working with technical experts from the bureaucracy—engage in relatively quiet bargaining and negotiation that are essential to success. Usually these negotiations result in limits on the original redistributive potential of the proposal but some such potential often still remains.

～7～

Foreign and defense policy

THE NATURE OF FOREIGN AND DEFENSE POLICY

CONGRESS HAS the potential to be heavily involved in many aspects of foreign and defense policies and it has been actively using this power during the 1970s and seems to be in a mood to continue an activist stance into the 1980s. The quiescent position of Congress in the late 1950s and early 1960s in many of these areas was deceptively atypical (on the changing role of Congress in foreign and defense policies in general see Carroll, 1966; Frey, 1975; Kolodziej, 1975; Lanouette, 1978; Manley, 1971; and Moe and Teel, 1970).

Unfortunately, most of the literature on the involvement of Congress in foreign policy—and on the relationship between Congress, the President, military and foreign policy bureaucracy, and interest groups— treats foreign and defense policy as a single, undifferentiated area. We argue, however, that there are three different kinds of foreign and defense policy, distinguishable by the kinds of politics surrounding each. Tables 1–3 and 4–1 and the discussion of those tables have previously laid out the shape of these three areas in summary fashion.

The characteristics of *structural policy* (which occurs in noncrisis situations) are virtually the same as in domestic distributive policy: subgovernments composed of actors from bureaus, subcommittees, and small units in the private sector (individuals, corporations, small interest groups) dominate policymaking on the basis of mutual noninterference and logrolling. The relationship among the actors in these subgovernments is stable, and their decisions are implemented in a decentralized fashion, usually at the bureau level.

In *strategic policy* (which also occurs in noncrisis situations) the pattern is somewhat similar to domestic regulatory policy, with the major difference being that interest groups and especially bureaus and subcommittees have a reduced role. The major decisional locus is centralized in portions of the executive branch, especially the presidency, which deals basically with the whole Congress. Implementation of policies tends to be only partially decentralized.

In *crisis policy* the basic decision making structure is very simple: it is the President and whomever he chooses to consult. Usually he will consult only a few of his top advisors; sometimes he will bring in leading individual members of Congress or occasionally "peak association" leaders. The issues are defined quickly, debated in private by the executive actors, and responded to quickly in a highly centralized fashion through executive (presidential) action. Of course, the decisions may provoke considerable public debate after they are announced.

THE CONGRESSIONAL-BUREAUCRATIC RELATIONSHIP IN FOREIGN AND DEFENSE POLICY

The relationship between members of the executive branch (at the bureau level) and individuals in Congress (at the subcommittee level) will vary depending on the kind of foreign and defense policy being dealt with. In the case of structural policy, we expect that the subgovernment relationship will be the most important source of decisions that emerge, and that those decisions will not be altered in subsequent stages of the formal legislative process. The subgovernments will deal with a wide range of aspects of the issues within their jurisdiction. There is a high degree of cooperation between bureaucrats and congressmen because each is motivated to serve clients, but if there are differences of opinion they will generally be resolved by the members of the subgovernment themselves, without involving a large number of participants. Both parties have a high degree of motivation to reach some form of compromise between their initial positions to prevent "outsiders" such as the Secretary of Defense or the President or a congressional party leader from intervening. The compromises they reach are likely to contain more subcommittee preferences than bureaucratic preferences, although the interests of neither (nor of their clients) will be badly treated.

In strategic policy we expect the importance of the subgovernment relationship to be greatly reduced. Only a few narrow aspects of an issue will be dealt with at the bureau-subcommittee level and very few final decisions will be made there. Most will instead be made in the higher reaches of the executive branch, where strategic-regulatory policy usually originates. Conflict based on ideological differences between congressional and executive branch actors may occur; it is not usually resolved at a subgovernment level but is simply passed along to a higher level for final decisions. At that higher level, conflict is either resolved by a broad compromise between contending positions or it may remain unresolved. Executive branch views typically dominate final decisions.

In the case of crisis policy we expect that the subcommittee-bureau level of interaction essentially will not be a factor in the decision making process. Major decisions are made within the confines of the presidency with the participation of those few individuals the President chooses to include. There is little chance for either cooperation or conflict, except in the confines of the small group summoned by the President. Conflict between the President and Congress may develop after an event, of course. Formal statements of either cooperation or conflict after the event usually take the form of either congressional resolutions disagreeing with or supporting presidential action or Executive Orders that either formalize a course already being followed or that simply impose a solution despite congressional dissent. Genuine compromise on controversial actions is generally not reached (largely because it is irrelevant since decisions have already been made and actions have already been taken). Sometimes sham compromise is effected in the name of "national unity." Some differences of opinion are, in effect, eliminated through an imposed solution (either a congressional action with teeth or an executive order). Generally, the presidential view of issues left in controversy prevails in one way or another.

STRUCTURAL POLICY

The defense budget

Many aspects of the defense budget, especially those related to ongoing procurement decisions, provide good examples of structural policy. Of course, the defense budget contains items with strategic impact —for example, the choice of a major new weapons system—and these items represent decisions that get made in the executive branch and sometimes get debated in Congress, usually on the floor of the House or Senate. The items of a more purely distributive nature, such as decisions to fund existing procurement contracts, typically get decided in the interaction between relevant subcommittees and parts of the Pentagon with more perfunctory ratification by the entire House and Senate.

We will investigate congressional-bureaucratic interactions in defense budgeting by examining a number of patterns of interaction that both enhance subgovernments' domination of many decisions and reflect that dominance. Three of these patterns relate specifically to procurement aspects of defense budgeting, and the remaining ones pertain to distributive aspects of the defense budget in general.

Procurement subgovernments. Very close links exist between Pentagon procurement officials, nongovernmental contractors, and members of the House and Senate whose states and districts benefit from defense contracting. The close ties and shared benefits reinforce the attitudes of other participants to proceed quietly to disburse more than $20 billion a year to procure military hardware. Contractors are approached by defense procurement officials and jointly they work out the specifications to be met. Members of Congress are kept abreast of the progress of such negotiations and often are given the privilege of announcing awards of contracts in their districts and states.

When two weapons systems are put into competition, sometimes, in effect, rival subgovernments will spring up. Typically each of the competing systems will have a Pentagon sponsor (usually one service favoring one system and a different service favoring a competing system), favored contractors as allies, and members of the House and Senate linked with given contractors for geographical reasons as additional allies. The Pentagon rivals will deliberately seek to mobilize the largest group of allies, even though such mobilization involves nonexperts in decisions that have strategic impact (see Armacost, 1969).

When a system has been decided on there may still be competing contractors with their respective congressional supporters giving them at least ritualistic support. Once the basic decision about what kind of system is going to be developed is made, however, the Pentagon has a relatively free hand in making the final choice of contractors although, over time, these decisions are made to build as large a constituency for military programs as possible (see Smith, 1973).

The decentralized nature of governmental procurement, especially within the Defense Department, enhances the latitude of groups of interacting DOD officials, contractors, and Senators and Representatives. In the absence of a central clearinghouse, defense procurement subgovernments operate with a high degree of autonomy. The federal procurement structure (of which defense procurement expenditures represent two thirds) was described by a former head of the General Services Administration as a "garage sale," with no one in charge.

In 1974 a new Office of Federal Procurement Policy was established in OMB by legislation to centralize federal procurement policies and practices. The Pentagon lobbied against the bill as did OMB itself. But in this case industry, supported by the House and Senate Government

Operations Committees, supported the bill. This institutional development seems to have made little difference in the way military procurement has worked.

Congressional priorities within the defense budget. Congressional
activity on the defense budget tends to concentrate on procurement
and research and development items (which constitute about 40 percent of the total defense budget) and to place much less emphasis on
personnel and operations and maintenance categories (these comprise
about 60 percent of the total). In the areas on which they concentrate,
the input of congressional defense appropriations subcommittees is
significant and has also been more in accord with the views of the individual services than with the views of the Secretary of Defense,
where those views have differed. The congressional focus on these
areas is enhanced by the deliberate appeals of Pentagon officials for
allies, even though they grant those allies some impact on strategic decisions. Kanter (1972) suggests that Congress is deliberately used by
the military services to provide critical support so that military preferences themselves will dominate (although given interservice rivalries,
any one service is likely to suffer some temporary setbacks).

The motivations of Pentagon officials, particularly the military services, to seek congressional support reflect the great importance they
attach to procurement and research and development. Their own values lie in these two areas (Kanter, 1972: 135).

The tendency by Congress to focus on procurement and research
and development items within the defense budget has continued beyond the period from 1960 to 1970, which Kanter (1972) described.
Data for the 1970s show the same concentration on changes in procurement and research and development items in the President's budget, and also a continued tendency to defer to the requests of the military. For example, in 1974, in both the bill authorizing procurement
and research and development and also in the defense appropriations
bill, Congress exhibited support for the subcommittee-military service-
contractor subgovernments.

In dealing with the procurement and research authorization bill in
1974 the House uniformly upheld the judgments of the House Armed
Services Committee (a consistently strong supporter of Pentagon views
on policy questions) and rejected all amendments aimed at cutting or
limiting controversial weapons systems. Overall, the House bill provided the services with 97.5 percent of their requested $23,139,139,000
authorization. In the Senate the experience was the same—with the
full Senate consistently upholding the Pentagon's views and defeating
restricting and limiting amendments. The Senate bill was only slightly
more restrictive than the House bill, granting 94.4 percent of the original request.

The appropriations bill approved by Congress in 1974 for fiscal 1975 (which contained all military funds except those for construction), although it reduced the total request by about $4.5 billion, still provided 94.9 percent of the funds requested by the administration and provided $3.6 billion more than in the previous year. More importantly, Congress supported all major weapons systems that were requested, making minor cuts in only a few of them.

The pattern of authorization and appropriations bills for defense procurement and research in 1978 was similar to the 1974 pattern. The President vetoed the first procurement and authorization bill, and Congress did not override the veto. The issue was whether an additional nuclear carrier, which the President opposed, would be authorized in the bill (the carrier's price tag was almost $2 billion). Not at issue was whether the Defense Department would retain claim to the disputed amount; the money was to remain in the defense community.

The President's veto of the first bill constituted a temporary, but not insurmountable, setback for the proponents of the carrier. It is worth noting that the Navy admirals continued lobbying for the carrier despite the presidential opposition. The second bill, which the President signed, was virtually identical to the vetoed bill with the exception that the offending carrier was removed. Overall, even with the carrier cut, Congress still provided almost as much authorization in dollar terms (over $36 billion) as the President requested. To achieve this total Congress added monies in some other areas not favored by the President but favored by various interests in Congress, the Pentagon, and the defense supply industry. It is symbolic that in the revised bill the only change, in addition to the deletion of the carrier, provided authorization of $209 million to settle some contract disputes between the Navy and two of its largest contractors. These companies, backed by the Armed Services Committees, would now collect these sums based on previous negotiations with the Navy.

The Fiscal 1979 defense appropriations bill passed in 1978 provided virtually all of the money requested in the President's budget (interested parties had succeeded in getting the President to request much of what they wanted—he was not at serious odds with any of their requests). The President even announced that the $2 billion that had to be cut from the bill because the extra nuclear carrier had not been authorized (recall that money can be appropriated only if an authorization exists) would be requested again early in 1979 and would be allocated to other defense purposes. Thus the Department of Defense would have over $119 billion in new appropriations for Fiscal 1979.

The DOD congressional liaison structure. The congressional liaison structure of the Department of Defense promotes the development and maintenance of independent subgovernments (see Holtzman, 1970:

137–141 and 167–168; Pipe, 1966). Each service has its own very large liaison staff that works directly with relevant committees, subcommittees, and individual Senators and Representatives. In fiscal 1965, for example, the Army had 92 individuals involved directly in congressional liaison, the Air Force had 144, and the Navy had 70 (Pipe, 1966: 18). By contrast, the central DOD liaison operation in the Office of the Secretary had only 34 persons—hardly enough to compete with the services if they were pushing policy views and making alliances not in direct accord with policies favored by the Secretary of Defense. Holtzman (1970: 138) summarized the situation well:

> Each military department cooperated with the SOD [Secretary of Defense] in relation to the Congress when its interests coincided with his, but each attempted to play its own game when their interests conflicted. Control and coordination from the secretarial level were very difficult to impose, in large measure because key individuals in the Congress had long opposed such domination by the senior political executive within Defense. . . . when a military department was in rebellion against the policies of the SOD, that service's legislative liaison staff withdrew from the usual cooperative arrangements with the DOD liaison officer. Under such circumstances, the latter could not rely upon the service's liaison staff as a resource for intelligence or as an aid in working with the Congress.

DOD–OMB relations. The relations between the Department of Defense and the Office of Management and Budget facilitate strong subgovernments. OMB has deliberately (perhaps out of a sense of inevitability) structured its relations with DOD so that the latter has a freer hand in its budgeting decisions than the domestic agencies. OMB budget examiners work directly with Pentagon and service budget officers (usually working physically in the Pentagon) to arrive at a recommendation for the President. The Secretary of Defense and the White House still exercise some control but the vastness of the military establishment lends itself to the official recognition of fragmentation.

Conference committee procedures. The practices of the House and Senate conferees on defense authorization and appropriations bills maximize congressional support for certain military policies that are highly valued by either the House or the Senate. Kanter (1972) analyzed 161 differences between House and Senate positions on DOD appropriations bills that were resolved by conference committees between fiscal 1966 and fiscal 1970. In examining the relative influence of the two houses, he found that only about 20 percent of the time did the conferees adopt a "split-the-difference" approach to resolve a disagreement. Rather, the usual approach was to give each house all of what it wanted on some issues, but none of what it wanted on other issues. In this way both houses got what was most important to them without major compromises on those issues. Only the lower priorities were likely to suffer either in being compromised or in being cut. Thus the highest priorities of the military services and their contractor allies were likely to emerge unscathed.[1]

Reprogramming funds. The Defense Department has considerable leeway to reprogram appropriated funds within appropriation accounts during a fiscal year—that is, it can transfer money and use it for purposes other than those for which it was originally appropriated (see Fisher, 1974). Reprogramming maximizes the ability of the military parts of defense subgovernments to make decisions that allow them to pursue their highest priorities despite competing priorities that might be articulated by the President, the Secretary of Defense, or the whole House or Senate. The relevant committees have to be informed about most reprogrammings—but, of course, that keeps the information within the subgovernment and does not involve "outsiders." Typically, reprogrammings for procurement have to obtain prior approval from the Armed Services and Appropriations committees in both houses (and have to have at least nominal approval from either the Secretary of Defense or Deputy Secretary of Defense before being sent to the committees). Research and Development reprogramming has to have approval of the Armed Services committees—or at least notification has to be given. This practice is not insignificant—between fiscal 1956 and fiscal 1972, for example, it involved between $1.7 and $4.7 billion annually. Between 1964 and 1972 an average of over 100 separate reprogramming actions took place annually.

Weapons systems

Decisions about weapons systems have important strategic implications, and initial decisions and research are generally done within the Defense Department, usually by the services. Congress must approve or disapprove executive requests for new weapons, and interactions on these kinds of issues constitute strategic policy. But once a weapons system has been approved for "pilot testing" or prototype research, subsequent decisions regarding its continuation, expansion, or alteration take on patterns of structural policy.

The B-1 bomber. For a number of years the Air Force lobbied for the development and production of the B-1 bomber to serve as the suc-

---

[1] This same pattern of mutual deference was found in a study of congressional treatment of foreign aid in the period between 1951 and 1962 (Ripley, 1965). This similarity suggests that perhaps in foreign and defense policy congressional committees may work—maybe unconsciously—to maximize their impact through this logrolling pattern of bargaining, which is quite different from the normal "split-the-difference" compromises characterizing many domestic policy areas.

cessor to the B-52 as the mainstay of the manned bomber fleet of the United States. Some critics began to suggest a number of years ago that manned bombers are superfluous in the age of missiles. But until 1976 the Air Force pushed the case for the B-1, consistently supported by the House of Representatives, the makers of the B-1 and their sub-contractors (each plane would cost $100 million and profits could be expected to be high), and Presidents Nixon and Ford. Only in 1978—with a new president now opposed—did the Air Force give up on the B-1. Even when death (presumably final) came to the B-1 (false deaths had been reported on several previous occasions) many in Congress (though no longer a majority) remained loyal and, perhaps most important, the money did not vanish from the Air Force budget but was, in effect, transferred to other projects such as the cruise missile. Equally important, when the House finally sided with the President in early 1978 it did so in voting on a bill that contained considerable money (almost $8 billion) for various domestic projects close to the hearts of many members.

Two glimpses of decision making on the B-1 follow. In the first situation in 1973–74 the supporters were basically in control and had the President on their side. In the second situation in 1977 and 1978 the President chose to intervene in this structural matter by stressing its strategic aspects and thus claiming more presidential prerogatives.

1973–1974. In 1973 the Air Force requested an authorization of $473.5 million for the B-1 in order to continue funding of the development of prototypes. The House Armed Services Committee recommended the entire amount and an attempt on the floor to delete it was defeated easily by a vote of 96 to 313. The Senate Armed Services Committee recommended a reduction of $100 million, which was sustained on the Senate floor. However, an amendment adding $5 million to finance a study of alternatives to the B-1 was rejected. The Senate was willing to practice some economy but not at the expense of jeopardizing the whole project. The conference committee was even less inclined to economy, and the Air Force's B-1 finally emerged with only $25 million less than had been requested—with the added stipulation that the money could not be saved by firing employees of the contractor.

In 1974 the Air Force asked for $499 million for continued prototype development in fiscal 1975. The House Armed Services Committee again recommended the full authorization. The supportive stance of Chairman F. Edward Hébert was unquestioning: "No matter what it costs, if that's what we need, we've got to pay for it." (Quoted in *Congressional Quarterly Weekly Report,* May 2, 1974, p. 562.) On the House floor an amendment to delete all money for the B-1 was defeated 94–309, virtually the same vote as in 1973. The Senate Armed Services

Committee recommended a cut of $44 million from the Air Force B-1 request but in the report made it clear that the cut was not to be interpreted as showing lack of Committee support for the project. Rather they simply wanted to reduce the number of prototypes constructed from four to three. A floor amendment to cut another $225 million from the B-1 authorization was rejected 31 to 59. The conference committee adopted the Senate figure of $455 million. However, the Air Force really didn't lose anything as the remaining $44 million could be obtained by reprogramming funds as soon as the first prototype had been successfully flight tested. Congress gave the appearance of deferring slightly to the economizers and critics of the B-1, but in reality the support for the Air Force was virtually total. The defense appropriations bill contained virtually full funding for the B-1 ($445 million of the $455 million authorized).

The prime contractor for the B-1, Rockwell International, took pains in its lobbying of members of Congress to emphasize the public works nature of the B-1. During a period of rising unemployment they argued persuasively for the value of contracts and jobs, both nationally and in the individual states and districts containing subcontractors.

1977–1978. One of President Ford's last acts (after he was a lame duck because of his defeat in November 1976) was to order initial production of the B-1, even though incoming President Carter had already expressed opposition to the plane. Congress had stipulated that full-scale production would have to await the new president's review.

In his early months in office Carter was subjected to the arguments of both supporters and opponents about the value of the plane. By mid-1977 he had become firmly convinced that the money would be better spent on a cruise missile and he made his position public. He moved to rescind the $462 million appropriated in Fiscal 1977 for building the first two planes. The Senate, which had been increasingly skeptical of the plane for several years, went along with the President. However, in December 1977, the House refused to accept the rescission by a vote of 191 to 166.

For the next several months after this vote the administration orchestrated a concentrated campaign against the B-1. Gradually the administration had won over the Air Force and then had won over key pro-defense establishment figures in Congress, especially on the Defense Appropriations Subcommittee and on the Armed Services Committee. The basic method of winning these key people was to stress that the defense subgovernment (Air Force branch) would not lose these resources in any ultimate sense but that they would merely be shifted to other Air Force projects such as the cruise missile. Procedurally, the rescission was attached to an omnibus $7.8 billion supplemental appropriations bill that contained funding for an assortment of enterprises important to many House members. Thus, when the House voted on the rescission again in late February it upheld the President by a vote of 234 to 182. However, supporters (except, perhaps, for the contractors themselves) had lost little—they had simply bowed to technological inevitability (the increasing obsolescence of the B-1) that had been seized on by the President and his supporters. He had been more than willing to pay the price of not removing the resources from the Air Force subgovernment sphere of influence.

The F-111 and the A-7D. The case of the F-111 and the A-7D over recent years shows that subgovernment support for the procurement of a given weapons system does not die easily, even when the system in question has been purchased in sufficient quantities or becomes out-moded. In both 1973 and 1974 Congress added money to the defense appropriations bill for continued procurement of the F-111 (the con-troversial TFX during the 1960s) and the A-7D (an Air Force fighter plane), even though the Defense Department had not requested money for those planes because it had determined that the services already had a sufficient number of them.

The impetus of congressional generosity to insert the unrequested money ($250 million in 1973 and $320 million in 1974) came from the Texas delegations, and their motivation could be interpreted as pure pork barrel—both planes are manufactured in Texas, and the extra money would nearly all be spent in Texas. The Texans were aided by F-111 supporters in Congress who argued that as the only bomber be-ing made until mass production of the B-1 begins, the F-111 should not be allowed to go out of production.

The tenacity of the subgovernment was successful two years in a row and its work went largely unnoticed, except by one observer who labeled interaction between Congress and the Pentagon a "charade" (Getler, 1974: A28): "The Pentagon . . . knows that the urge of the Tex-ans in Congress to keep production going is so strong that if the Penta-gon does not put the plans in its budget and allows production to slow or stop, then the Texans in Congress will put the money in. That is basically what has happened for the past two years."

The President, supported by the full House and Senate, put a partial and at least temporary stop to the charade in 1975 by requesting a re-scission of appropriations that included funds for continued procure-ment of 12 F-111s. The House and Senate Appropriations committees (the Chairman of the House Appropriations Committee was a Texan), true to their Air Force allies and the supporters of the Texas contracts, rejected this part of the President's request. But the full House and Senate overrode the committees' decision and amended the rescission bill to disallow the F-111s.

The subgovernment supporters of both planes (and the contractors)

showed their resilience and inventiveness by continuing to procure revised versions of both aircraft during the first few years of the Carter
administration. The A-7D had been produced as a trainer, and the
F-111 has been altered into the FB-111H, a strategic bomber that is
generating its own controversy. The EF-111A, a plane loaded with
electronic jamming equipment, is another version of the F-111.

Reserve forces

Since World War II the subgovernment surrounding the size, status,
and prerequisites of the reserve military forces has operated in classic
distributive fashion (Levantrosser, 1967). A close liaison has been
forged between the chief interest group (the Reserve Officers Association), the Armed Services committees, other members of Congress who
are either members of or have an interest in the reserves, and members
of the executive branch—especially regular officers in the three military services. The concerns of this subgovernment have been to retain
a large reserve force and give its members generous pay, retirement,
and other benefits. Both ends have been accomplished.

The ROA is an interest group that functions directly as a policy-
maker. It initiates legislation in addition to monitoring legislation
emerging from the executive branch or from Congress. Its representatives participate directly in the "mark-up" sessions held by committees on bills pertaining to the reserve. It has a Legislative Advisory
Committee made up of members of Congress who are reserve officers,
and this Committee both aids in the passage of favorable legislation
and passes out various awards to particularly important and supportive
members of the House and Senate.

In the executive branch the ROA actively builds allies in the services by seeking regular officers as associate members. The ROA also
confers regularly with service officials following reserve legislation.

The one change that has occurred over the years is that the Department of Defense itself (at the level of the Office of the Secretary) has
disassociated itself from a close symbiotic tie to the reserve forces and
has been willing to take a more independent stand, not always interpreted as friendly by the ROA and its allies. But the essence of policy
has still not changed much, and ties with the services and Congress remain strong.

Food for Peace

Since its passage in 1954 the history of the Food for Peace program
(also known as Public Law 480) has been one of expansion in times of
domestic crop surpluses and one of contraction when those surpluses

have disappeared. P.L. 480 was designed as a means of disposing of surplus agricultural commodities abroad; the program has been used both for humanitarian purposes and for diplomatic and political purposes by the State Department and the administration. But from the viewpoint of the subsidized producers of farm commodities in the United States, P.L. 480 represents a major subsidy in years of surplus.

The supportive subgovernment has been consistently successful in continuing and expanding the program. The major members of the subgovernment have been bureaucrats in the Foreign Agricultural Service of the Department of Agriculture, most members of the relevant subcommittees of the House and Senate Agriculture committees, virtually all of the farmer interest groups, and the U.S. shipping interests, who get into the act by obtaining a guaranteed portion of the resulting shipping. Earl Butz, Secretary of Agriculture for Presidents Nixon and Ford, stated the viewpoint of the Department of Agriculture and the subsidized farmers succinctly when he referred to P.L. 480 as primarily a way of "getting rid of the stuff" ("stuff" refers to surplus food). (Quoted in *National Journal*, November 23, 1974, p. 1761.)

But the world of P.L. 480 is more complex than Secretary Butz' comment implies. P.L. 480 has both structural and strategic aspects, and a debate arose in late 1974 and 1975 over the purposes of the program and its uses. Commodity exports under the program have been increasingly used in recent years to reward political allies abroad (South Korea, South Vietnam, Pakistan) and to encourage desired behavior from other nations. Critics of the strategic uses of the program (who included Senator Hubert Humphrey [Dem., Minn.], one of the original sponsors of the program) opposed what they viewed as the excessive use of food aid for political and diplomatic purposes. They urged Congress to take initiatives that would put a stronger emphasis on the humanitarian aspects of the program (as well as on guaranteeing more stability in the level of subsidy to the American farmers—although that was not so widely articulated). These critics combined a focus on humanitarianism with an implicit focus on stabilizing the subsidy aspects of the program at home—perhaps an unusual but certainly not an uncomfortable stance. Opponents of the revision (who included Secretary of State Kissinger) were interested in more than just the U.S. image as a humanitarian nation and the stabilization of subsidies at home. They would have preferred to retain flexibility in the P.L. 480 program to use surplus commodities for diplomatic and political purposes.

As of early 1979 P.L. 480 was continuing unhampered, serving primarily the domestic purpose of buying agricultural surpluses and the foreign-policy purpose of rewarding the friends of the United States, such as South Korea, or at least trying to keep moderate governments in power in countries like Indonesia and Bangladesh. It seemed ill-suited to achieving these dual purposes simultaneously because of food market fluctuations. The problems with the program seemed even more acute when judged by humanitarian standards of whether the surplus food is actually gotten to the poorest people in the aided countries in a timely fashion (Rothschild, 1977; Bird, 1978). But the subgovernment supporting P.L. 480 seemed to be in no danger of having its favored program altered in any major way.

STRATEGIC POLICY

In general, the congressional posture in dealing with strategic issues of foreign and defense policy has been either to support the administration's requests (as in the case of the strategic implications of defense procurement decisions about new weapons systems, including the B-1, discussed above) or to register a competing point of view in such a way as not to remove all administration flexibility. In short, Congress usually gives either willing or at least grudging support to the administration's view of strategic matters. This does not mean that the congressional impact is missing, however.

Soviet trade

In 1973 and 1974 the expansion of U.S. trade with the Soviet Union was a high-priority item on the executive branch's agenda—including the personal agendas of President Nixon, President Ford, and Secretary of State Kissinger. Leading figures in Congress, however, especially presidential aspirant Senator Henry Jackson (Dem., Wash.), took the view that the United States should refrain from expanding trade until the Soviet Union altered its internal emigration policies to allow Jews to emigrate freely. The administration opposed linking trade and emigration, and a 20-month deadlock ensued. In October of 1974 a compromise was agreed upon that allowed passage of the administration's trade bill in the last days of the congressional session. Both the Secretary of State and the President were personally involved in the negotiations with Jackson and other members of Congress in reaching the compromise.

The compromise was complex, but it illustrates both the eagerness of Congress to have an impact on this strategic issue and at the same time the unwillingness of Congress to bind the executive too tightly. The trade bill denied most favored nation trade status to countries that do not permit free emigration. But the restriction was not ironclad. For 18 months following enactment the bill also allowed the President to request a waiver of the restriction if he received assurances from the country in question that its policies were leading to substantially free emigration, and if he informed Congress of those assurances. At the end of the 18-month period the waiver right could be renewed for a year at a time by the President with the approval of Congress. The waiver procedure was embodied in an amendment offered by Senator Jackson and adopted on the Senate floor 88–0. Kissinger and Jackson exchanged letters outlining the conditions that the Soviet Union would have to meet in order to qualify for the waiver provision.

The President did not request a waiver and the congressional imposition of the Jackson Amendment seemed, at least to the State Department, to inhibit the expansion of Soviet-U.S. trade, although it had resulted in no reductions. The Soviet Union publicly took the position that its emigration policies were reasonable and were not the proper concern of the United States anyway and that it would certainly not give the kinds of assurances required by the legislation. The State Department and the Treasury Department—which has special responsibility for negotiating trade expansion—were reconciled to living with the Jackson Amendment until after Jackson had completed his bid for the 1976 Democratic presidential nomination. Jewish voters in the United States were presumably impressed by Jackson's efforts on behalf of Soviet Jews, and few members of either party in either house were willing to risk appearing to be anti-Jewish by working actively for a modification or elimination of the Jackson Amendment.

At about the same time that the Jackson Amendment was being adopted, Congress extended the Export-Import Bank bill for four more years (this organization helps U.S. businesses sell their products overseas and finances U.S. export sales). The bill contained restrictions on the Bank's activities in general and especially limited its activities in the Soviet Union. The motivation seems to have been generated more by a desire to improve congressional oversight of the Bank's activities than to have been triggered by specific complaints about Soviet behavior.

In this bill, however, Congress again shrank from reducing executive flexibility in a strategic field. The bill set a ceiling on the amount of credit to be extended to the Soviets, with a subceiling set on the amount to be used for energy research and development (apparently Congress hoped a restrictive ceiling would encourage energy development at home). However, the ceiling limits can be raised by the President if he finds that an increase would be in the national interest and if both houses approve his request.

While thus allowing the President flexibility in regard to Soviet trade, the impact of the Bank bill overall (which severely limits the amount of funds available to the Bank) is to give Congress more opportunity to become involved in the Bank's investment decisions before those decisions become policy commitments.

Troop cuts

In recent years Congress has become increasingly restive about the size of the American military establishment. Considerable concern, for a variety of reasons, has also been expressed about the proportion and numbers of those troops stationed overseas.

One of the leading critics of a large American military contingent in Europe was Senator Mike Mansfield, the Democratic floor leader until his retirement from Congress in 1976. Over the years the sentiment in Congress for overseas troop reductions has been growing. Arguments have focused on the balance of payments problems, on the responsibility of allies for their own defense, and on the dangers of incidents that might lead to warfare. Despite efforts to reduce troops and to specify the location of those reductions, Congress has ultimately contented itself with specifying overall troop levels (usually representing at most only modest cuts from existing levels) and has not specified location decisions. In short, Congress has continued to leave the principal strategic decisions in the hands of the executive branch.

In 1974 the defense appropriations bill contained a provision requiring a total troop withdrawal of 12,500 from overseas locations by May 31, 1975 (about eight months after the passage of the bill). This reduced the total authorized U.S. troop strength abroad to 452,000. (By early 1975 about 300,000 were in Europe, 125,000 were in East Asia—principally South Korea, Japan, the Philippines, and Thailand—and 27,000 were in a variety of other locations.) The decisions on locations for the 12,500 pullback were left in the hands of the executive branch.

In reaching the decision to include a 12,500 mandated overseas troop cutback the conference committee reconciled the Senate bill, which required a cut of 25,000, and a House bill that had specified no cut. The · Senate Appropriations Committee indicated that it would have preferred to mandate the cuts specifically in Europe. But the Secretary of Defense and his staff had worked very hard to convince the conference committee that such a course of action was unwise.

The troop reduction issue had also been debated during the consideration of the 1974 authorization bill for procurement and research and development funds for the Defense Department. In the House the Majority Leader, Thomas P. O'Neill (Dem., Mass.), proposed an amendment reducing overseas troops by 100,000 by the end of 1975. This amendment was defeated 163 to 240. The House Armed Services Committee had recommended against unilateral troop withdrawal from Europe. (Their motivation was tied to a provision in the 1973 defense procurement act, relating to the balance of payments deficit, a domestic economy problem.)

In Senate consideration of the defense procurement bill, a large troop reduction (125,000) was defeated by a vote of 54 to 35. The vote came on an amendment offered by Mansfield and was defeated in part because of the strenuous activities of high-ranking administration officials, including both Secretary of State Henry Kissinger and Secretary of Defense James Schlesinger. The Senate barely defeated a second proposal—also made by Mansfield—to set the level of pullback at 76,000. The vote on this was 44 to 46.

The one provision dealing with overseas troop strength in the defense procurement bill adopted in 1974 required a reduction of 18,000 support troops specifically from Europe—but at the same time allowed the Secretary of Defense to replace them with combat troops and gave him until June 30, 1976, to accomplish the reduction (6,000 would have to be removed by June 30, 1975). The Senate bill had set the reduction at about 23,000 but the conference committee reduced the figure. Again the twin urges of Congress are apparent: the desire to have an impact on a strategic issue and the desire not to bind the executive branch too tightly.

In 1977 and 1978 some members of Congress exhibited an opposite concern when President Carter announced a phased withdrawal of U.S. ground troops from South Korea (scheduled to be completed by 1982). The opponents of this move did not generate any concrete activity, however (in part, because the Joint Chiefs of Staff had been successful in getting the President to accept some conditions surrounding the withdrawal: withdrawal in a manner that would not "destabilize" the military situation between North and South Korea, a public renewal of American obligations under a mutual security treaty with South Korea, and a statement to the effect that the United States intended to remain a military power in the Pacific area). Thus the congressional reaction was essentially symbolic. In 1977 language was added to the bill authorizing funds for the State Department declaring that U.S. policy toward South Korea should "continue to be arrived at by joint decision of the President and Congress" and that implementation of the phased troop withdrawal plan should be "carried out in regular consultation with Congress." In 1978 the military aid appropriations bill contained a provision that it was the sense of Congress that additional withdrawal of U.S. troops from South Korea might upset the military balance in the region and that such moves require full consultation with Congress. But these provisions put no effective limits on the administration's power in this strategic area. Rather, they simply served notice on the President that Congress was watching this area carefully and might become troublesome in the future if members did not receive appropriate stroking.

More important, in votes on concrete matters Congress supported the President. By a vote of almost two to one the House rejected an amendment to the defense authorization bill that would have barred a reduction in U.S. troops in South Korea to a level lower than 26,000. The military aid bill contained a provision allowing the President to give weapons of U.S. units in Korea to the Koreans as the U.S. units depart (about $800 million worth of weapons were covered).

Turkish aid

Two hostile ethnic communities (Greeks and Turks) occupy the island of Cyprus, and Turkey and Greece have long disputed which country has rightful claim to the island. In July of 1974 Turkey invaded the island, using in part weapons supplied through the U.S. military foreign assistance program. This violated the provisions of the military assistance statutes prohibiting the use of the weapons for other than defensive purposes.

During the autumn of 1974 Congress engaged in a running battle with the administration over what response the United States should make to this action. As is the case when Congress gets heavily involved in domestic regulatory issues the level of final decision was the full floor of the House and Senate rather than in a quiet bureau-subcommittee setting. As was true in the case of Soviet trade restrictions, Congress also got involved in part because of the presence of a group of American voters—those of Greek extraction, who were vocal in demanding anti-Turkish action (there was no competing set of American voters of Turkish extraction). In this case, despite the fervent protests of the President, Secretary of State, and other high-ranking executive branch officials, Congress made the strategic policy decision that a cutoff of military aid to Turkey (presumably coupled with U.S. mediation of the Greek–Turkish dispute over Cyprus) would be a better means of forcing a solution to the military situation on Cyprus than quiet diplomatic moves alone. But as in the Soviet trade and troop cut decisions, there was enough self-doubt in Congress about this strategic decision that it still allowed the administration some flexibility by giving it the option to postpone the cutoff date.

The parliamentary maneuvering over Turkish aid from mid-September through mid-December 1974 was elaborate and intricate. Each house took numerous roll call votes on the issue and always took an anti-Turk, anti-administration position. The entire story of the maneuvering throughout the autumn need not be told here, but the kinds of compromises that were reached are interesting and show the reluctance of Congress to be overly rigid on strategic issues when caught between the cross-pressures of voters, moral principle, and forceful arguments from the President and Secretary of State that the national interest and national security demand a minimum of overt restriction on a valued and important ally.

The first restriction voted by Congress and accepted unhappily by the administration was contained in a temporary law—an appropriations continuing resolution—signed in mid-October. The key congressional concession was to delay the aid cutoff until December 10, thus giving Ford and Kissinger time to put diplomatic pressure on the Turks so that the cutoff of aid would be moot. The final Ford agreement to the compromise came in a telephone call to the House Minority Leader. The language of the bill allowed the President to delay imposing the ban as an aid to working through negotiation on the Cyprus question as long as Turkey observed the cease-fire on the island and did not add either troops or U.S. weapons to its forces on Cyprus.

The same kind of debate resumed when Congress reconvened after the 1974 elections for a "lame duck" session as proponents of an aid cutoff sought to add mandatory language to the foreign aid and military assistance authorization bill, thus making the cutoff part of permanent law rather than just a continuing resolution. Both houses voted for the cutoff, although the House insisted on making the cutoff take effect December 10. However, the Senate passed a provision allowing the President to suspend the cutoff until February 14, 1975, in the interest of giving the President and Kissinger more latitude to continue quiet work with the Turks and Greeks. The conferees chose February 5 as the cutoff date and both houses approved. The new law provided that if the cutoff took place on February 5 it could be lifted if the administration could certify that "substantial progress" was being made toward a solution to the Cyprus problem.

As February 5 approached Kissinger met with four Democratic leaders of the cutoff forces. He asked them to arrange another extension of the deadline in the interests of national security and to avoid jeopardizing American bases in Turkey and the Turkish–American alliance, but he indicated he could not certify substantial progress in the Cypress negotiations. The Senator and three Representatives present refused and indicated that the cutoff would have to take effect on schedule. They also indicated, however, their support for a speedy resumption of aid once the certification of substantial progress could be made.

When the cutoff of military aid to Turkey went into effect on February 5, 1975, the administration continued to press for a lifting of the ban. In the next three months an impressive coalition was built in the Senate that included the Majority Leader, the Minority Leader, the Minority Whip, the chairmen and ranking minority members of the Foreign Relations Committee and the Armed Services Committee. These individuals cosponsored a bill allowing resumption of aid but retaining an active oversight role for Congress, which the Senate narrowly passed, 41 to 40. The House narrowly upheld (223–206) the ban in late July 1975, however, and the Turkish government retaliated by ordering American bases closed.

In October 1975, Congress agreed to a partial lifting of the arms embargo in order to give the President latitude in negotiations to prevent the Turks from making the base closings permanent. Reporting requirements preserved an important congressional role in monitoring U.S. relations with both Greece and Turkey. The permitted sales were to be related to NATO defenses.

In his 1976 campaign, Jimmy Carter supported the partial arms embargo, but as President in 1978 he took the position that the partial embargo should be lifted because it was threatening Turkey's continued membership in NATO and because Turkey was threatening to make the U.S. base closings permanent. (See Maxfield, 1978a, 1978b, 1978c, 1978d, 1978e on the details of the 1978 struggle.) Turkey had not, however, changed its position on Cyprus and remained in control of about 40 percent of the island. In early June 1978, the President labeled his request for repeal his number one foreign policy priority. The President personally lobbied members of the House and Senate and was aided by other high-ranking officials such as NATO commander General Alexander Haig, Secretary of State Cyrus Vance, and Secretary of Defense Harold Brown.

The denouement of the 1978 debate took place along lines familiar to strategic issues: decisions in congressional committees had no finality—final decisions were made on the floors of the House and Senate after heated debates. Those decisions required compromises that left Congress with the illusion of being important in continued decision making on the subject, and the President got the essence of what he wanted.

In the Senate the Foreign Relations Committee voted against ending the embargo 8 to 4. When the issue came to the Senate floor it was clear that some compromise language to accompany the repeal would be needed. The Majority Leader and others offered such language, which provided that when the President requested any funds for Turkey, Greece, or Cyprus he must simultaneously certify that U.S. goals for resolving the conflict over Cyprus were being achieved. The language also noted disapproval of continuing Turkish military presence on Cyprus. The President was required to report to Congress every 60 days on progress toward a solution to the Cyprus question.

The House had always presented a tougher pro-embargo stance than the Senate. The International Relations Committee narrowly voted

18–17 to end the embargo but only because two pro-embargo members did not vote.

On the House floor the pro-embargo forces would have won had not an even more "pro-Congress" compromise than the one the Senate had forged been found. Even it passed only 208 to 205. This compromise, drafted by the Majority Leader (working with the White House), did not formally repeal the embargo but instead allowed it to be put aside by the President if he certified to Congress that resumption of aid was in the "national interest of the United States and in the interest of NATO." He also had to certify to Congress that Turkey was "acting in good faith" in settling a number of the Cyprus-related issues on a permanent basis. Like the Senate, the House required the President to report every 60 days.

The Conference Committee took the harder House line in framing the final bill—calling it a "de facto repeal" rather than an outright repeal. This was done probably to avoid another bruising and perhaps losing battle on the House floor.

The importance of the Greek–American community in generating congressional interest in a cutoff and in sustaining such a cutoff despite strong appeals from the President and Kissinger in 1974–1976 should be stressed (see *Washington Post,* October 25, 1974, p. A5). This has never been a politically active community before and yet on this issue an impressive organization was put together to lobby members of the House and Senate. There were also several members of the House and Senate willing to take the lead in pressing the issue, including several members of Greek extraction. Of course, the issue was more complex than simple ethnicity, but the strength of the Greek–American lobby was important in sustaining congressional interest in an aid cutoff.

CRISIS POLICY

The typical pattern in crisis decision situations is one of post hoc congressional legitimation of presidential action. There is not enough congressional participation in most instances to warrant more than a sentence or two in a book on congressional-bureaucratic interaction or even in a book on congressional-presidential interaction. For example, President Johnson ordered air strikes against North Vietnam in August 1964, after North Vietnamese attacks on two U.S. destroyers were reported. He used the alleged attacks as a basis afterwards for obtaining the Gulf of Tonkin resolution from Congress, which both he and President Nixon used to justify executive expansion of the war in Vietnam.

Other patterns exist, however. Occasionally, the post hoc reaction of Congress is not one of legitimation. This was the case, for example, with the decision by Johnson in 1965 to send U.S. marines to the Dominican Republic, allegedly to prevent a communist takeover (see Evans and Novak, 1966, chapter 23). He had not engaged in even symbolic consultation with any members of Congress ahead of time, but instead simply told some of the leaders an hour after the landing was ordered that the decision had been made. No formal congressional legitimating action was either requested or received. In fact, the event marked the public defection of the Chairman of the Senate Foreign Relations Committee, William Fulbright (also a Democrat), from the President's foreign policy in general—both in the Dominican Republic and then in Vietnam.

There is also the possibility that congressional leaders will be consulted before action is taken in a crisis situation. When consulted they may, of course, take a variety of positions—either with or without effect. Two incidents, briefly described here, illustrate different kinds of response when Congress is consulted in a crisis situation. In the first case, involving a decision about Vietnam in 1954, the congressional response to the administration proposal was critical and negative in the sense of wanting no action rather than the proposed action; the administration finally wound up bowing to the congressional view (although other factors intervened too). In the second case, involving the U.S. response to the discovery of Soviet offensive nuclear-armed missiles in Cuba in 1962, congressional response was also critical and negative, this time in the sense of wanting more action than that proposed by the administration. But in this instance the President remained firm and proceeded with his initial decision.

In an effort to prevent a repetition of U.S. involvement in a foreign war because of executive action without congressional consent, Congress in 1973 passed the War Powers Act, which required the President to consult with Congress when making decisions involving the commitment of U.S. forces abroad. The Act was envisioned by its supporters as a tool for ensuring congressional participation in crisis decisions involving armed forces before they became policy commitments. The last of the examples looked at in this chapter focuses on a recent partial application of the War Powers Act.

Vietnam, 1954

In 1954 the administration pondered becoming involved militarily in Southeast Asia in support of what proved to be the losing French effort to keep Indochina French and non-Communist (see Roberts, 1973). In April of that year the Secretary of State, John Foster Dulles, called a meeting attended by five Senators and three Representatives—leaders from both parties in both houses—and a few Defense Department officials, including the Chairman of the Joint Chiefs of Staff, Admiral Arthur Radford. Basically what Dulles proposed at this meeting was that Congress pass a resolution giving the President the authority to use American sea and air power to support the French in Indochina. The members of Congress who had been summoned gave both Dulles and Radford hard questioning. Two key points were established: first, that the other members of the Joint Chiefs of Staff did not agree with Radford that military action was essential and, second, that the United States had not consulted any allies about their support for the move. As events spun out, the United States could not generate support—especially critical support from Great Britain—and Dien Bien Phu (the French stronghold in Southeast Asia) fell before further action was taken.

The lesson of this episode should not be overstated. This was, after all, primarily a crisis for the French and it did not have to become a crisis for the United States unless we chose to define it so. Radford and Dulles tried unsuccessfully to establish such a definition, but the congressional leaders' resistance and hard questioning convinced President Eisenhower to shrink from action until Dien Bien Phu had fallen, at which time action became moot. Nevertheless, it shows that when top administration officials consult congressional leaders the questions and/or advice they receive might have considerable impact.

Cuban missiles

On October 16, 1962, President Kennedy received undeniable proof that the Soviet Union had established offensive missile bases in Cuba. He and his closest advisors viewed this as a grave threat to American security and pondered their response for six days before deciding on a naval quarantine and a demand that existing bases and missiles be dismantled and returned to the Soviet Union. If the Soviets did not bow to these demands the President was prepared to take direct military action against the bases. And, in his own private calculations, he figured the chances of a general nuclear war with the Soviet Union at between 1 in 3 and 1 in 2. But he thought that what was at stake demanded such a gamble and his advisors agreed.

Until he had decided to make a public announcement concerning the U.S. reaction to the discovery of the missiles, President Kennedy's consultations had been limited to a small group of less than 20 individuals from the highest levels of the executive branch (Kennedy, 1971: 8). Although some congressional critics had been claiming knowledge of the existence of Soviet missiles in Cuba for more than a month before the President was convinced of their presence and had been demanding strong action, the President did not consult with anyone from Capitol Hill until he had made his decision and was ready to announce it to the American people. Shortly before making the announcement, the President met with leaders of Congress to inform them of the course of action he was to take. Robert Kennedy described that meeting (Kennedy, 1971: 31–32):

> Many congressional leaders were sharp in their criticism. They felt that the President should take more forceful action, a military attack or invasion, and that the blockade was far too weak a response. Senator Richard B. Russell of Georgia said he could not live with himself if he did not say in the strongest possible terms how important it was that we act with greater strength than the President was contemplating.
>
> Senator J. William Fulbright of Arkansas also strongly advised military action rather than such a weak step as the blockade. Others said they were skeptical but would remain publicly silent, only because it was such a dangerous hour for the country.
>
> The President, after listening to the frequently emotional criticism, explained that he would take whatever steps were necessary to protect the security of the United States, but that he did not feel greater military action was warranted initially. Because it was possible that the matter could be resolved without a devastating war, he had decided on the course he had outlined. Perhaps in the end, he said, direct military action would be necessary, but that course should not be followed lightly. In the meantime, he assured them, he had taken measures to prepare our military forces and place them in a position to move.

The Mayaguez incident and the War Powers Act

After disillusionment with Vietnamese policy had set in strongly, many individuals in Congress were discontented with the minimal role of Congress in crisis situations involving the use of armed force. Even if that use began on a limited basis it always posed the threat of expanding. Thus in November 1973, Congress passed, over a presidential veto, the War Powers Act. In broad terms this law provided that the President must report overseas commitments of American troops to combat within 48 hours. He must order the end of such combat after 60 days unless Congress has given specific approval for continuation, although he is given the power of extending the period for 30 more days if he determines that American troops are in danger. The Act also provides that the President should "in every instance possible . . . consult with Congress" before ordering actions that might risk military hostilities.

An early test, fortunately a limited one, of the impact of the War

Powers Act on congressional involvement in a crisis situation occurred in May 1975, when forces of the new Communist government of Cambodia seized an American merchant ship, the *Mayaguez*, in waters claimed by the Cambodians but interpreted by the United States to be international waters.

The President, as is typical in crisis situations, consulted with officials from the White House, State Department, and Defense Department and then informed a few leading members of Congress of his decision. The President opted for a limited use of force, although somewhat more force than that counseled by the Defense Department. He used Marines to seize the ship and rescue the crew from an island where they were being held. He also ordered bombing of selected Cambodian mainland targets as a preemptive measure to prevent retaliation.

However, in arriving at a decision, the consultation suggested by the War Powers Act did not take place. As Senator Mansfield said, "I was not consulted. I was notified after the fact about what the administration had already decided to do. . . . I did not give my approval or disapproval because the decision had already been made." (Quoted in *Congressional Quarterly Weekly Report* May 17, 1975, p. 1008.) The Republican floor leader in the Senate, Hugh Scott, agreed that he had not been consulted either—he said he had merely been advised of the administration's intentions after they had already been decided. It was not until after the administration members had themselves decided on a course of action that any members of Congress were informed by White House congressional liaison officials.

The President, although not consulting, complied with the reporting requirements of the Act by sending a letter to the full Congress explaining the provocation and the course of action. By the time the letter was received the incident was over and the *Mayaguez* and her crew were rescued, although close to 20 American servicemen had died in the process. Congressional reaction to the letter was moot since the hostilities had already ceased.

The reaction from Congress to the President's handling of the crisis was generally congratulatory. Except for some not-too-seriously voiced skepticism about having been "informed" rather than consulted, and despite a few skeptics who questioned whether negotiation had been explored sufficiently before force was used, the praise for the President was general from both parties and from members of all ideologies and included a superfluous resolution of support from the Senate Foreign Relations Committee.

There is not agreement within Congress itself on what the War Powers Act of 1973 is supposed to do. On the one hand, critics of the Act argue that if consultation with Congress were taken literally, executive flexibility to maneuver in a crisis would be seriously reduced. Supporters of the Act argue that at a minimum it guarantees Congress the right to review executive decisions involving armed forces and to decide whether or not to continue them. Potentially, the War Powers Act gives to Congress a greater role in crisis decision making, but the *Mayaguez* incident does not reflect any change from the usual post hoc involvement of Congress. The euphoria of having escaped a serious international incident, perhaps a war, was so great that serious reflection on the efficacy of the War Powers Act seems to have escaped attention.

After he left the presidency, Gerald Ford reflected on the use of the War Powers Act in his administration (Ford, 1977). He made it clear that the provisions really had very little impact on how he conducted himself in six specific incidents, including the *Mayaguez* case. The most accurate comment on the War Powers Act, given Ford's testimony and what else we know of the six cases he mentions (there were no incidents to which the Act would have been applicable in 1977 and 1978), is that it remains an unclear and probably ineffective congressional attempt to control warmaking powers. It is at least a symbol of congressional frustration in facing a world in which a genuine large-scale crisis could destroy much of the world's population in a matter of minutes or a few hours at most.

CONCLUSIONS

In general the expected patterns of congressional-executive interaction can be observed in the illustrations chosen for this chapter. Subgovernments are very important in structural decisions, although when those decisions also have major strategic implications (as in the case of most major weapons systems) the scope of conflict may be widened. Congress as a whole typically gets involved in strategic decisions, although the tendency to defer to the executive branch or at least to preserve considerable flexibility for the executive branch is very strong. In crisis situations congressional participation tends to be only symbolic if it is present at all. The War Powers Act potentially claims more for Congress, but the *Mayaguez* case at least raises the question of whether anything has really changed. There is a serious question whether significant congressional involvement in any crisis situation is likely except for involvement in the form of endorsing presidential action. On the other hand, a president who is genuinely willing to consult congressional leaders before action is decided on and who is willing to listen to what they say may be swayed toward a different course of action than he would pursue if he had not asked or listened. Often, however, the press of events does not seem to allow time for consultation or the president involved is simply not disposed to consult.

The largest deviation from our expectations is the degree to which Congress gets involved in strategic decisions. This can be explained largely on two grounds. First, there is often a blurring between structural and strategic issues. The defense budget presents a number of structural decisions to Congress each year, but some of the decisions, particularly those on new weapons systems, are also strategic in impact. At the nadir of congressional willingness to challenge the executive branch, a period from roughly 1955 to 1965 (see Ripley, 1978: 379–386), when such issues were mingled, the tendency was for Congress to back off from any involvement. Now Congress is much more willing to get involved, even though strategic matters are at stake.

Second, if domestic political considerations are involved, then Congress is usually more willing to render judgments on strategic issues that may vary from those coming from the executive branch and the services. This tendency was illustrated when Jewish voters and interest groups influenced the tie made between expanded U.S.–Soviet Union trade and Soviet emigration policy for Jews and when Greek–American voters and interest groups influenced the Turkish aid ban. It is also apparent—although not in terms of an identifiable potential voting bloc—in the case of troop cuts where balance of payments deficits, tied to the domestic economy, are one of the principal motivating factors behind the congressional drive to reduce the number of U.S. troops stationed abroad. But in all of these cases there was also congressional concern for allowing the executive branch, and particularly the President, flexibility in his decision making.

Presidents wishing to have an impact on structural decisions can enhance their chances of success by stressing the strategic aspects of those decisions. When Congress wishes to intervene in strategic matters it is most likely to oppose the President, at least in part, when it focuses on structural aspects or when there are domestic lobbies and groups of voters pushing in such a direction.

~8~

Congress, the bureaucracy, and the nature of American public policy

IN GENERAL, American public policy can be characterized as slow to change, as more responsive to special interests than to general interests, as more responsive to the privileged in society than to the underprivileged, and as tending to be defined and treated as distributive when possible. The reasons for this situation are rooted in the basic dominance by subgovernments of much of American policymaking, the great premium placed on cooperation between Congress and the bureaucracy, the lack of meaningful congressional oversight on a continuing basis for many policies, and the greater strength of forces pushing for no change or minimal change in policy as opposed to the forces pushing for greater change in policy.

Yet, given that the world is gray (rather than black or white) and that features of man-made institutions, processes, and policies are manipulable rather than inevitable, our examination of the congressional-bureaucratic relationship has also found some exceptions to these generalizations. The policymaking system in operation supports these generalizations more often than not, but at times counter-pressures can also develop that produce different results.

It is our aim in this final chapter to summarize the principal analytic themes we have developed in the preceding chapters in order to explain both the predominance of slow-changing, largely distributive policy catering mainly to special interests and the more privileged members of society and the exceptional conditions that produce some policies that do not fit the predominant mold. We also wish to under-score some normative concerns in the course of the discussion, al-though we do not pretend to have pat answers to the problems we see in the general shape of American public policy.

In the sections that follow we will first address in summary fashion the relative influence of various participants in different policy areas. Second, we will discuss the rewards of cooperation compared to the rewards of conflict in policymaking. Third, we will offer some final thoughts on congressional oversight of bureaucratic policy perform-ance. Fourth, we will summarize the relative strength of the forces pushing for stable policy and the forces pushing for changed policy.

PARTICIPANTS, INFLUENCE, AND ISSUES

The argument has been made in Chapters 4 through 7 that different relationships have varying degrees of importance in determining final policy statements depending on the kind of issue at stake. That argu-ment is summarized graphically in comparative terms in Figures 8–1 through 8–6. These figures address the relationships between five clus-ters of actors in each of the six policy areas that have been identified. The five clusters of actors are the President and centralized bureauc-racy (the President personally, his top advisors and cabinet appoin-tees); the bureaus (symbolizing the bureaucracy in its decentralized state); Congress (as a whole); subcommittees (symbolizing Congress in its decentralized state); and the private sector (with actors including individuals, corporations, interest groups, and peak associations).

Figures 8–1 through 8–6, when coupled with the material in Tables 1–3 and 4–1, present an overview of the relative influence of all par-ticipants in the six different policy areas and also specify the changing role of the bureau-subcommittee-private sector subgovernments from area to area. The expectations we summarized in Table 4–1 were, in general, supported by the cases we examined. Thus it would be accu-rate to say that ordinarily subgovernments dominate distributive pol-icymaking, both in domestic and non-domestic spheres (which we have called distributive and structural policy). They play lesser roles in the other four policy areas but do not disappear altogether except in crisis situations involving foreign and defense policy. They play a moder-ately important role in protective regulatory policy and are at least sporadically important in handling redistributive issues and strategic foreign and defense policy questions. Given that there is both a natural tendency for all domestic issues to be defined or redefined as distribu-tive if possible and for strategic foreign and defense issues often to involve some structural aspects this creates a very large role for sub-governments indeed.

Figure 8–1: Relative importance of relationships for
determining distributive policy

Key

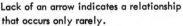

= Very important relationship.

= Moderately important relationship.

= Relatively unimportant relationship.

Lack of an arrow indicates a relationship
that occurs only rarely.

Some would argue that the dominance of subgovernments in much
policymaking is good and works in the public interest because genuine
experts are placed in charge of issues. In addition, it is sometimes argued that the mechanisms for redressing any excesses of subgovernment self-indulgence exist because access to various pressure points
is open.

We would not entirely agree with this sanguine view both because
the incentives for using the mechanisms of redress are low most of the
time and because the self-defensive mechanisms possessed by most
subgovernments are so strong. We certainly would not argue that
subgovernments can or should be eliminated from the policymaking
process in the United States. However, we think that often better and
more responsive public policy and changes in public policy result from
both broader oversight of subgovernment functioning and the involve-

Figure 8–2: Relative importance of relationships for
determining protective regulatory policy

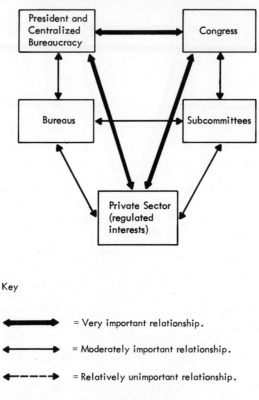

Key

= Very important relationship.

= Moderately important relationship.

= Relatively unimportant relationship.

Lack of an arrow indicates a relationship
that occurs only rarely.

ment of "outsiders" in at least some subgovernment deliberations. At
a minimum, the policies of distributive subgovernments have implications for many sectors of the society and economy beyond the direct
beneficiaries of the policies, and expanding the participants in subgovernment deliberations would help to spell out those impacts (sugar
subsidies on the grocery store price of sugar, price supports on the
cost of various foods, water resources subsidies on the environment,
airline subsidies on the cost of plane tickets) and also might help to
relate the disaggregated policies of numerous dispersed subgovernments into a more coherent pattern. Bargaining, negotiation, and compromise are, indeed, the hallmarks of the American decision making
system on public policy. Our preference is to open the bargaining and
negotiation that occur within subgovernments more broadly than is

Figure 8–3: Relative importance of relationships for
determining redistributive policy

Key

= Very important relationship.

= Moderately important relationship.

= Relatively unimportant relationship.

Lack of an arrow indicates a relationship
that occurs only rarely.

often the case, particularly in the distributive areas of both domestic
and nondomestic policy.

One general pattern we found that did not quite conform to our initial expectations in Table 4–1 was that Congress in general (not only
at the subcommittee level) was a more important actor in all areas
than the literature had led us to expect. In the protective regulatory
area, for example, members of Congress get involved not only in seeking weaker regulation for favored interests but also, in some cases, in
seeking stiffer regulation, often stiffer than that being favored by the
relevant regulatory agencies. In the redistributive area we found, as
expected, that presidential initiation was often essential to action and
that vigorous presidential support was virtually always essential to
action. However, in several of the redistributive cases we observed an
important role for Congress in quiet negotiations during the critical

Figure 8–4: Relative importance of relationships for
determining structural policy

Key

= Very important relationship.

= Moderately important relationship.

= Relatively unimportant relationship.

Lack of an arrow indicates a relationship
that occurs only rarely.

decision making stages of the development of new or altered redistributive policy. These quiet negotiations often took place directly
within what might be called a redistributive subgovernment—individuals from relevant congressional committees and subcommittees, bureaus, and interest groups (often peak associations). This role for subgovernments is not nearly as frequent as in distributive policy, but it
was often necessary at some critical juncture during a debate that
might already have lasted for years.

In the foreign and defense policy areas Congress played an unex-
pectedly large role in strategic decisions both because there was a blurring of strategic and structural issues and because domestic political
considerations often motivated congressional involvement. Even in crisis situations it was suggested that individuals from Congress—senior
leaders from the foreign policy and defense-oriented committees and

Figure 8–5: Relative importance of relationships for determining strategic policy

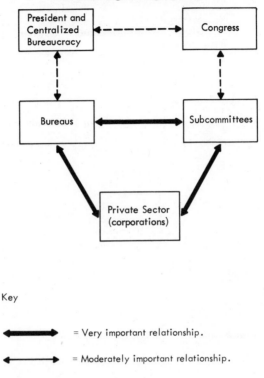

Key

= Very important relationship.

= Moderately important relationship.

= Relatively unimportant relationship.

Lack of an arrow indicates a relationship that occurs only rarely.

the party leaders—might give relevant advice that could be important *if* the President chose to ask for the advice in the first place and chose to listen to it in the second place. Presidents often have neither the time nor the disposition to ask or listen but the potential is there. The War Powers Act is at least a paper reminder from Congress that it would like to be consulted and a stronger reminder that it does not again wish to abdicate its power of declaring war as it did in Vietnam.

Some analyses of the role of Congress in policymaking proceed as if the source of the initiation of legislative ideas is all that matters and that somehow Congress and the executive branch are involved in a zero-sum game over initiation. The conclusion is usually drawn that since the executive initiates more than Congress it has "won" the game and the importance of Congress in policymaking has declined. At least three things are wrong with this often repeated formula. First, Con-

Figure 8–6: Relative importance of relationships for
determining crisis policy

Key

= Very important relationship.

= Moderately important relationship.

= Relatively unimportant relationship.

Lack of an arrow indicates a relationship
that occurs only rarely.

gress can and does get involved in initiation on a broad range of issues
(see Chamberlain, 1946; Moe and Teel, 1970; and Orfield, 1975). For
example, Congress was responsible for initiation in the following policy areas in recent years: Medicare, Social Security disability insurance, pension reform, the 18-year-old vote, political campaign reform,
air pollution (including automobile pollution), reduction and cessation
of the U.S. role in the Indochina war, chemical additives in foods,
the creation of a consumer protection agency, mandatory automobile
safety standards, food programs for the poor, and increases in the minimum wage (see Rich, 1975). Congress also initiated major investigations of the drug industry, multinational corporations, organized crime,
and labor racketeering.

   Second, and more important, Congress does much more than initiate. Even granting that the executive branch initiates a great deal on a

piecemeal basis and that the President is probably the only possible source for a genuinely comprehensive and integrated legislative program, the power that Congress has and uses to legitimate, or amend, or reject executive and presidential initiatives is both extensive and extremely important.

Third, and perhaps most important, congressional-executive relations cannot reasonably be interpreted as a zero-sum game. Congress and the executive branch (both the President and the bureaucracy) can be creative together or can fall on their faces together, but in most instances policymaking involves at least some efforts from both of them —it is a cooperative venture.

A more systematic way of thinking of the interaction of the executive branch and Congress in making policy involves positing four basic "models" of the relationship (see Ripley, 1978: 28–30, 372–386).

The first model is one of *executive dominance*. In this relationship the executive branch is the principal source of the initiation of legislative ideas and also shapes most of the details. Congressional participation in the shaping of details is low. Legislation does result.

The second model is one of *joint program development*. In this relationship either the executive branch or Congress can be the principal source of initiation. Both branches are heavily involved in shaping the details of the final decision. And, again, legislation results.

The third model is one of *congressional dominance*. In this relationship Congress provides the chief source of initiation and also shapes most of the details of the final legislation (which is passed).

The fourth model is one of *stalemate*. In this relationship principal initiative can come from either branch. Often it comes from both branches (but moves in different substantive directions). Both branches get involved in shaping details—but again they do not agree. The short-term result is that no legislation results because the disagreements are too great.

Table 8–1 summarizes these models of policy formulation and legitimation. Table 8–2 lists examples of domestic cases from recent years that generally fit each model (see also Anderson, Brady, and Bullock, 1978, for many more examples).

COOPERATION AND CONFLICT BETWEEN
CONGRESS AND THE BUREAUCRACY

In Chapter 1 we specified six conditions that promote either cooperation or conflict between Congress and the bureaucracy, depending on the state of the conditions at any given time. These included the level of personal compatibility, the level of ideological or programmatic agreement or disagreement, the level of genuine congressional

Table 8–1: Models of policy formulation and legitimation

Model	Principal source of initiation	Degree of congressional participation in shaping details	Degree of executive participation in shaping details	Final legislative product
Executive dominance	Executive	Low	High	Yes
Join program development	Executive or Congress or both	High	High	Yes
Congressional dominance	Congress	High	Low	Yes
Stalemate	Excutive or Congress or both	High	High	No

Source: Ripley (1978: 30).

Table 8–2: Examples of recent domestic policymaking generally fitting different models

Executive dominance
  Economic Opportunity Act, 1964
  Model Cities, 1966
  Juvenile Delinquency, 1963

Joint program development
  Area Redevelopment Act, 1961
  Humphrey-Hawkins Bill, 1978
  Appalachia program, 1964
  Food stamps, 1963
  Aid to airports, 1950s and 1960s
  Mass transit, 1960s and 1970s
  Numerous education programs, 1940s–1960s

Congressional dominance
  Air pollution control, 1950s–1970s
  Water pollution control, 1950s–1970s
  Strip mining regulation, 1977
  Health research, 1950s, 1960s

Stalemate
  Housing, early 1970s
  Aid to elementary and secondary education, 1940s–early 1960s
  Medicare, 1940s–early 1960s
  Creation of an Urban Affairs Department, 1961–1962
  Welfare reform, 1970s

participation in decision making, the level of salience of an issue to constituents and organized groups, the nature of party control of the executive branch and Congress, and the relative aggressiveness of agencies in requesting support for expansion and the relative aggressiveness of Congress in engaging in oversight. We can now suggest that some of these conditions are most important in some types of policy and others are more important in other types of policy. Specifically, in reflecting on the material presented in this volume, it can be suggested that smooth subgovernment relations are dominant in the distributive and structural policy areas because personal compatibility is high, programmatic agreement is high (with ideology being almost totally irrelevant to all parties), the level of congressional participation is high, the issues are salient to constituents and organized groups that congressional and bureaucratic figures in key positions are anxious to serve, there are mutually agreed on levels of agency expansion and congressional oversight (or, usually, non-oversight) and—given all of the above—differing party control of the two branches is often only a minor irritant.

In the protective regulatory, strategic, and redistributive arenas there is more likely to be ideological or programmatic disagreement; the executive branch may try to exclude Congress or at least diminish its role; the salience of issues is likely to encompass larger groups and sets of individuals rather than small, tightly knit groups with common interests; desires for expansion and/or oversight will be articulated without prior agreement; and—given the above—differing party control of the two branches makes increased conflict much more likely.

Cooperation is certainly needed or else effective government cannot exist in the United States. Thus we do not denigrate the values of cooperation. But we also do not denigrate the values of conflict. Conflict can produce harder questions about public policy, more oversight and evaluation of program performance, and more awareness of what is at stake in public policy decisions. The desire of most participants, however, is for cooperation whenever possible and sometimes at all costs. The price that is paid for this desire is often an uncritical attitude about specific public policies on the parts of public officials, both elected and nonelected. The incentives are heavily loaded in favor of cooperation. As suggested in Chapter 2 the background of our officials, both in Congress and in the executive branch, is such that a fairly homogeneous group of mostly middle-aged, middle class white males make most decisions. This may mean that there is an inbuilt bias to see things from a single perspective. This is not to suggest a conspiracy but only that relative homogeneity in a set of officials helps produce relative homogeneity in outlook on some crucial policy questions.

Even more important, as suggested in Chapter 3, a number of institutional incentives contribute to the desire to see policy in a nonconflictual light. Both members of Congress and members of the bureaucracy usually have more to gain from cooperation than from conflict (see also Ripley, 1978: chapter 10, on this point).

LEGISLATIVE OVERSIGHT

Why oversight is less than systematic: resources and motivations

Oversight as a congressional activity can be thought of in two senses. In a random and nonsystematic sense, oversight can be described as a continuous activity, because there are many opportunities for individual members and for subcommittees and committees to inquire into specific activities of the bureaucracy, and these opportunities are exercised. However, in a more systematic and continuous sense—such as would occur in a "rational," constant evaluation of program performance and/or impact—oversight by Congress happens only occasionally. Some of the reasons for this have already been suggested: Members of the House and Senate have a variety of interests, and the motivation to engage in detailed, continuous oversight is often missing or weak at best.

Ogul (1973: 2–3) discusses specific legislative oversight activities in terms of these motivations (see also Ogul, 1976, 1977):

> When any action is perceived to contribute directly and substantially to political survival as well as to other legitimate functions, it is likely to move toward the top of any member's priority list. Extra incentives to oversee come from problems of direct concern to one's constituents or from issues that promise political visibility or organizational support. Conversely, problems not seen as closely related to political survival are more difficult to crowd onto the member's schedule. . . .
>
> Not all congressional activity is linked directly to political survival. A congressman seems to gain interest in pushing oversight efforts onto his active calendar under the following conditions: New executive requests are forthcoming calling for massive new expenditures or substantial new authorizations in controversial policy areas; a crisis has occurred that has not been met effectively by executive departments; the opposition political party is in control of the executive branch; he has not been treated well either in the realm of personal attention or in the servicing of his requests; he has modest confidence in the administrative capacity of departmental or agency leaders.

Ogul also points out that when a member has high confidence in a set of leaders and/or agrees with the policies they are pursuing the motivation for oversight lessens. If favored policies are being ignored or contradicted, however, the member has relatively high incentive to get involved with the bureaucracy in such a way as to try to alter their policy behavior in a desired direction.

Davis (1970: 133–134) adds some reasons that oversight is weak and sporadic:

> For all the formal power of Congress, Congress does operate under important restraints in playing its role of administrative overseer. Congress is relatively small compared to the executive branch; it does not meet continuously, it is made up (at best) of intelligent laymen, and it has limited staff. These characteristics mean that Congress is unable to review the performance of executive branch organizations in any regular and systematic way. Because of its limited staff Congress cannot collect all the information it would need to review agency performance systematically and, if it could collect the needed information, it could not analyze and interpret it. Congress can at most spot-check what is going on in the executive branch. It can react to complaints, respond to fires. But it may be able to spot fires only when they have reached considerable proportions. . . .
>
> An additional limit on Congress's ability to oversee administration is the potential ability of a government executive to avoid the close examination of his organization and its budget by maintaining friendly personal relations with relevant committee chairmen. If a bureau chief can build an atmosphere of confidence and trust, then Congressmen may not ask him many questions and may accept on faith his answers to any questions asked.

Ralph K. Huitt (1966: 20), a careful student of Congress and a former Assistant Secretary of Health, Education, and Welfare, reaches much the same conclusion as Davis about the extent of congressional oversight and also indicates the conditions under which it is most likely:

> . . . not much "oversight" of administration, in a systematic and continuous enough manner to make it mean very much, is practiced. The appropriations committees probably do more than the legislative committees. . . . Most legislative oversight occurs when hearings on new bills or authorizations occur. Closer scrutiny is likely to result from the personal interest of a chairman or ranking member, the sudden interest of the public in a program or a member's hunch that interest can be aroused, or the relationship (amounting virtually to institutional incest in a separation-of-powers system) which arises when a chairman fills the agency's top jobs with his own former staff members. The individual member's interest in administration is likely to be spurred by a constituent's protest, which subsides when the matter is taken care of.

Surprisingly, only a few systematic studies of congressional oversight have been undertaken. One such study is of the relations between three congressional committees and seven independent regulatory commissions for the period from 1938 to 1961 (Scher, 1963). Another is a study of the relations between the Senate Banking and Currency Committee and three agencies (the Small Business Administration, the Federal Reserve Board, and the Housing and Home Finance Agency) from 1954 through 1962 (Bibby, 1966). The Scher study supports the Davis and Huitt positions by observing that long periods of time would pass between serious reviews of the various agencies by the committees. The Bibby study examines specific conditions promoting greater oversight. These include the presence of a committee chairperson devoted to "serving" the other members of the committee rather than imposing personal views on the committee; a relatively high degree of subcommittee autonomy within the committee; a sufficient and aggressive staff for the committee; members highly interested in the work of the committee and experienced in Congress and in interacting with the executive branch; and a committee with a basic orientation toward oversight of the administration of existing statutes rather than the development of new basic legislation. Since few committees meet all of these conditions very often or for very long periods of time the relative paucity of systematic oversight is easy to understand and explain.

A study by Ogul (1976) of three House committees (the full Post Office and Civil Service Committee, a Judiciary Subcommittee, and a Special Subcommittee of the Government Operations Committee) in the mid and late 1960s produced similar findings: only one of these three committees had much oversight impact and that was a short-term special subcommittee. He also summarizes the conditions most likely to foster oversight, although the presence of any one or even all of these conditions in no way guarantees a strong oversight performance (Ogul, 1976: 21–22). His general conclusion is that nothing can guarantee effective oversight, and idiosyncratic features probably explain a great deal about its occurrence.

A thorough study of the intergovernmental grant system—one of the largest and most important sets of domestic programs—concluded that congressional oversight performance in this area, despite verbiage showing interest, had been "disappointing" (Advisory Commission on Intergovernmental Relations, 1978: 86). Specifically, a provision for periodic review of grants contained in the Intergovernmental Cooperation Act of 1968 has simply been ignored by Congress.

General and special revenue sharing also present new challenges to already weak oversight. Since these programs are not directly controlled or implemented by federal bureaucracies, but are instead controlled largely by seemingly innumerable state and local governments, Congress has great trouble in getting a "handle" on how to oversee them and also has little incentive to do so. The performance of Congress in reauthorizing one major special revenue sharing program—the Comprehensive Employment and Training Act (CETA)—in 1978 (it had first been passed in 1973) suggests that little meaningful oversight had taken place. Such programs are now quite large (CETA alone, for example, cost over $10 billion in Fiscal 1978).

Even in the area of covert intelligence, in which extremely disturbing revelations about the practices of the Central Intelligence Agency, the Federal Bureau of Investigation, and other agencies have been made, protestations of changed congressional attitudes toward the intelligence function—which took considerable time to develop (see Ransom, 1975, and Elliff, 1977)—seem to have been followed up with little concrete in the way of sustained oversight (see Marro, 1977, and Horrock, 1978). Both houses have shown interest by creating Select Committees on Intelligence but continuing productivity of these committees is far from assured.

One very concrete problem Congress faces in trying to oversee many fields is that the delegations of power by Congress to the executive branch agencies are so broad that they contain no standards against which performance can be measured, even at a very general level (Woll, 1977). Broad delegations of power also blur the intended focus of oversight, and as a result oversight can ask widely varying questions, focusing on issues such as management efficiency, bureaucratic procedures, programmatic impact on clients and beneficiaries, degree of programmatic goal achievement, or justification for a program, for example. Yet another obstacle to oversight is an attitude among legislators who agree that oversight is necessary and important but who do not want their pet programs to be the object of oversight activities. This can lead to reverse form of backscratching—"you don't investigate my program and I won't investigate yours"—that diminishes the incentives for and the frequency of oversight.

In short, oversight does not come naturally or easily to Congress, and there is no reason to expect that it ever will.

Altering the patterns of resources and motivations to perform oversight

Broadly, the reasons described in the preceding section for sporadic or absent congressional oversight relate both to the capacity and resources of Congress on the one hand, and to the motivations of congressmen on the other. Problems of capacity or resources are difficult but are easier to affect than problems of motivation.

Resources. At both the verbal level and the formal statutory level Congress has shown considerable interest in oversight since World

War II, and that interest had intensified in the 1970s (on the verbal in-
tensification see Freed, 1975, and Havemann, 1975).

The first explicit congressional legislative attempt to create both an
oversight mandate and capacity came in the Legislative Reorganization
Act of 1946. In that Act (which also reduced the number of standing
committees, rationalized their jurisdiction in relation to the governmental agenda in 1946, and provided professional staffs for committees
and members) all committees were charged with "continuous watch-
fulness" of executive branch performance in administering public laws
and with studying agency reports submitted to Congress. The Government Operations Committees in both houses were given a special mandate to make sure that all government programs were meeting the twin
traditional criteria of economy and efficiency.

In the Intergovernmental Cooperation Act of 1968 committees were
specifically required to oversee the operations of federal grant-in-aid
programs to states and localities, including those that had no firm
expiration dates in the initial statutes. As already indicated, Congress
has ignored this provision. The Legislative Reorganization Act of 1970
gave oversight capacity, at least in principle, to the General Accounting
Office (GAO) and the Congressional Research Service. It also required
virtually all committees to report every two years on their oversight
activities.

In 1974 Congress passed two statutes that showed substantial concern with oversight. The Congressional Budget and Impoundment
Control Act created the staff capacity in the two budget committees
and the Congressional Budget Office. In addition, GAO was mandated
to establish an Office of Program Review and Evaluation and to recom-
mend to Congress methods to be used in such review and evaluation.
The Treasury and the Office of Management and Budget in the executive branch were also required to provide special information to
committees, to the GAO, and to the Congressional Budget Office.

Perhaps most important, the Budget Act got at least some members
of the House and Senate themselves—the members of the budget committees—intimately involved in the details of the federal budgets. This
involvement could lead to a greater concern with systematic oversight.
And, given the procedures of the Budget Act requiring some critical
resolutions on the budget each year passed by the entire House and
Senate, there was at least some potential in the Act for creating a
similar concern in all members of the House and Senate.

One critical resource Congress has done well in providing itself in
recent years is adequate and high-quality professional staff (Fox and
Hammond, 1977). Staff limits are no longer a major constraint on oversight potential in most areas. Individual Senators and Representatives
and all committees and subcommittees have sizable staffs.

In addition, Congress has created some new central support offices and strengthened some preexisting ones in an effort, in part, to create a more professional staff structure that could help sustain more effective and continuous oversight. The Congressional Budget Office has already been mentioned as one new office that has some potential for enhancing congressional oversight. Another new office with at least limited potential is the Office of Technology Assessment, although in its early years it was mired in charges of political empire-building and had not built a constituency supporting it that would help guarantee some attention to its analytic products.

An old organization, the Congressional Research Service, was required by the 1970 Legislative Reorganization Act to provide committees of Congress (in effect, chairpersons) with lists of expiring legislation and also with "a list of subjects and policy areas which the committees might profitably analyze in depth." Another established organization, the General Accounting Office, was authorized by the same law "to review and analyze 'the results of government programs and activities, including the making of cost benefit studies,' on its initiative or when ordered by either house or a committee." The use of the GAO is not governed by a rational plan, however. A Wisconsin Republican member of the House, William Steiger, complained that GAO "is not used properly because there is no comprehensive, rational approach to how it should be used. By and large, a congressman will tell GAO, 'Here's a problem, look at it and report back.' There's no understanding of the types of questions that should be asked or how programs should be evaluated." (All quotes in this paragraph are from Congressional Quarterly Weekly Report, March 22, 1975, pp. 597 and 598.)

Both houses have reorganized their committee systems in the last few years—the House in 1974 and the Senate in 1977. The Senate reorganization had no particular relationship to oversight potential. In the House one provision required standing committees with more than 20 members to set up special oversight subcommittees or to require their standing subcommittees to engage in oversight. It also gave special oversight responsibilities and powers to seven standing committees (Budget, Armed Services, Education and Labor, International Affairs, Interior and Insular Affairs, Science and Technology, and Small Business). These committees were specifically authorized to cross normal jurisdictional boundaries in pursuing their oversight duties. It's not clear, however, that this formal requirement has improved either the quality or quantity of oversight.

Motivations. A more subtle and difficult problem in improving oversight lies in altering the motivations of members to conduct it. Staffs can be enlarged and upgraded—but the motivations of members are set in institutional contexts that are considerably less flexible, although fortunately not totally impervious to change. One way to increase the amount of oversight that gets done would be to stress the linkages between oversight and other higher priority tasks of legislators. This would help improve members' motivations to perform oversight. The performance of oversight should have payoffs for members' other priorities or goals—such as getting reelected. For example, constituents' problems raise issues that spark legislative oversight. By seeking out patterns among constituents' problems with agencies' programs (for example, Social Security eligibility and payments) more systematic oversight of client-oriented programs would result.[1]

Another way of creating motivation for legislative oversight would be to tie oversight to the desire of members to initiate and develop legislation. Because most members feel a pride and accomplishment in authoring legislation, that pride of parenthood might be tapped to motivate the members of a committee involved in creating legislation to follow through on oversight of the implementation and impact of that legislation. This would be facilitated if the legislation mandated stiff reporting and evaluation requirements for the administering agency, which would provide the input automatically for congressional attention to the subject (and Congress is increasingly including such requirements in its legislation).

It can certainly be observed that in those areas in which Congress has been most important in initiating it has often been most aggressive in oversight. Air and water pollution legislation offer a good example. In short, we disagree at least partially with Huitt (1966) and Bibby (1966) when they suggest that there is a necessary trade-off between performing oversight and developing new legislation and that a committee interested in the latter will not have much time for the former. This may be true if the committee is not subsequently forced, in effect, to consider performance because of the receipt of agency reports and

---

[1] Congressional perception of the public mood may help stimulate oversight, as many journalists at the beginning of the 96th Congress (1979–80) were speculating. But we would argue that what results is toothless oversight, more concerned with appearance than substance. At the close of the decade of the 1970s (a period of rising inflation and high unemployment) public opinion was concerned with issues like government efficiency, quality of administration, and federal overspending. In such an atmosphere some legislators may engage in oversight activities—or at least the appearance of oversight—in order to win points with the folks back home and demonstrate that they too are concerned with government efficiency, administration, and overspending. Aside from the problem that such oversight is motivated more by imagemaking than by substantive concerns is a larger problem that hamstrings effective oversight—local constituents (the folks back home), like legislators themselves, believe that it is always other federal programs, not the ones in their own districts, that should be cut because of inefficiency. They don't want their federal subsidies cut, and protest vigorously if cuts are threatened.

evaluations. But with the automatic, scheduled receipt of such reports and evaluations the opportunity for oversight would be created and we would place our bets on the most aggressive initiating committees also performing most aggressively as overseers.

An additional provision of new statutes that might also enhance oversight would be an automatic termination date coupled with reporting and evaluation requirements that would simply force the committee to consider the statute periodically and at the same time provide data and agency views that would be considered in the deliberations about whether to terminate, extend, or amend a program (see Lowi, 1973b).

Some members of Congress, particularly some Senators, have been pushing the creation of such "sunset" legislation that would add termination dates to all statutes creating major programs. One version of this bill, authored by Senator Edmund Muskie (Dem., Maine), was passed 87 to 1 by the Senate very late in the 95th Congress (1978)—so late that it was clear that the vote was only symbolic and that the House would not take action. This version of the sunset bill required automatic termination of funds for most federal programs if the programs had not been specifically reauthorized after review every ten years. Muskie had spent three years trying to get his bill to the floor and had met all sorts of roadblocks. As one Muskie aide commented: "Muskie's experience on sunset has been like reading the Kamasutra. You find out you can get screwed 130 ways" (quoted in *Congressional Quarterly Weekly Report*, October 14, 1978: 2951).

Through a combination of attention to developing congressional resource capacity and to increasing members' motivations for performing legislative oversight, the quality and continuity of oversight that gets performed could improve. No magic formula will cure all problems, however, and congressional oversight is never likely to become everything critics want.

FORCES FOR AND AGAINST CHANGE

As already indicated, there are a number of powerful forces working against change of policy of any sizable magnitude. And yet some sizable changes do occur, which suggests that there also may be individuals and forces working for it. In considering the range of institutions and individuals in both branches with which we have dealt in this volume the identity of the contending forces in most cases becomes clear.

The status quo forces are most likely to be higher civil servants, especially those in older, larger, well-established agencies, and members of Congress and staff members working on the subcommittees related to the individual agencies and their programs. Their disposition to make only moderate or small changes in policies that exist is seconded by the impact of the representatives of already advantaged interest groups working in the same substantive field. These individuals are all characterized by long service and usually by long-established patterns of personal interaction. They are highly specialized in the substantive business of their particular subgovernment. And their loyalties tend to be primarily institutional (that is, to the subcommittee or agency itself) or, in the case of members of Congress, to a limited electoral constituency (that is, the "most important" voters in a district or state).

The forces that are more likely to be mobilized in support of substantial programmatic change on at least some occasions consist of a few bureau officials, a few congressional staff members, a few members of Congress (usually outside of the subgovernment dominating policy in the area), and—selectively—the President and some of his appointees in relevant portions of the executive establishment. These individuals tend to have a shorter tenure (this is most evident in the case of presidents and their appointees) and probably do not have long-established patterns of personal relations with one another (that is, the forces that coalesce to work in favor of major change are likely to do so on an ad hoc basis, whereas the subgovernments supporting the status quo with only minor changes tend to be more institutionalized and permanent). The degree of specialization is much lower than for the members of the typical subgovernment. And the principal loyalties of these individuals are more likely to be ideological or programmatic (that is, to a vision of "good policy") than narrowly institutional. The President (and perhaps ambitious Senators who want to be President) also presumably takes some major policy initiatives with a national electoral constituency in mind.

The sheer complexity of getting new policies adopted in the United States when compared to a number of other developed countries with open political systems also helps explain why "new departures" seem to be relatively rare in the United States. After studying regional development and population distribution policy in the United States, Great Britain, France, Italy, the Netherlands, and Sweden, one careful student of policymaking (Sundquist, 1978: 79) reached these conclusions: "Because the institutional structure of policymaking in the United States is more complex and pluralized than those of the other industrial democracies of the Atlantic community, because the policymaking circle is broader and more amateur and less disciplined, public participation more intense, and the points of potential veto of policy innovation more numerous, and because political parties are weaker as integrating mechanisms, a higher degree of national consensus and a more intense commitment of political leadership are necessary before new departures can be developed and approved, and a narrower range of innovation can be successfully attempted at any one time."

A CLOSING WORD

We end this chapter and this book both on an analytical note and on a moderately hopeful note. The analytical note is that conservatism in the sense of support of the status quo is dominant in the national policies of the United States for reasons that we hope we have made clear: The pervasive need for compromise built into the system, the widespread desire to minimize conflict, and the desire to protect personal careers on the part of individuals throughout the executive and legislative branches. The hopeful note is twofold: Not all of the status quo is bad or undesirable policy, and more important, the status quo policy is not completely rigid, nor are the status quo forces completely dominant. Bursts of creativity can and do occur and may come from either branch. Too much is often claimed for the "genius of American government." Likewise, indictments are often too sweeping. Conservative, distributive policies are likely to prevail unless deliberate action to the contrary is taken. Even though the system does not encourage such deliberate action, it at least permits it when men and women of energy with differing policy commitments become policy actors.

References

Aaron, H. J. (1972) Shelter and Subsidies. Washington, D.C.: Brookings.

Aberbach, J. D., and B. A. Rockman (1976) "Clashing Beliefs within the Executive Branch: The Nixon Administration Bureaucracy." American Political Science Review 70 (June): 456–468.

——— (1977) "The Overlapping Worlds of American Federal Executives and Congressmen." British Journal of Political Science 7 (January): 23–47.

——— (1978) "Bureaucrats and Clientele Groups: A View from Capitol Hill." American Journal of Political Science 22 (November): 818–832.

Advisory Commission on Intergovernment Relations (1978) Categorical Grants: Their Role and Design (publication A-52). Washington: U.S. Government Printing Office.

Anderson, J. E. [ed.] (1970) Politics and Economic Policy-Making. Reading, Mass.: Addison-Wesley.

Anderson, J. E., D. W. Brady, and C. Bullock, III (1978) Public Policy and Politics in America. North Scituate, Mass.: Duxbury.

Armacost, M. H. (1969) The Politics of Weapons Innovation. New York: Columbia University Press.

Arnow, K. S. (1954) The Department of Commerce Field Service. Indianapolis: Bobbs-Merrill. ICP Case #21.

Asher, H. B. (1974) "Committees and the Norm of Specialization." Annals of the American Academy of Political and Social Science 411 (January): 63–74.

Bendiner, R. (1964) Obstacle Course on Capitol Hill. New York: McGraw-Hill.

Bernstein, M. H.   (1955)   Regulating Business by Independent Commission. Princeton: Princeton University Press.

——— (1958)   The Job of the Federal Executive. Washington, D.C.: Brookings.

Bibby, J. F.   (1966)   "Committee Characteristics and Legislative Oversight of Administration." Midwest Journal of Political Science 10 (February): 78–98.

Bird, K.   (1978)   "Food for Peace—Or Politics?" Washington Post (January 4): A19.

Bonafede, D.   (1979)   "The Tough Job of Normalizing Relations with Capitol Hill." National Journal (January 13): 54–57.

Carper, E.   (1965)   The Reorganization of the Public Health Service. Indianapolis: Bobbs-Merrill.

Carroll, H. N.   (1966)   The House of Representatives and Foreign Affairs, revised edition. Boston: Little, Brown.

Cater, D.   (1964)   Power in Washington. New York: Random House.

Chamberlain, L. H.   (1946)   The President, Congress and Legislation. New York: Columbia University Press.

Cohen, R. E.   (1974)   "Senate Seeks to Modernize Workings of the Patent Office." National Journal (March 30): 475–482.

——— (1976a)   "When Congress Takes on Antitrust Reform, Anything Can Happen." National Journal (March 20): 354–359.

——— (1976b)   " 'Motherhood' Issue Survives Long Test in the 'Antitrust Congress.' " National Journal (June 19): 853–854.

——— (1976c)   "Maritime Industry Keeps Afloat on Seas That Are Often Stormy." National Journal (September 4): 1252–1258.

——— (1976d)   "It Was a Fight to the Finish When Congress Passed the Antitrust Bill." National Journal (September 25): 1353–1355.

Congressional Quarterly   (1965)   Congress and the Nation, 1945–1964. Washington: Congressional Quarterly Service.

Cooper, A.   (1978)   "Congress Approves Civil Service Reform." Congressional Quarterly Weekly Report (October 14): 2945–2950.

Corrigan, R.   (1977a)   "The Senate Plays 'Let's Make a Deal' With Carter's Energy Plan." National Journal (September 24): 1486–1489.

——— (1977b)   "Lobbyists Are Putting the Blitz on Carter's Energy Program." National Journal (November 26): 1836–1840.

——— (1978)   "Chalk One Up for the President's Energy Lobbyists." National Journal (September 30): 1556–1559.

Corrigan, R., and D. Kirschten   (1978)   "The Energy Package—What Has Congress Wrought?" National Journal (November 4): 1760–1768.

Corson, J. J., and R. S. Paul   (1966)   Men Near the Top. Baltimore: Johns Hopkins.

Davidson, R. H.   (1967)   "Congress and the Executive: The Race for Representation," in A. De Grazia (ed.) Congress: The First Branch of Government. Garden City, N.Y.: Doubleday.

——— (1969)   The Role of the Congressman. New York: Pegasus.

——— (1972)   The Politics of Comprehensive Manpower Legislation. Baltimore: Johns Hopkins.

——— (1975)   "Policy Making in the Manpower Subgovernment," in M. P. Smith et al. Politics in America. New York: Random House.

——— (1977)   "Breaking Up Those 'Cozy Triangles': An Impossible Dream?," in S. Welch and J. G. Peters (eds.) Legislative Reform and Public Policy. New York: Praeger.

Davidson, R. H., and W. J. Oleszek   (1977)   Congress against Itself. Bloomington, Indiana: Indiana University Press.

Davis, J. W.   (1970)   The National Executive Branch. New York: Free Press.

Davis, J. W., and R. B. Ripley   (1967)   "The Bureau of the Budget and Executive Branch Agencies: Notes on Their Interaction." Journal of Politics 29 (November): 749–769.

Dodd, L. C., and B. I. Oppenheimer (eds.)   (1977)   Congress Reconsidered. New York: Praeger.

Donovan, J. C.   (1973)   The Politics of Poverty, 2nd edition. Indianapolis: Pegasus.

Downs, A.   (1967)   Inside Bureaucracy. Boston: Little, Brown.

Drew, E. B.   (1970)   "Dam Outrage: The Story of the Army Engineers." Atlantic (April): 51–62.

Eidenberg, E., and R. D. Morey   (1969)   An Act of Congress. New York: Norton.

Elder, S.   (1978)   "The Cabinet's Ambassadors to Capitol Hill." Congressional Quarterly Weekly Report (July 29): 1196–1200.

Elliff, J. T.   (1977)   "Congress and the Intelligence Community," in L. C. Dodd and B. I. Oppenheimer (eds.) Congress Reconsidered. New York: Praeger.

Evans, R., and R. Novak   (1966)   Lyndon B. Johnson: The Exercise of Power. New York: New American Library.

Feingold, E.   (1965)   "The Great Cranberry Crisis," in E. A. Bock (ed.) Government Regulation of Business. Englewood Cliffs, N.J.: Prentice-Hall.

Fenno, R. F., Jr.   (1959)   The President's Cabinet. New York: Vintage.

——— (1966)   Power of the Purse. Boston: Little, Brown.

——— (1973)   Congressmen in Committees. Boston: Little, Brown.

——— (1978)   Home Style: House Members in Their Districts. Boston: Little, Brown.

Fiorina, M. P.   (1977)   Congress: Keystone of the Washington Establishment. New Haven, Conn.: Yale University Press.

Fisher, L.   (1974)   "Reprogramming of Funds by the Defense Department." Journal of Politics 36 (February): 77–102.

Ford, G. R.   (1977)   "The War Powers Resolution: Striking a Balance between the Executive and Legislative Branches." Reprint #69. Washington: American Enterprise Institute.

Foss, P. O.   (1960)   Politics and Grass. Seattle: University of Washington.

Fox, H. W., Jr., and S. W. Hammond   (1977)   Congressional Staffs: The Invisible Force in American Lawmaking. New York: Free Press.

Freed, B. F.   (1975)   "Congress May Step Up Oversight of Programs." Congressional Quarterly Weekly Report (March 22): 595–600.

Freeman, J. L.   (1965)   The Political Process, revised edition. New York: Random House.

Frey, A.   (1975)   A Responsible Congress: The Politics of National Security. New York: McGraw-Hill.

Friedman, K. M.   (1975)   Public Policy and the Smoking-Health Controversy. Lexington, Mass.: Lexington Books.

Friedman, L.   (1969)   "Social Welfare Legislation." Stanford Law Review 21 (January): 217–247.

Fritschler, A. L.   (1975)   Smoking and Politics, 2nd edition. Englewood Cliffs, N.J.: Prentice-Hall.

Froman, L. A., Jr.   (1968)   "The Categorization of Policy Contents," in A. Ranney (ed.) Political Science and Public Policy. Chicago: Markham.

Getler, M.   (1974)   "The Great Warplane Charade." Washington Post (September 20): A28.

Gist, J. R.   (1978)   "Appropriations Politics and Expenditure Control." Journal of Politics 40 (February): 163–178.

Green, H. P., and A. Rosenthal   (1963)   Government of the Atom: The Integration of Powers. New York: Atherton.

Greenberg, D. S.   (1967)   The Politics of Pure Science. New York: New American Library.

Greider, W.   (1978)   "After Squeezing through Hill Pipeline, Gas Bill Now Skewed toward Industry." Washington Post (July 30): A14.

Harris, J. P.   (1964)   Congressional Control of Administration. Washington, D.C.: Brookings.

Haveman, R., and P. Stephan   (1968)   "The Domestic Program Congress Won't Cut." Reporter (February 22): 36–37.

Havemann, J.   (1976)   "Congress Tries to Break Ground Zero in Evaluating Federal Programs." National Journal (May 22): 706–713.

———   (1977)   "Congress Opens Floodgates in the SBA's Disaster Loan Program." National Journal (December 31): 2001–2003.

———   (1978)   Congress and the Budget. Bloomington, Indiana: Indiana University Press.

Hayes, M. T.   (1978)   "The Semi-Sovereign Pressure Groups: A Critique of Current Theory and an Alternative Typology." Journal of Politics 40 (February): 134–161.

Heclo, H.   (1972)   "Review Article: Policy Analysis." British Journal of Political Science 2 (January): 83–108.

———   (1977)   A Government of Strangers: Executive Politics in Washington. Washington, D.C.: Brookings.

———   (1978)   "Issue Networks and the Executive Establishment," in A. King (ed.) The New American Political System. Washington, D.C.: American Enterprise Institute.

Hines, W. (1974a) "How the 'Great Chicken Massacre' Was Almost Bailed Out." Washington Post (April 21): A20.

———— (1974b) "Senate Votes Aid to Chicken Growers." Washington Post (April 24): A1.

Holtzman, A. (1970) Legislative Liaison: Executive Leadership in Congress. Chicago: Rand McNally.

Horn, S. (1970) Unused Power: The Work of the Senate Committee on Appropriations. Washington, D.C.: Brookings.

Horrock, N. M. (1978) "Intelligence Oversight: Congress Tries Again." New York Times (February 12): E3.

Huitt, R. K. (1966) "Congress, the Durable Partner," in E. Frank (ed.) Lawmakers in a Changing World. Englewood Cliffs, N.J.: Prentice-Hall.

Huntington, S. P. (1952) "The Marasmus of the ICC: The Commission, the Railroads, and the Public Interest." The Yale Law Journal 61 (April): 467–509.

———— (1961) The Common Defense. New York: Columbia University Press.

———— (1973) "Congressional Responses to the Twentieth Century," in D. B. Truman (ed.) Congress and America's Future, 2nd edition. Englewood Cliffs, N.J.: Prentice-Hall.

Jantscher, G. R. (1975) Bread upon the Waters: Federal Aids to the Maritime Industries. Washington, D.C.: Brookings.

Jensen, M. C. (1978) "Tobacco: A Potent Lobby." New York Times (February 19): F1, F4.

Johannes, J. R. (1976) "Executive Reports to Congress." Journal of Communication 26 (Summer): 53–61.

Jones, C. O. (1967) Every Second Year. Washington, D.C.: Brookings.

———— (1977) An Introduction to the Study of Public Policy, 2nd edition. North Scituate, Mass.: Duxbury Press.

Kanter, A. (1972) "Congress and the Defense Budget, 1960–1970." American Political Science Review 66 (March): 129–143.

Keefe, W. J., and M. S. Ogul (1977) The American Legislative Process, 4th edition. Englewood Cliffs, N.J.: Prentice-Hall.

Kennedy, R. F. (1971) Thirteen Days. New York: Norton.

Kilpatrick, F. P., M. C. Cummings, and M. K. Jennings (1963) The Image of the Federal Service. Washington, D.C.: Brookings.

King, S. S. (1977) "Sugar Game: Consumer Loses." New York Times (November 13): section 3: 1, 4.

King, W. (1978) "Documents Indicate Corps Misled Congress on Major Southern Canal." New York Times (November 26): 1, 32.

Kirst, M. W. (1969) Government without Passing Laws. Chapel Hill: University of North Carolina Press.

Kluger, R. (1976) Simple Justice. New York: Knopf.

Kofmehl, K. (1977) Professional Staffs of Congress, 3rd edition. West Lafayette, Indiana: Purdue University Studies.

Kohlmeier, L. M. (1975) "Shipping Subsidies Defy Trend." National Journal (May 31): 826.

Kolodziej, E. A. (1975) "Congress and Foreign Policy: The Nixon Years," in H. C. Mansfield, Sr., (ed.) Congress against the President. New York: Academy of Political Science.

Landis, J. M. (1938) The Administrative Process. New Haven: Yale University Press.

Lanoutte, W. J. (1978) "Who's Setting Foreign Policy—Carter or Congress?" National Journal (July 15): 1116–1123.

Lawrence, S. A. (1965) "The Battery Acid Controversy," in E. A. Bock (ed.) Government Regulation of Business. Englewood Cliffs, N.J.: Prentice-Hall.

——— (1966) United States Merchant Shipping Policies and Politics. Washington, D.C.: Brookings.

LeLoup, L. T. (1977) Budgetary Politics. Brunswick, Ohio: King's Court.

Levantrosser, W. F. (1967) Congress and the Citizen-Soldier. Columbus: Ohio State University Press.

Levitan, S. A. (1969) The Great Society's Poor Law. Baltimore: Johns Hopkins.

Lewis, E. (1977) American Politics in a Bureaucratic Age: Citizens, Constituents, Clients, and Victims. Cambridge, Mass.: Winthrop.

Light, L. (1979) "White House Lobby Gets Its Act Together." Congressional Quarterly Weekly Report (February 3): 195–200.

Loftus, J. A. (1970) "How the Poverty Bill Was Saved in the House," in J. E. Anderson (ed.) Politics and Economic Policy-Making. Reading, Mass.: Addison-Wesley.

Lowi, T. J. (1964) "American Business, Public Policy, Case-Studies, and Political Theory." World Politics 16 (July): 677–715.

——— (1967) "Making Democracy Safe for the World: National Politics and Foreign Policy," in J. N. Rosenau (ed.) Domestic Sources of Foreign Policy. New York: Free Press.

——— (1972) "Four Systems of Policy, Politics, and Choice." Public Administration Review 32 (July/August): 298–310.

——— (1973a) "How the Farmers Get What They Want," in T. J. Lowi and R. B. Ripley (eds.) Legislative Politics U.S.A., 3rd edition. Boston: Little, Brown.

——— (1973b) "Congressional Reform: A New Time, Place, and Manner," in T. J. Lowi and R. B. Ripley (eds.) Legislative Politics U.S.A., 3rd edition. Boston: Little, Brown.

——— (1979) The End of Liberalism, 2nd edition. New York: Norton.

Lytle, C. M. (1966) "The History of the Civil Rights Bill of 1964." The Journal of Negro History 51 (October): 275–296.

Maass, A. A. (1950) "Congress and Water Resources." American Political Science Review 44 (September): 576–593.

Manley, J. F. (1970) The Politics of Finance. Boston: Little, Brown.

——— (1971) "The Rise of Congress in Foreign Policy-Making." Annals of the American Academy of Political and Social Science, number 337: 60–70.

Marmor, T. R. (1973) The Politics of Medicare, revised edition. Chicago: Aldine.

Marro, A. (1977) "Watching over Intelligence Involves New Fears and Doubts." New York Times (March 22): E2.

Maxfield, D. M. (1978a) "Carter Plan to End Turkey Arms Sale Embargo Faces Tough Opposition in House." Congressional Quarterly Weekly Report (April 15): 872–873.

——— (1978b) "Carter Steps Up Lobbying for Turkey Arms Sales." Congressional Quarterly Weekly Report (June 10): 1464.

——— (1978c) "Senate Backs End to Turkey Arms Embargo." Congressional Quarterly Weekly Report (July 29): 1919–1920.

——— (1978d) "House Votes End to Turkey Arms Embargo." Congressional Quarterly Weekly Report (August 5): 2041.

——— (1978e) "Military Aid Bill Cleared Authorizing $2.8 Billion; Turkey Arms Ban Lifted." Congressional Quarterly Weekly Report (September 23): 2561.

Mayhew, D. R. (1974) Congress: The Electoral Connection. New Haven: Yale University Press.

Meier, K. J. (1979) Politics and the Bureaucracy. North Scituate, Mass.: Duxbury.

Meier, K. J., and L. G. Nigro (1976) "Representative Bureaucracy and Policy Preferences: A Study in the Attitudes of Federal Executives." Public Administration Review 36 (July/August): 458–469.

Meisol, P. (1978) "Has the Disaster Loan Program Hit Its High-Water Mark?" National Journal (September 16): 1462–1463.

Mintz, M. (1969) "FDA and Panalba: A Conflict of Commercial, Therapeutic Goals?" Science (August 29): 875–881.

Moe, R. C., and S. C. Teel (1970) "Congress as Policy-Maker: A Necessary Reappraisal." Political Science Quarterly 85 (September): 443–470.

Moreland, W. B. (1975) "A Non-Incremental Perspective on Budgetary Policy Actions," in R. B. Ripley and G. A. Franklin (eds.) Policy-Making in the Federal Executive Branch. New York: Free Press.

Morgan, R. J. (1965) Governing Soil Conservation. Baltimore: Johns Hopkins.

Morrow, W. L. (1969) Congressional Committees. New York: Scribners.

Munger, F. J., and R. F. Fenno (1962) National Politics and Federal Aid to Education. Syracuse: Syracuse University Press.

Nadel, M. V. (1971) The Politics of Consumer Protection. Indianapolis: Bobbs-Merrill.

Nelson, G. (1975) "Change and Continuity in the Recruitment of U.S. House Leaders, 1789–1975," in N. J. Ornstein (ed.) Congress in Change. New York: Praeger.

Neustadt, R. E. (1954) "Presidency and Legislation: The Growth of Central Clearance." American Political Science Review 48 (September): 641–671.

—— (1955) "Presidency and Legislation: Planning the President's Program." American Political Science Review 49 (December): 980–1021.

—— (1973) "Politicians and Bureaucrats," in D. B. Truman (ed.) Congress and America's Future, 2nd edition. Englewood Cliffs, N.J.: Prentice-Hall.

Noone, J. A. (1974) "Great Scrubber Debate Pits EPA Against Electric Utilities." National Journal Reports (July 27): 1103–1114.

Ogul, M. S. (1973) "Legislative Oversight of the Bureaucracy." Paper prepared for the Select Committee on Committees, U.S. House of Representatives, 93rd Congress, 1st session. Washington, D.C.: Government Printing Office.

—— (1976) Congress Oversees the Bureaucracy. Pittsburgh: University of Pittsburgh Press.

—— (1977) "Congressional Oversight: Structures and Incentives," in L. C. Dodd and B. I. Oppenheimer (eds.) Congress Reconsidered. New York: Praeger.

Oleszek, W. J. (1978) Congressional Procedures and the Policy Process. Washington, D.C.: Congressional Quarterly Press.

Orfield, G. (1975) Congressional Power: Congress and Social Change. New York: Harcourt Brace Jovanovich.

Pelham, A. (1978a) "Gas Pricing Bill Passes Second to Last Test." Congressional Quarterly Weekly Report (September 30): 2615–2616.

—— (1978b) "Energy Bill: The End of an Odyssey." Congressional Quarterly Weekly Report (October 21): 3039–3044.

Phillips, J. G. (1975) "Unexpected Obstacles Hinder Ford Plan for Coal Conversion." National Journal (May 31): 816–822.

Pincus, W. (1974) "Reforming Oversight Functions." Washington Post (December 23): A14.

Pipe, G. R. (1966) "Congressional Liaison: The Executive Branch Consolidates Its Relations with Congress." Public Administration Review 26 (March): 14–24.

Polsby, N. W. (1968) "Institutionalization in the House of Representatives." American Political Science Review 62 (March): 144–168.

Price, H. D. (1971) "The Congressional Career—Then and Now," in N. W. Polsby (ed.) Congressional Behavior. New York: Random House.

Rankin, B. (1977) "House Gives Carter Major Energy Victory." Congressional Quarterly Weekly Report (August 6): 1623–1628; 1694–1695.

Ransom, H. H. (1975) "Congress and the Intelligence Agencies," in H. C. Mansfield, Sr. (ed.) Congress against the President. 32 Proceedings of the Academy of Political Science: 153–166.

Rich, S. (1975) "Congress Has Lead in Major Programs." Washington Post (February 14): A2.

Rieselbach, L. N. (1977) Congressional Reform in the Seventies. Morristown, N.J.: General Learning Press.

Ripley, R. B. (1965) "Congressional Government and Committee Management." Public Policy. Volume 14: 28–48.

—— (1969a) Power in the Senate. New York: St. Martin's.

——— (1969b) "Congress and Clean Air: The Issue of Enforcement, 1963," in F. N. Cleaveland and Associates, Congress and Urban Problems. Washington, D.C.: Brookings.

——— (1972) The Politics of Economic and Human Resource Development. Indianapolis: Bobbs-Merrill.

——— (1978) Congress: Process and Policy, 2nd edition. New York: Norton.

Roberts, C. M. (1973) "The Day We Didn't Go to War," in T. J. Lowi and R. B. Ripley (eds.) Legislative Politics, U.S.A., 3rd edition. Boston: Little, Brown.

Rothschild, E. (1977) "Is It Time to End Food for Peace?" New York Times Magazine (March 13): 15, 43–48.

Rudder, C. E. (1977) "Committee Reform and the Revenue Process," in L. C. Dodd and B. I. Oppenheimer (eds.) Congress Reconsidered. New York: Praeger.

Russell, M. (1978) "Nader's Tactics and the Defeat of the Consumer Bill." Washington Post (February 10): A1, A5.

Ruttenberg, S. H., and J. Gutchess (1970) Manpower Challenge of the 1970's: Institutions and Social Change. Baltimore: Johns Hopkins.

Salisbury, R. H. (1968) "The Analysis of Public Policy: A Search for Theories and Roles," in A. Ranney (ed.) Political Science and Public Policy. Chicago: Markham.

Schattschneider, E. E. (1960) The Semi-Sovereign People. New York: Holt, Rinehart and Winston.

Scher, S. (1963) "Conditions for Legislative Control." Journal of Politics 25 (August): 526–551.

Scott, A. (1977) "Veterans' Clout Extracts Extraordinary Benefits." Washington Post (November 1): A1, A10.

Seidman, H. (1975) Politics, Position, and Power, 2nd edition. New York: Oxford University Press.

Sharkansky, I. (1965a) "Four Agencies and an Appropriations Subcommittee: A Comparative Study of Budget Strategies." Midwest Journal of Political Science (August): 254–281.

——— (1965b) "An Appropriations Subcommittee and Its Client Agencies: A Comparative Study of Supervision and Control." American Political Science Review (September): 622–628.

Smith, R. A. (1973) "TFX: $7 Billion Contract That Changes the Rules," in M. H. Halperin and A. Kanter (eds.) Readings in American Foreign Policy. Boston: Little, Brown.

Stanley, D. T. (1964) The Higher Civil Service. Washington, D.C.: Brookings.

Stanley, D. T., D. E. Mann, and J. W. Doig (1967) Men Who Govern. Washington, D.C.: Brookings.

Strickland, S. P. (1972) Politics, Science, and Dread Disease. Cambridge, Mass.: Harvard University Press.

Sundquist, J. L. (1968) Politics and Policy. Washington, D.C.: Brookings.

——— (1978) "A Comparison of Policy-Making Capacity in the United States and Five European Countries: The Case of Population Distribution," in M. E. Kraft and M. Schneider (eds.) Population Policy Analysis. Lexington, Mass.: Lexington Books.

Talbot, R. B., and D. F. Hadwiger (1968) The Policy Process in American Agriculture. San Francisco: Chandler.

U.S. Civil Service Commission (1976) Executive Personnel in the Federal Service. Washington, D.C.: Government Printing Office.

Welch, S., and J. G. Peters (eds.) (1977) Legislative Reform and Public Policy. New York: Praeger.

Wildavsky, A. (1974) The Politics of the Budgetary Process, 2nd edition. Boston: Little, Brown.

Wilensky, H. L. (1967) Organizational Intelligence. New York: Basic Books.

Wilson, G. C. (1978) "Corps of Engineers Consulted in China." Washington Post (December 17): A6.

Wilson, J. Q. (1975) "The Rise of the Bureaucratic State." Public Interest (Fall): 77–103.

Witmer, T. R. (1964) "The Aging of the House." Political Science Quarterly 79 (December): 526–541.

Woll, P. (1977) American Bureaucracy, 2nd edition. New York: Norton.

Wolman, H. (1971) Politics of Federal Housing. New York: Dodd, Mead.

Index

Bernstein, M. H., 14, 145
Bibby, J. F., 14, 68, 224, 228
Bird, K., 197
Bonafede, D., 55
Brookings Institution, 72
Brown, Harold, 203
Block grants, 13–14; see also Revenue
    sharing
Budget process, 19–20, 66–67, 76–78
Bureau of the Budget; see Office of
    Management and Budget
Bureau of Reclamation, 101, 103
Bureaucrats, as policy actors, 5–7,
    chapter 2
Bureaucracy
    models of interaction with Congress,
        219–20
    relations with Congress; see also Co-
        operation and conflict between
        Congress and bureaucracy
    actors in relationship, chapter 2
    bureaucratic techniques, 80–86
    impact of role, 48–59
    motivations for interaction, 61–65
    occasions for interaction, 66–69
    resources for interaction, 62–65
Business Roundtable, 140
Butz, Earl, 196

C

Cancer Act of 1971, 114
Cancer research, 112–15
Carper, E., 74
Carroll, H. N., 184
Carter, James E., 55–56, 68, 101, 103–4,
    108, 120, 126, 141–44, 166, 180–82,
    193, 200
Casework in Congress, 69
Cater, D., 8, 117
Census Bureau, 79
Central Intelligence Agency, 225
Chamberlain, L. H., 218
Change, forces for and against, 229–31
Cigarette Labelling and Advertising
    Act of 1965, 105
Civil Aeronautics Board, 24, 121
Civil Rights Act of 1964, 166–70
Civil Rights Commission, 169
Civil servants; see Bureaucrats, as pol-
    icy actors
Clayton Act, 122, 139
Clean Air Act, 122, 145
Cohen, R. E., 109, 115–16, 139
Committees, congressional; see Con-
    gressional committees
Communications Satellite Act of 1962,
    43
Community Services Act, 161

Community Services Administration,
    161–62
Competitive regulatory policy, descrip-
    tion, 23–24
Comprehensive Employment and
    Training Act of 1973, 158, 172–76,
    225
Confirmation of presidential appoint-
    ments, 78–79
Congress
    models of interaction with bureauc-
        racy, 219–20
    relations with bureaucracy; see also
        Cooperation and conflict be-
        tween Congress and bureaucracy
    actors in relationship, chapter 2
    congressional techniques, 69–80
    impact of role, 48–59
    motivations for interaction, 61–65
    occasions for interaction, 66–69
    resources for interaction, 62–65
Congress of Racial Equality, 167
Congressional Budget and Impound-
    ment Control Act of 1974, 66, 72,
    75, 81, 226
Congressional Budget Office, 72, 226,
    227
Congressional committees
    individual committees
    Ad Hoc Select Committee on En-
        ergy (House), 141–43
    Agriculture, 65, 96, 98, 105, 118
    Appropriations, 20, 50–52, 65–66,
        68, 70, 72, 74, 78, 81, 85–86, 98–
        99, 101, 105, 113, 148, 191, 193–
        94, 199
    Armed Services, 188–95, 199, 203,
        227
    Banking and Currency, 132, 224
    Budget, 227
    Commerce (Senate), 132
    Education and Labor (House), 157,
        227
    Energy and Natural Resources
        (Senate), 143
    Finance (Senate), 66, 182
    Foreign Relations (Senate), 203,
        205, 208
    Government Operations, 72, 132–
        34, 224, 226
    Governmental Affairs (Senate), 68
    Intelligence (Select), 225
    Interior and Insular Affairs, 125–
        31, 137–39, 227
    International Affairs (House), 203,
        227
    Interstate and Foreign Commerce
        (House), 132, 142

This book has been set in 10 and 9 point
Melior, leaded 2 points. Chapter numbers are
48 point Melior Bold and chapter titles are 18
point Melior Bold. The size of the type page
is 27 by 46 picas.